CYPRUS PORTRAITS 2005-2013

by Peter Rutkoff

Other titles by Peter Rutkoff can be found at xoxoxpress.com, amazon.com

D and friend in the Old City

CYPRUS PORTRAITS 2005-2013

by Peter Rutkoff

XOXOX
PRESS

Gambier, OH 43022 | xoxoxpress.com

Andrea and D, and Elena, taverna chanteusse in South Nicosia

For Costas and Roula
and Cem and Seray
and Chara and Dileck
and Andrea and Fez
and Rena and Ruth
and Yiorgous and Meltem and Marios
and Constantinous and Mustafa and Daniel
and Charis and Ipek and so many other Cypriots
who have made my life richer. I hope those who
read this book will learn from you as well.

Introduction: Beginning At the End

This journal, begun during my stay on Cyprus in the fall of 2005 and continued on subsequent visits, tells stories of passages. It is both a series of intimate portraits and the record of my own intellectual and cultural journey back and forth across the Green Line.

06 | 05 | 2011

Do you think that I have earned the right to share my opinions over the "so-called" Cyprus question? After all, I have visited and lived in Cyprus four times in the past six years. Yes, I am only a visitor whose understanding remains only as complete as you allow. In that respect, my position is just as I imagined it when I first applied for a Fulbright in 2004 — that of an outsider trying to understand another culture. I even called myself a boundary crosser in that application, believing that decades of trying to learn about African-American life and culture might well equip me to try to excavate your Cypriot site — of which I knew absolutely nothing. Ah, the dangers and arrogance of amateur ethnography. Zora Neale Hurston, the great novelist and anthropologist, even warned us: "Don't expect to learn anything more of the people you feel so compellingly passionately about than they will allow you to learn." Couple that with the advice Daniel Hadgitoffi, the Cyprus Fulbright Commission Director, offered on my first day there in 2005. Smilingly — always smilingly from Daniel I came to learn — he warned: "Do not become involved in Conflict Resolution."

Of course, when I first arrived I heeded that advice. For about three days. Then it occurred to me that you, your history and your culture, are incredibly fascinating precisely because of the intractability of your problem. Take away the bitter conflict between north and south, between Greek and Turkish Cyprus, between Orthodox and Muslim, and what's left? In one sense, only another sun-soaked Mediterranean island. Surely that's the Cyprus as seen from the outside — a place of tourists strolling amidst cheerful locals, donkey carts and souvlaki, mustaches and open-toed sandals. But your Cyprus, the one you have allowed me to glimpse, is another place entirely.

Careful, I say to myself. I must not romanticize the very things that bring you so much anguish. I am reminded of the astounding Orthodox Monasteries, like the one at Kykkos, tucked remotely away in the mountains. Stone sanctuaries so well hidden that your most intrepid EOKA-B guerrillas found refuge there in the 1970s. They have existed, some of them, for a thousand years, as if to say we can outlast whatever human excess you may unleash. But these religious safe places also existed precisely because of the special brand of tolerance of the Turkish rulers of the island for more than 400 years. They granted relative autonomy to the Orthodox church in return for collecting taxes. They are magical places, these Monasteries, perched almost in the clouds, both strong and independent.

In contrast, so many of you live in the Cyprus of never-forgotten pain, of past injuries, offenses, of loss. You carry it within you, a terrible burden, as it corrosively shapes your consciousness and even your identity. This Cyprus is the place that your political leaders depend on, that they manipulate, that divides you so deeply. This "Cyprus Problem," which so many of you say is imposed by outsiders — by Greeks, Turks, British and Americans — seems to have no end. Your island is divided, your capital is divided, your peoples are divided.

You know, it feels like Alice in Wonderland, your Cyprus. Inhabited by memories and fears and fantasy, yet all disguised by your incredible warmth, hospitality, generosity, and humanity. This, in fact, is the real Cyprus problem. You are as wonderful a people as I have ever met. And by YOU I mean Turkish Cypriots, Armenian Cypriots, Greek Cypriots, Russian-Greek Cypriots, South African-Greek Cypriots, Turkish-English Cypriots, Turkish-American Cypriots, Maronites, Cretin-Turkish Cypriots, Sri Lankans, Filipinos, Yoruba, Buddhists and Hindus. Your laughter rings in my ears, your smiles shine in my memories, your wine and meze, your actual cosmopolitanism — and above all your friendship — all remain indelible.

But as long as you insist on a version of Cyprus that pretends there is only one Cyprus, one Cypriot entity, one culture, you have landed back in Wonderland, back in a place that sees everything inside out, magnified by the distortions of enmity, ethnocentrism, and never-to-be healed injury. I wish you better, far better.

Ali in Famagusta, 2005

A cafe owner in Famagusta, 2011

Across the Green Line: 2005

09 | 05 | 2005

Today we had our first foray into the Old City of Nicosia, Cyprus — that is, to the Turkish Community of the Old City. The Old City, halved by a so-called Green Line that keeps Greek and Turkish Cypriots apart, divides, in fact, two countries. No, make that two places. But that doesn't tell the whole story.

Two political entities share a single geographic space on the island of Cyprus. It is home to a complex Greek-Turkish Cypriot culture that seems partly European and partly middle-eastern, in turn Byzantine, Venetian, Ottoman and English. The Old City — until 1974 a single-walled city of narrow streets, khaki sand-stone buildings, weathered doorways protected by ornate wrought iron gates, surrounded by a massive-walled Venetian fortification — has an architectural unity that modern commerce has only partially transformed.

We walk into the TRNC, the Turkish Republic of Northern Cyprus, the Turkish half of the Old City of Nicosia, now called Lefkosia, through their version of Check-point Charlie. Razor-wire-like strands of rusted Christmas lights drape rooftops and doorways while faded sandbags spill out of the gaping windows of abandoned buildings in this "neutral" zone. Policed by the United Nations, the treeless, naturally dry soil of the buffer zone looks now like a dry gulch in New Mexico, sandy and baked hard by the sun, commanded by an old hotel, eight or ten stories high, clearly a once-grand Old City landmark. The Ledra Palace hotel serves as home to whomever has chosen to hang white and pale blue shirts and sheets from the decaying yet elegant balconies. I wonder if this is where the UN soldiers live. It makes me think of an old New York Lower East Side welfare hotel.

Our passage between the two states that have carved up this single city on this remarkably beautiful island is uneventful. (They use the word "communities" to avoid calling Cyprus and north Cyprus by other names.) Greek-Cypriot guards wave us by, scarcely looking up from a mid-morning mouthful, and their Turkish counterparts only ask us to sign a form that they check against some kind of computer list of undesirable names before nodding us down the street.

Limes and apples in north Nicosia

No photographs

The southern portion of the Old City is filled to overflowing with T-shirt shops, electronics, shoes and then more shoes, ice-cream stands, a thriving McDonalds, and the old Woolworth's building that now houses a small department store, Ermes.

The northern, Turkish part of the city looks like what the whole city must have looked like for the last 200 years. Families live in crumbling buildings, in ground floor apartments whose doors open to catch the rare breeze as the temperature climbs above 40, that is, 110. The broiling sun forces us to the sides of the streets for shade. Shaded and cool courtyards promise something, a hidden well perhaps, while dark eyes mysteriously observe as we parade by.

The streets are barely wide enough to allow a car to pass, and tiny shops open into dark rooms that reveal a cooler filled with beer and soft drinks, or a dozen random packets of cigarettes sitting oddly on the counters. As we walk we see a very old man pushing a fruit cart. A small boy, perhaps eight years old, matches him stride for stride while whispering into his grandfather's ear. The old man is surely blind, he never lifts his head, but calls out his wares, a dozen lemons and limes, a few apples, as he moves down the street. I catch the boy's eye, motion with my camera, asking permission, and he smiles, whispers, and nods. After I take his picture he grins again and gives me five.

My wife D reminds me that it would be generous to buy a lemon. We turn and catch up with them, offer a coin, and the boy grins and whispers again, and hands us a lemon. Two hours later we see them again in the open-air market that winds through the center of the old city, calling and whispering. The fruit on the cart has disappeared. Perhaps they are headed off to restock at the sprawling covered bazaar overflowing with fruits, Turkish delights, cheap Italian designer shirts hung from rafters, and evil eye charms.

We wander, making pictures of women in the street, and of Ali, a hair dresser who sells us a cell phone case in a shop that belongs to someone else. We photograph a shoe store owner who has lovely sandals, and teaches us to say "thank you" in Turkish. He writes it out and says proudly, "We say just like we write. Not like English." Part of the word is "ederim" and it sounds like Hebrew to us. He sends us on our way, this courtly and polite man, whose warmth shines from his dark beaming face.

The place Ali recommends for lunch is a tiny take-out on a triangular stone intersection with three or four tables under a canvas roof where the breeze

Ali the hairdresser

from a noisy ceiling fan begins to evaporate the sweat from our faces. It must have reached well above 40; we are soaked and starving. We sit for half an hour, hungrily eating two chicken sandwiches, munching fresh-made Halvah, and sipping water — simple and revitalizing — at this oasis.

We think it's time to leave, to return to the "other side." This part of the Old City feels like a well worn and poor neighborhood — in American terms, a black neighborhood. The cars are old and battered, the shops filled with people talking and gesturing and unfailingly warm and welcoming. We struggle just to remember the word for thank you. But they love it when we try. "How much," I ask, about lunch. "Three million," the waiter replies. Three Turkish Lira — they clearly had a substantial devaluation recently — which makes it about a dollar for the whole show.

As we walk back to the checkpoint, the Moslem call to prayer floats overhead, minor and sweet. And then a heap of a white car, maybe a Fiat or a Ford, pulls up. Two teenage boys sit in the front, the windows down, the bass all the way up, sharing the hip-hop music that has them nodding their heads up and down. A split second later a cell phone rings. I recognize the tune. It's "Micha Mocha" from the Jewish Sabbath service. That seems to say it all.

05 | 09 | 2005

Our fourth-floor flat is in the new city, the bursting, car dealer filled, ATM'd, euro-style Mediterranean city, its neighborhoods sprouting pastel-colored six-story condominiums amidst occasional vacant lots strewn with sand, an occasional dead cat, and other detritus. Our own local dead cat greeted us on arrival. It lies on its side alongside a concrete wall, across the street from the spanking new computer store. In fact, the city is filled with cats, usually scrawny, slinking everywhere — in doorways, alleys, vacant lots — wherever people leave handfuls of dry food. Like the cats, cars park themselves randomly everywhere, on sidewalks, empty street corners, in driveways. "We love rules," my new department head, a psycho-linguist tells me. "But, if we find they are in our way, you know, not right for us, well, then, we have to change them." He announces this as we search for a space at a restaurant adjacent to the University of Cyprus, and bounce up on a curb, two wheels on the street, two on the piece of sidewalk that extends for a few meters.

We knock at number 51 upstairs. Our neighbors are slow to come to the door. We can't tell if the door bell is working; it's a small plastic toggle switch in the hall next to an identical plate that turns the light off and on for a minute at a time. The TV inside their flat is broadcasting something in Greek. We can't understand that either. The door opens finally, and a small man with gray mustache, yellow golf shirt and a new pair of sport sandals peers up at us. His smile lights up the dim hallway, but his eyes say, who are you, what do you want? We explain that we are from the apartment below and want to pay our "common charge" (not that we have a clue what that is). We ask, "Me latte Anglika?" do you speak English, one of the four Greek phrases we have mastered in our first few days. He grins, eyes clear, calls out in English to his wife, "Roula, the Americans are here."

Costas and Roula take us in. We are fed, proffered coffee, water, and fruit. They tell us about their three married children, two of whom attended college in Ohio, their family business operating Timberland and Nautica stores in Cyprus and Romania, Costas'career as an accountant for AT&T and then NCR in Dayton. And, as so often seems to happen, the conversation becomes serious, political. It's not that their warm and open demeanor changes, but something changes — it is as if they are searching to see if we will understand their story. The same thing happened to us the day before, when the head of the Cyprus Fulbright Commission, a lovely man named Daniel, told us about his father's disappearance in 1974 just on the heels of the Turkish "invasion" of the northern part of the island. Sharing political stories carries with it here, we think, the same confessional weight as personal intimacy does in contemporary American culture.

Roula and Costas came to the southern, Greek half of Nicosia more than thirty years ago. As newlyweds they had lived in north Nicosia, driving to work in the city from their home just beyond the walls of the Old City. The division of the island after 1974 left them displaced, "refugees." They abandoned their house and land north of the Old City and did not return to see it for a generation. Only after the border slowly and painfully opened to visitors from either side did they gain access to the home they had once owned in the north.

As Roula told it, in contrast with her husband's sense of getting on with it, the memories have never receded. They moved to South Nicosia, raised three children, led a good and prosperous life. Only the year before last, when the

Roula and Costas with his two sons

first check point opened to allow Cypriots to venture back to "The north," did Roula and Costas return to their house — just to see it, just for a moment.

"It was all there. My furniture. Everything," Roula remembers. Her face shows her spirit, generous and kind, proud of her children, even prouder of her grandchildren. "We had a big lemon tree at that house. Very big." And when Roula asked the Turkish Cypriot woman who had been living in the house for more than thirty years if she could see the tree, the woman told her it was gone. "Why? It was so beautiful," Roula asked. "Too big," she was told.

They have not gone back to the house. It makes me think, and I'm not really sure why, about Tim O'Brien's book, *The Things They Carried.* I will teach it to my Greek Cypriot students this term in my American Studies course at the University. O'Brien repeats a moment when an American soldier in Vietnam, one of O'Brien's platoon, steps on a land mine. "Lemon Tree," O'Brien calls him, his body parts hanging from the jungle branches.

09 | 11 | 2005

We are invited to a Sunday dinner in a tiny village on the west coast of Cyprus. It's a two-hour drive along the motorway from Nicosia, but it takes us another half hour to find our way through the labyrinth of narrow streets and stone buildings of the village of Ineia. Some men, sitting at an outdoor cafe — a kind of open balcony above a limestone wall — smile each time we drive by. On our third pass they look out and laugh. "That way," they point, to the intersection that we have managed to miss each time around. They grin when we wave back.

At dinner, our hosts serve a meal with enough food for three days. But the heart of the event is a Slouva, a roast goat on open fire — large chunks of coal that burn white and send waves of shimmering heat rising into the summer air. An electric spit turns the joints of goat for hours until the pieces are crisp and deep brown and dripping. I ask my host if I may use my hands to pick up the meat and he grins. "Mr. Peter," a common use of the polite and the formal, "We have a saying here on Cyprus. You use your hands for two things. Slouva and women." He glances at my wife to see her reaction. But Maroula, a Greek-speaking woman who claims not to know any English, bats him across the arm as he raises it to protect his face. She's laughing and so is he.

This ancient village looks down on the sea. It is nestled high in the foothills of a mountain plateau — the Trodos — that dominates the western half of Cyprus. When we drive closer we have a sense of the drama of the landscape. The coast curves out below us, a crescent stretching as far as the eye can see southward to Paphos, an old-new tourist city, with white low buildings hugging the shore line. From our perch, about 2,000 feet high, Paphos looks miniature. It is an English-dominated beach resort, our host tells us. We pass sign after sign proffering Paphos district villas, seaside cottages, and Mediterranean estates that creep up on the arid outskirts of these traditional Greek-Cypriot villages. Only time and a new highway will allow for real development, I think. Then look out — Home Depot, Wal-Mart, here we come.

We slow down to watch a shepherd, bent over, leaning on his staff, loping up down up down as he guides his flock across a field beside the narrow road. The cannon-ball sized white rocks that are everywhere, sharing the dry soil with scrub brush and olive trees, have been gathered up to form wonderful irregular walls that separate us from the shepherd. He belongs to a traditional world, one we imagine that shares the region with the men at the cafe.

He's dressed in black, like the olive picking woman down the road. But as we stop and snap his picture and he smiles radiantly at the camera, I see that his clothing is of a single piece. He has wrapped it round his waist, like a skirt, and then brought the end between his legs and tucked it into the material at his mid-section, making legs out of the skirt. His weathered face, deeply lined, squints back at us and he continues on his way.

This is the Cyprus of the postcards and tourist books. Not busy and cosmopolitan Nicosia, but clearly a vanishing Cyprus. No. I know better. It's a shrinking Cyprus, but these small villages and stone streets and tiny churches and traditional ways of cultivation and dress will, I am absolutely sure, find ways to survive. Even in the face of British golf courses and retirement communities.

09 | 17 | 2005

The kitchen of our fourth floor apartment faces north. The balcony — we leave the door open all day and night to catch the breeze — serves as storage for mops, the spare gas canister for our stove, garbage, and the rickety clothes-drying rack that hangs out over the awning a story below. Sitting in the kitchen I can always see the rugged mountains in the north. They are like knuckles, dark and jutting and crooked, that carve the horizon into jigsaw shapes. If they were not there I'm sure we could see all the way to the north coast, about 30 kilometers, all the way into the sea that separates Cyprus from Turkey.

The view does allow us to see into the Old City, Lefkosa the signs now proclaim, past the new six-story apartments with balconies like ours that boast roof-top arrays of electronic gear — antennas, satellite dishes, solar panels, tubular water tanks — that would make a battleship proud. The low, brown, small and venerable houses of the Old City, north and South, offer a curious illusion. Their diminished size, compared with our suburban scale, makes them look tiny and very far away, much smaller and further than they actually are. And yet looming above them, about three quarters of the way up the tallest knuckle in the gray-black mountains to the north, the TRNC has constructed a mural of a Turkish-Cypriot flag on the hillside. It seems as big as twenty square Old City blocks, looming overhead. Its red crescent moon and star on a white field looks down on all of us. We see it all day. And I wonder about its presence — provocative or proud or taunting — when I see it every morning. Someone tells us that it appeared overnight, on some Greek Cypriot military holiday celebration, and subsequently made it into the Guinness Book of World Records as the world's largest flag. It feels like a finger in the eye to me.

We travel twice this week to the north, both times in a car through a different checkpoint. Same story, however, as our first time — indifferent and bored guards, curious tourists, and UN officials in too-big cars driving too fast. One difference: some hustle has been created to have us purchase separate automobile insurance for any ventures into north Cyprus. So, next to the passport booths at the Turkish entry position, jovial men sit selling a piece of paper for the equivalent of 50 dollars that will presumably protect us from mishap for 90 days. We schmooze with one about his cousin in Milwaukee who complains about the winters. Then we are on our way.

The guide books tell us that north Cyprus remains poor. It looks poor. White and uniform and sitting on sandy lots in open flat fields, government housing vies for space and visual attention with massive billboards. Our favorite, Taitles Casio, a gigantic red and gray affair, becomes in our minds a sign for "the Tasteless Casino." But the roads are straight, there is little traffic, and we follow the valley all the way to the eastern-most part of Cyprus and the city of Famagusta.

Famagusta, once the tourist pride of Cyprus, has fallen on difficult times. The grand old seaside hotels have closed and stand empty, like a ghost town in the American west. In their place has risen a new university, a whitewashed cinder block campus accented with steel and glass, whose halls admit 11,000 new students. Eastern Mediterranean University, as it is now called, is integrated into the Turkish University system. It looks out over the sea, towards Lebanon, but the area between the campus and the beach is rough terrain, torn up and disheveled. The Turkish army maneuvers there, we are told; sometimes tank turrets point into the faculty dining room. It feels very different from my other academic home, in the south, the University of Cyprus. Eastern Mediterranean University is an entirely English-speaking, large, and comprehensive university; the University of Cyprus, despite its standing as a national university, is small, with instruction in Greek, and a Greek-run English literature and linguistics program. At Famagusta, at EMU, we are introduced to the English department, a collective of about 6 middle-aged men, American and British academics, a bit forlorn, a bit bedraggled, who are led by a dynamo.

Loriannia Pinnell, she is called. She reminds me of Honor Blackman from one of the Bond films, but with a long and sharply-featured face that I'm sure, at first, is Greek. Turns out she's Scottish — another ex-pat at the university. Loriannia has pazazz, a dash of charisma; in addition to chairing the English Department, she is also Dean of Humanities. I readily agree to give four talks at her school over the course of the semester.

Our venture north would give us courage to return two days later — this time to the beach. For now, we head back to the Nicosia-Lefkosia checkpoint, and drive north, right into the dark mountains that sport the Turkish-Cypriot flag. The only clouds we have seen in three weeks on Cyprus hang, puffs on a necklace, around the ragged peaks. We speed across the plain that extends from the city to the foothills, and then start to climb in a long upward swooping curve through a pass between two jagged hilltops. And as we hoped, when we clear the pass, Kyrenia, a port city, lays spread out at our feet, a tumble of white that spills into the sea, the dark blue glistening Mediterranean.

They tell us that on a clear day one can see Turkey from Kyrenia, but for us, the sea extends north to the horizon. It is enough. Kyrenia turns out to be very, very English. They are everywhere, in the taverns that have tables along the horseshoe-shaped stone harbor that dominates the town's center, on queues for day boat trips to fish or snorkel, and in the ramparts of the local castle, a lumbering affair constructed by some French noble who got lost on the way to one of the Crusades. Inside the castle, in one of the chambers, they display the hull of a Greek ship lost at sea in 300 BC and only recently recovered. It's a knockout, allowing our imaginations to walk down its gangplank, to see the hold filled to overflowing with pottery containers of wine and almonds, to visualize life on these islands almost 2,500 years ago.

With tables outside by the water, a kitchen on the periphery in the street-level buildings that circle the harbor, each restaurant has its glib tickler. They stand, these dark boys, smiling, and invite us to dine, to sail, to jabber. They could be along any tourist route in Paris, or Florence, or even New Orleans. But here, next to the water, framed by hulls of old and sturdy fishing boats, they really seem picaresque. "Just call me Charlie," one calls out.

Directions are not the forte of Cypriots, Greek or Turkish. Maybe it's just a reflection of our own culture, where every Uncle Bob has his "better" way of getting there — to the movies, the funeral home, to the beach. Here, we spend hours trying to find a tiny key shop, "two traffic lights, then left. Only thirty meters." It is three lights, and three hundred meters. So, driving west along the north coast of Cyprus, Kyrenia in our rearview mirror, we have no expectations. My wife has three maps and guide books spread out on her lap and at her feet. They all show little umbrellas stamped on the side of the road, but as we drive all we can see are dirt streets leading to yet another Tasteless Casino or Sea-View Villas Estates Development — unfinished, baking in the sun, brick and concrete skeletons that will one day house a dozen more British retirees.

Finally we find the beach. Or, a beach — and it's perfect. Perfectly low key, low rent. And Turkish-British. Picture two dozen faux-wicker umbrellas, green ones, stabbed into small concrete-filled Michelin tires, each shading a pair of wood chaise-lounges. For 8 Lira, about 1.5 Cyprus pounds or three dollars, they are ours for the day. A young boy drags out two blue mats for comfort, flops them on the lounges and points to the concrete patio behind us. It is covered with a grape arbor and attached to a cinder-block bunker which is also a kitchen. Plastic tables and chairs are scattered across the patio. Later, we eat an absolutely smashing cheese sandwich and salad in the shade of that arbor.

The Mediterranean — that is something to behold, to hold, to savor, to indulge. Warm but fresh, a sweet breeze blowing straight from Turkey, the bottom sandy and firm, the sea tells us to relax, to swim or float, to dream. This is why they have been coming here for 4,000 years. Is it also what they have been fighting over, I wonder? Why bother if you can just take in the sun and salt and let your body tingle with delight. There's got to be enough coastline, probably 500 miles of it all around, for everyone.

We have noticed — in fact it is impossible to ignore — that along this stretch of coastline, perhaps 25 kilometers west of Kyrenia, the Turkish military is deeply entrenched. Military bases rush up to us along the road every few minutes, almost with the same frequency as the concrete mixer trucks that barrel along past us in the other direction.

One local Greek Cypriot tells us just after we return from Kyrenia that Cyprus is "just like America, just smaller." Well, it's a lot smaller, but he may just have something. Take the map of Cyprus and turn it about 20 degrees to the south and you have the outline of something like the United States, in miniature. In this sense, Nicosia is akin to St. Louis, while Kyrenia is near Chicago. The long peninsula in the north, Karpas, becomes Maine; Paphos corresponds to San Diego; Larnaca to St. Petersburg and Limassol to Houston. Easy when you see it this way. Thing is, it takes about 5 hours to drive coast to coast on Cyprus, compared to the five days to cross the States.

09 | 23 | 2005

Our upstairs neighbors, Costas and Roula, take us out to dinner. An informal joint in the neighborhood with a dozen outdoor tables, a Margaritaville bar in the center. It's called the Calypso Restaurant. They order for us REAL souvlaki, kebabs on a stick, fresh and sweet, and joints of lamb, grilled and succulent. We sit and talk for hours. They have become our friends, somewhere between mentors and an aunt and uncle.

Costas talks this night, and Roula listens, hanging on every word. He's a gifted storyteller, gets an avuncular twinkle in his eye, and rolls his "r"s with sweet élan. He grew up in a farming village north of Nicosia, he tells us, but had neither gift nor inclination for the land. He knew he wanted to make it to the city, and needed a wife to make the journey with him. So, as I struggled in the 1950s to "get to second base" with any number of girls with elbows as sharp as their tongues, he studied accounting by correspondence courses from England, preparing for his migration.

His life changed one day when the village priest told him of young woman who lived near Nicosia and asked if Costas might be interested in meeting her. He was. They met under the supervision of the priest and both their families. "Impossible," he says twinkling, "to even touch her hand." He touches the back of her arm with such sweetness at that moment that I swear she blushes, sitting there in the cool evening forty years later. "I'll never forget the first time I saw her," he remembers, and this time her eyes twinkle. "She was so lovely."

After The Invasion — that's how they talk about it, in capital letters, The Turkish Invasion of 1974 — they fled to the South. Their home and property in the north was given to a Turkish-Cypriot family. They have visited twice in the last few years. Roula says, "You know, I can not hate them, the family who lives in our house — they still have my dining room. No, it is not their fault. They didn't do this." There is no glitter in her eyes when she talks about this. "We will take you there," she announces. I wonder what that will be like, traveling back in time with them.

09 | 25 | 2005

Time to start recording the date in Cyprus style. We attend our second football match. This week between APOEL, the Nicosia-based team that our friends support, and their rivals from Limassol, a city to the South on the coast. As we walk up to the stadium, a modern curved concrete and steel structure built just off the main highway, we see rings of barbed wire strung along the sloping walkways that curl up toward the field. Crowds pour into the area, on foot, on motor scooters and motorcycles, mostly men, many teenaged, team scarves draped around their shoulders. Young men, lots of energy, bouncing on the balls of their feet, running ahead, high-fiving their pals. Between the concrete banister and the crowd stand clusters of armed soldiers, many resting their translucent plexiglass shields on the ground, at their feet. When I ask what they are for, Costas, whose son is the treasurer of the local team (and hence the source our wonderful tickets high up in the stands on the 50 yard line) tells me simply, "in case of trouble." Later, his son Michael says that the government charges the Cyprus Football League about a million pounds a year for "protection." Double that to get dollars.

APOEL versus Limassol – “SING LOUD”

As the game evolves, I forget about my fantasy/memory of some Central American soccer war about 20 years ago. I get caught up in the spirit of the game. It's fun. And exciting. The fans, all the energy-loaded young men, have gone to the end-zone all decked out in the teams' colors, bright orange (actually the colors are green and yellow, but they "sell" orange gear). There they stand, chant, wave banners, tell Limassol's "fanatics" in the other end zone seats that they are "bastards." Like "Boston Sucks," I say smartly to my host, who went to college in the States. He smiles. So, as the game on the field continues, the fans at both the goal-ends of the stadium keep up a constant beat, each trying to exhaust the other.

When our team scores a questionable goal (questionable because it was a penalty shot in the last minute based on a foul that some think never happened) the Limassol fans erupt. While our fans scream and cheer and set off flares and rockets, 150 yards across the length of the field, the kids from Limassol push and shove their way towards the part of the stadium, along both sidelines, where the rest of us sit. It's not mayhem — not yet — but it's inching there. Only then do we see a squadron of riot police file down the steps along side goal-line seats, shields up, batons raised, to cordon off the entire section. They will not allow the Limassol fans to leave until all the Nicosia supporters have gone home. I wonder if any will lay in wait. The game ends in a tie, and on the radio afterwards, the German coach of Limassol tells the audience in English that he wuz robbed. "We can't allow ourselves to be defeated by a questionable penalty."

09 | 29 | 2005

I give my first talk of four at Eastern Mediterranean University in Famagusta today. We arrive an hour early and drive into the center of the city of Famagusta, wiggling our way to the old sea port and up to the Venetian Walls, a small replica of the walls around Nicosia. Othello's Castle reads one sign, and then Desdemona's Bar and Grille. So, this is where Shakespeare set his play. The city had once been the center of Mediterranean raunch, the guide book informs us. No longer. Clearly Famagusta is a poor town, its once-fabled beach hotels abandoned, its tiny streets poor and broken. A large Orthodox church, the color of sand and roofless, has been transformed into a Mosque. A Minaret juts up from inside like a weed. Even the tall windows have been covered by painted wood shutters, with hundreds of tiny slits cut for light and ventilation.

We wander the street a bit, finding a small table inside an Turkish Cypriot coffee bar, owned by a couple who smile to beat the band and speak no English. They point proudly to the old black and white photograph on the wall, "Ataturk." These folks are tiny, almost copper in color, and remind me of the painting that the artist Achile Gorkey did of his Armenian parents. The phone rings and the man busies himself pouring two demitasse cups of coffee. He places them on a tray alongside two glasses of water and then, tray in hand, walks out the door, down the street. Home delivery. We see this all the time in the Old City, in Nicosia/Lefkosia.

A bit further down the street D stops to admire a barren banana tree and an older man comes out of his shop to explain that some kids had picked the fruit just the night before. He looks at us — I love his face, long and deep and smiling — and points disapprovingly at the paper under his arm. "No one understands," he says choosing his words carefully. "No one who is not from here. Turkey is playing with the EU. But we are not the same here. They are Greek and Christian, we are Turkish and Moslem." The gist is that Turkey will, one day soon, abandon its protection of the north to join the EU. I've been wondering about that myself. He takes us inside his shop, which turns out to be a soft-drink factory, and offers us a glass of Bubble Up! He's been bottling it for 20 years in partnership with a company in Baltimore. "But we can't compete with Coke and Pepsi," he tells us. "So, I sell." Ali Eyup, educated as an engineer in Istanbul, soft drink maker in Famagusta, will soon start producing "old" carved wood objects in the new industrial park on the outskirts of the city.

The room they have me speak in today is called the Blue Hall, a large auditorium filled with deep blue-velvet upholstered theater chairs. It is also called the Ralf Denktash room, in honor of the leader of the Northern Republic who began his political career in the mid-1950s as a Turkish-Cypriot partisan leader opposing Enosis, Cypriot unity with Greece.

Denktash has been at the forefront of Turkish Cypriot politics for almost half a century. He has only recently been replaced by a younger man, one they say is more committed to reconciliation and unification.

I speak to a room full of students and faculty from all over. They are mostly first-year students who seem alternately attentive and glazed when I play them the blues of Muddy Waters. It's curious trying to teach American Studies out of context. I need to explain everything, and so I go slower, even slower than in the South. But, in contrast to my students at the University of Cyprus, these Turkish students come in all shapes, sizes, and colors — Africans, north Africans, Arabs, Turks, Turkish Cypriots — and speak many flavors of English. I can't tell if any of them have heard the blues before, so I stand before them, sweating in the close heat, and give it my best.

D tells me it went really well. I remind her about the shopkeeper the other day who told me that I spoke Greek well. Three words including "gizmo" for mixer came out of my mouth. But, I am usually not the best judge of my teaching efforts, and seem to need several repeats before I become comfortable. I wonder how it will go next time. And I wonder what my colleagues at EMU thought of my presentation. I genuinely want the feedback, in part because I sense that it wasn't perfect, and in part because I want to "learn" that it actually was perfect.

09 | 30 | 2005

It is six a.m. The building across the street is coming alive. They have finished the brick work and are now mixing concrete to cover the joints, which makes a racket. The building is directly across the street, but a vacant lot sits between our avenue, Kennedy, and the building site. This is where the dead cat has lain for the past 5 weeks, black and stretched out, its tail just edging into the driveway of the shop next store. Everyone in our building, and that now includes us, tries to park in the hard sand and gravel of the lot that is clearly part of the building site. If all the "spaces" are taken, some just block the rest of us in. The lot is about 200 feet deep, connecting our street to the new building. In the middle of the lot another car, long-term parking we think, sits untouched, unclaimed. It has been gathering dust since we arrived here. We imagine ghoulishly that the driver was on that Helios jet that crashed near Athens just before we flew in.

The day seems to me to show the contradictions of Cyprus — part first world, part third. The cat perfectly preserved by the dry heat doesn't even seem to smell, as if it can't rot. Next door to the cat is a computer shop, one of six that line our street, cheek by jowl with the other appliance, TV, DVD and electronic stores that are everywhere. Almost as many shops as stray cats. These scrawny, under-fed cats roam around, tails high, shopping for scraps. What kind of metaphor is that, I wonder? And where do the workers who climb the scaffolding every day, dark and sweaty, where do they live?

It rains for the first time since our arrival almost five weeks ago. Dark clouds, claps of thunder, white lightning strikes over the mountains to the north, so dark between strikes that it obliterates the Turkish Cypriot flag engraved on the hillside. And the drops come slowly at first, big full drops, eight inches apart, plopping drops of water, the most precious resource on this dry arid island surrounded by the sea. They tell us that not a single drop of rain on Cyprus can find its way to the sea, it is all trapped, dammed, sluiced and saved in cisterns and reservoirs. And still the land in the east, from Nicosia/Lefkosa to the far shore, north and south, looks thirsty.

As I walk around the city this morning, dodging cars that speed down local streets like as if it were Le Mans, and then stepping around others parked randomly half on the sidewalk, half on the street, all the way on the sidewalk, vertically, horizontally, any which way, I muse about boundaries. The Green Line that divides north and south, with still only a few checkpoints open for workers, tourists, or gamblers, serves surely as a gnawing and painful boundary for people in both communities. Roads end arbitrarily, red signs tell all they cannot pass, oil cans and barbed wire run along streets that once belonged to both sides, and now belong to only one. In fact, there were no “sides” then, regions, districts, neighborhoods perhaps, but not sides. The Republic of Cyprus, the South, simply ends. The Turkish Republic, legal only in the eyes of Turkey, barely even exists. No wonder Cypriots ignore other boundaries, it’s a kind of freedom for them to not play by the rules. The rules have always been someone else’s rules.

10 | 03 | 2005

We wander up into the mountains this weekend, the range that seems to sit in the middle of Cyprus, between Nicosia and Limassol. Our guidebook directs us to Lefkara, the home of the island's lace artisans. It feels like an Italian hill town, built high in the mountains with narrow streets, stone-paved, with tinges of blue wash on the doors, faded green shutters, and corners that can't be seen around. There must be hundreds of these villages in Cyprus, places where people lived forever, since before Nicosia became such a big deal, commerce and automobiles dominated, international travel and education proliferated. And, as far as I can tell, this world is only a single generation in the past. One day last week, our landlord came to visit and help fix a few things. He sat with us and drank the Cypriot (aka Turkish) coffee that my wife D learned to make. Suddenly the doorbell rang. A man from the phone company arrived to install our internet modem. They greeted each other, our landlord and the phone technician, like long-lost brothers. "We come from the same village," Andreas explained. "I helped coach his football team." It felt like a bond second only to that of family, and reminded me that much of modern Cyprus is probably less than 40 years old. So much, then, has changed so fast, and not just politically either.

In Lefkara we wander in and out of lace shops in whose doorways sit elderly women sewing patterns, eager to invite "lady, and you, gentleman" in. "Just for a look. No obligation," they announce sweetly yet very aggressively, even flirtatiously. But one shop is somehow different. The woman in this doorway is sewing, but really intently. When I ask to take her photograph she nods but keeps working. Then her husband strides over. He's a tall and well proportioned muscular man of indeterminate age. I think 70, which makes him older than I; my wife D thinks 57, making him younger.

He asks if we like Cyprus, where we are from, and if we recognize the photograph perched on the glass display case. It is of a soldier in his 40s, a green-beret type. A Colonel. "That is me. I am still in the reserves," he says proudly. "I am called Glenn. Yes. Glenn." Colonel Glenn, I think — sure has a ring to it.

As happens to us so many times, Glenn turns our conversation to politics almost immediately. He quizzes me. The burden of his rhetoric being They have told us what to do for too long. They, of course, were the English and are now the Americans. As Pogo said, "They are us." I understand him in terms of the history of Cyprus I've been reading. Everyone seems to have had a stake in Cyprus. Turks, Greeks, English, Americans to be sure — but NATO and the UN and now the EU as well. Remarkably, Glenn's take is simply (of course it's not simple) — "Give us back control of our lands and we'll find a way to live together."

"And now, my dear lady," he says, taking my wife's hand, "I will teach you about lace." And he does for a half hour — patterns and stitching, and the local old ladies who do the work and how to tell what's good. It turns out he has an office in Nicosia, just down the street from where we live. We promise to phone him there to talk more.

11 | 03 | 2005

We pile into the car and drive all the way east in Cyprus, this time in the north and east, up the Karpas peninsula, which juts about 50 miles into the corner of the Mediterranean where Turkey meets Lebanon ("A dagger into the heart of Turkey," is how that old goat Winston Churchill once put it). It's a long ride because the road is narrow and winding and because it climbs the mountains that run east and west for almost the entire stretch of the northern portion of the island. The peninsula can't be more than 10 kilometers wide and it's virtually deserted. I don't think to speculate why. Large farms stretch along both sides of the road, each for many kilometers. Some farms reveal freshly disked fields and many more have sheep and goats and wild donkeys grazing peacefully. There is not a soul in sight. We climb up and down the hairpin turns. Except for the spine of the mountains that continue to extend all the way east, it looks a bit like the remote part of Cape Cod, scrubby and sandy. Blue Mediterranean water appears all around, as the peninsula narrows. Finally a sign, small and hand painted, like something from a kids lemonade stand:

HASSANS — OK FOR CARS

It marks a hard packed sand road that leads about half a mile to the beach, to a row of a dozen umbrellas and plastic lounge chairs with perhaps eight people sitting, sunning, sleeping. Another clump of the same, maybe half a mile south, and that's it. The entire beach, called Golden Beach, clear, white sand 300 yards deep, runs for miles. It's a glorious Sunday afternoon, warm with bright sun that makes the water into trembling pale aqua carpet. It is remote, beautiful and empty, and only Hassan, a Turkish-Cypriot marine biologist who studies local sea turtles, seems to live there. He also runs a generator-supported food joint/cozy-cabin motel in a grove of trees back from the water. Hassan, who looks like Mister Clean, is lively and muscular. He invites us to have a drink, sitting in the shade. But once he sees we are not interested in anything more, he retreats behind the bar and busies himself washing dishes.

We have come to Paradise, we agree later. We slip into the water and feel the salt envelope us, caressing our skin. The dried apricots and fresh almonds we bring in tiny plastic bags taste as sweet as if they have been sent by the gods. The bright sun glows toward our left, just beginning its descent that will take it behind the mountains we have just crossed. Paradise. Except there is no one around, and the more I think about it, the more eerie it feels.

10 | 03 | 2005

Lillias, the youngest daughter of Costas and Roula, meets us for coffee at the Hilton Hotel down the street from our place. It is a grand Imperial-style palace, crowded with well-turned-out clientele, about as far from Hassan's as one can imagine — white coated bellhops, quadrilingual managers in sharp gray suits with silver ties, shops that sell Bulgari and Rolex, and in the late afternoons a piano bar. It's an island on this island, and we go there daily to work out and swim. Lilia, who lives in the suburbs and works as the marketing director with her father in the multi-store Timberland business they operate on Cyprus, comes to the Hilton once a week while her daughter has swimming lessons.

She asks, and really is interested, about our weekend. I begin with great enthusiasm to describe the trip to Golden Beach, on the Karpas peninsula. But I hold back, not wanting to hurt her feelings about "the other side." And it's a good instinct. When I say, clumsily, that she might put aside politics and really enjoy this place, she looks away. It's not about politics, she says slowly, and her eyes find the mountains. They are the ones we see from our kitchen window, with the Turkish Cypriot flag on them, the ones I have called knuckles, and just

Lilia

learned are actually the Pentadactyl mountains, the five-fingered mountains, part of the chain that run east-west across the island and out to the Karpas peninsula. We see these all the time, she says, and we have been to Kyrenia once since they opened the border, "but it is..." She pauses and can't find the right word. But we can see it is something inside her, something powerful, perhaps beyond words. She is not sad, but reflective. She was born the year that Cyprus changed, in 1974, the year of "The Invasion." Her children play at her feet, and we sit at a poolside table on a lovely October afternoon, and she finishes. "It is something emotional. I can't quite explain it better." And I understand, I think, how painful is the fact of this divided land to the people who live here.

10 | 03 | 2005

The chair of the English department at the University of Cyprus just told me that at 4 a.m. today the EU approved the process by which Turkey will be admitted to "Europe." This will have a major impact on Cyprus' future, and maybe even an end to the partition that so vexes everyone on this, the Greek Cypriot, side. On the other hand, maybe it's just another larger entity emerging to dictate Cyprus' fate.

There is a story going around about 1974, just after the Turkish Invasion of the north, when the Greek-Cypriot mayor of Nicosia invited a host of diplomatic big wigs to dinner. They feasted, enjoyed cigars and brandy, and then asked to use the rest room. The mayor had to inform them that due to the partition the sewage system of the city no longer functioned. The important people left horrified. Within a month both sides of the Green Line in Nicosia had their waste and sewage connected. This was 32 years ago, where, at least in Nicosia, shit runs both ways.

10 | 03 | 2005

We spent the weekend on an exquisite Greek island, Santorini, a blue/white gem in the Aegean. Our hotel looked out over the crater of a now-extinct volcano, a view that was breathtaking in its drama and beauty. The babble of languages — Greek, English, German, Swedish, Finnish, and French — seemed endless, with Australian, South African, British, Canadian, Indian, and American accents tossed in for good measure. More than European, it seemed like a world center of upper-middle-class tourism. I strike up a conversation with the young man who staffs the desk of the hotel, and it enlivens when he learns that I am living on Cyprus. "They are very nice, the Cypriots. But they are not Greek," he announces. "What do you mean?" I ask. "They are too, how shall I say, Anglo-Saxon," he says. I look as if I understand what he is saying. In fact, I think I do. "You know," he continues, "when they check in here, they do not register in Greek, in our script, but in English." "So you feel they are a bit snooty?" I say, leading the witness. "Exactly." It gives me pause, this question of cultural identity. Everyone on Cyprus whom we have met, and that means educated middle-class Greek Cypriots, has gained professional status and certification from Britain: aircraft pilots, academics, accountants, a singer and mime, a diplomat, an electrical engineer, a film critic, and even a barber. Its more than an imperial overlay, more than the Cyprus Raj, I'm beginning to think; it's part of a public cultural identity, one that is not identical with the private — in this case Greek —one. I'm not sure yet what that means.

10 | 03 | 2005

Today I spend much of the day wandering through the Old City, the Greek side of the Old City of Nicosia. I take photos where I can — of old men sitting a tiny curb-side cafe, an even older man just standing in the shade of the narrow road, and later of a place where the street ends abruptly. There, oil drums piled two stories high cast a long shadow across the ancient cobblestones, and yet more barbed wire looms overhead. The street, the city, the official nation of Cyprus, all tumble down an old street into a 30-year-old barricade. For the first time I see the wooden frames that soldiers jammed into the seams between rows of sandbags to allow their guns a wide field of fire. I know it's there — the Green Line runs right through the Old City, east to west — but it's still a shock to come around a corner and be confronted by the end. It is a deep scar that won't go away. A Greek Cypriot soldier, a kid, slouches against the wall and tells me not to take the photograph that I have just snapped.

The streets, crooked and so narrow that one can almost stretch one's arms and touch the buildings on both sides, hide the late afternoon sun. Shadows fall everywhere, cutting across the dusty plate glass windows of shoe makers

Sandbags along the Green Line

and sandal shops, of hand laundries and tiny housewares stores whose displays of stainless Turkish coffee pots glint in the irregular sunlight. Old-fashioned clothing shops — not the glittering and hip stuff you find outside the Old City — sell bolts of material, black or black with just a hint of white or purple in small geometric shapes, that one sees on elderly ladies in the neighborhood — local women with great faces, with so much character that I can almost feel the engraved texture of their skin with my eyes.

Lefkonos is the street that meanders parallel to the Green Line. We have become friends with Leo and Soteria, a couple who run a film-screening place on Lefkonos called the Weaving Mill. It feels like it ought to have been in Paris in 1960 — but far too low-rent for that city today. The Weaving Mill is an informal bohemian cultural center, with sofas and directors chairs scattered about so we can watch films comfortably, furnished with up to date technology, wood shelves filled with DVDs and books on film, coolers stocked with beer and soft drinks, and a coffee bar. The Weaving Mill shows films — some serious and cultural, some simply for entertainment — most nights during the week. It's a safe place, we learn, a place for Greek and Turkish Cypriots to gather and talk, for experimental filmmakers, photographers and poets. It's located in a series of three old shops that are now one continuous space, with a loft upstairs that houses offices and yet more equipment.

Leo shows a set of films for my class on some Wednesdays. The students pile in — remarkably, some have never been to the Old City before — from the suburbs and collapse into the deep old leather chairs, light up (everyone in Cyprus seems to smoke) and watch. We saw "Guess Who's Coming to Dinner" this week. They seem to have loved it. I put it up for a segment on feminism and they were equally divided over how "really feminist is it when Spencer Tracy has the last word."

When I wander in around noon this day Leo and Soteria are hard at work. I want to photograph them. It's warm out already and Leo is schlepping boxes down from the loft. He wants no part of my request. "Look, I'm hot and sweaty, no movie star." He bends down with a box and looks up and grins. I take his picture. Soteria, on the other hand, sits for a minute, and I can see she loves the camera. I get three shots before she jumps up. "Enough. I don't really like to do this," she says and she's off. D and I like them, find them engaging and interesting. He's full of blarney and she is clearly the organizational brains of the outfit. A good team, it seems to us.

10 | 14 | 2005

A small adventure. We "discover" a lunch joint downtown in Nicosia, just outside the walls of the Old City, near the Fulbright office. It is simple and small, a cafeteria with a steam table that serves three or four home made dishes for lunch — Mousakka, stuffed grape leaves, Pasticcio, grilled chicken. After our third visit we are greeted like old friends, offered coffee, try to communicate. Trouble is, Irene, who runs the place, speaks about as much English as we do Greek, and only about half of that overlaps. But somehow she tells us that she has another restaurant in a village outside of Nicosia and that we should come on a Friday or Saturday. She writes down the name of the village, Veftera, on her card. Of course there are all these consonants in Greek that sound like something different in English. P's and B's or, it occurs to me late, V's and D's.

We are almost in our car and decide to check the map. There is no such place on as Veftera. But there is a town called Deftera and it seems relatively easy to get to. We decide to call, and, since Irene can't do English with us or we Greek with her, someone else takes the call. "Just in the center of town," the voice tells us, "near the church… in Deftera."

Of course it's night, we can't read the signs easily, the impatient Cypriot drivers do not at all tolerate our slowing and then speeding up at each intersection — we can tell this by the constant honking of horns and flashing of lights. I take it personally, a simple New Yorker's defensive reaction to criticism. But since they, the other drivers, can neither hear me nor see my hands, I do nothing in response. I'm feeling good about exercising this kind of restraint.

In a real gender bender, I stop the car in the middle of no place we've ever been before and say to my wife, "Can you ask how near we are to Deftera?" She's been urging me to keep going, that it's bound to be right ahead. But, she gets out and goes across the street for what seems to be a half-hour of conversation. Then she's back in the car and a white BMW with dark windows pulls along side, the window rolls down and a kid — a girl maybe 12 — begins to ask a question. My brain is already saying, "Look, I'm a dumb foreigner, I have no idea how to get where you want to go." Instead, she says in beautifully American-accented English, "Just follow us we'll take you to the restaurant." Despite the fact that the restaurant is only about three blocks away, it is clear that we'd have never found it on our own. My wife had simply called and they sent out a car to find us.

We are introduced to everyone — handshakes and kisses exchanged with cousins, uncles, mothers and grandfathers and the girl from the car. She is Andrea, Irene's niece. They all work at the restaurant, a small six-table souvlaki place. Andrea tends our table, translates for her aunt, the owner, and bustles around proud as proud can be. She's got a great smile and an open face. Finally we ask how she came to speak such good English, and she tells us that she's spent a lot of time in Houston, even a year once, and then other times for "checkups." I play a hunch, "At the Anderson Clinic?" Indeed, "for a transplant." Her dark eyes match her hair. She looks radiant.

The dinner, surrounded by table of Greek Cypriot men talking and gesturing loudly, a big screen TV is raucously broadcasting yet another football game. We have taken along another American couple, promising them an adventure, and they are up for it. Salads, yogurt and tahini and olive condiments followed by chicken and pork souvlaki, fresh pita and "patates," which turn out to be really crisp and tasty French fries. And beer and wine and a local schnapps called zivania and a heaping plate of fresh fruit. Throughout the several hours it takes to plow through this feast, different members of the family stop by and sit with us, Grandpa and Grandma, who cook and clean and wait, then the "boss" Irene, who shows us pictures of her four children. Irene looks 30, but her eldest daughter is 25 and about to have a child. Irene is small, slight, charming with a grin that lights up a room. Her English is good for numbers, names of food, and "how are you." But gestures, good will and laughter, and her niece Andrea, get the job done. Her younger sister, Andrea's other aunt, sits down and tells us, "Now you will have to come to our house. One Sunday for lunch." We give them our phone number and I get up and walk with her to the entry to the small dining room which opens right onto the small town square, so small you can almost reach out and touch the church across the street. Quietly, delicately I think, I ask for the bill. I know it will be modest even with all the alcohol we have consumed. Irene's father, the man who fetched us, who is planning to go to Houston with his granddaughter for her next check-up in November, hears me. "The first time," he smiles, his pencil mustache and bushy eyebrows jumping in two directions, "the first time is free, no charge."

We repeat the round of hugs and kisses on both cheeks. I hold Andrea's hands and give her a soul shake, knuckles to knuckles. D holds Irene and then

Pools of light and conversation — night-time Souvlaki on Kennedy Avenue

Andrea close. There is something compellingly tender about all of them, and D finally asks what we've all been thinking. "How are you doing," D smiles glowingly at Andrea, her question fragile and light. "Are you holding the transplant?"

Andrea smiles, unself-conscious and self-possessed. It is getting late, but there is no fatigue on this girl's face and her smile still glows with a sense of being at peace in the world. It's something inward, some special gift that has graced Andrea. We talk about the operation, until it becomes clear that she has had a bone-marrow transplant. When D asks about how she is feeling, I think she is really asking about rejection. Andrea tells us that the transplant is working. Her voice is matter of fact, her smile constant. After all, she informs us, she had a Turkish Cypriot donor. No rejection.

I've been thinking about this for two days. About culture and race and politics and about overcoming. I had my class hold hands and taught them to sing "We Shall Overcome," about two weeks ago. It still brings tears to my old/new left-wing eyes. We are talking and reading about Civil Rights. But I'm not at all sure that "The Movement" is a real guide to help the people on this wonderful and so very troubled island. Then again, I'm not sure that it isn't.

11 | 15 | 2005

As my friend Fred, back in the States, says, "The hits keep coming." We returned to the Turkish side of the Old City yesterday and walked around for three or four hours, talking to people like Mustafa, the shoe shop owner who was once an electrical engineer, and Ehemit, the shadow puppet artist who sells us a wooden flute and invites us back for a show next week. As we leave the quarter, I realize that we are only about 20 feet north of the Weaving Mill, on the "other" side, just beyond the sandbags and oil drums and barbed wire, "just over there," across the street that is now a wall. It will take about an hour to walk there now, across the UN "buffer zone" and through the checkpoint where customs officers will glance at our crumpled paper visas with about as much attention as a checkout girl at an American supermarket who tells you "have a nice day" right into her fingernails. I'm still thinking about Andrea's transplant, about the genetic match, as I wonder about these geographical and cultural and political distances.

We stop at a Turkish rug shop right before the buffer zone and spend about

Mustafa, electrical engineer and shoe shop owner

Cem and Seray at the Turkish rug shop

an hour with the owners, a couple who also take us into their world. Coffee and juice on trays, talk about where we live in "the states," and the man, Cem, pronounced Gem, disappears for a moment. He comes back as his wife Seray beams – she is a vivacious young woman who is a special education teacher and jewelry maker, beams. In his hands he holds a magnificent instrument, he calls it a Kanun. It looks familiar to us, although we have never heard the name before. He plays this 78-string zither for us, plays it beautifully and tells us that he's going to buy a new one that will cost $7,000. He has more music on the web and promises to burn a CD for us when we return in a week or two with our payment for the two rugs we have also purchased. Like their Greek counterparts across the line, Cem and Seray are warm and gracious and open and generous. "I am a patriot," he tells us, explaining that his family in Turkey (and Santa Monica) are all carpet merchants. They feel like a match for Costas and Roula in the "Greek community." It turns out that, in fact, Cem is Turkish to the core, not Turkish-Cypriot.

10 | 18 | 2005

My American Studies class at the University of Cyprus is moving along nicely. I'm having fun. The kids are all sweet and interesting, all the Elenas and Irenes, all 36 of them, with three male students thrown in for good measure. But now that I'm getting to know them better, these Greek Cypriot English majors in their last year at the University, I can see they are less heterogeneous than I had first imagined. Many come from mixed cultural backgrounds, English and Greek parents, Greek and Palestinian parents, Russian and Cypriot parents, Christian and Orthodox, a lone young man from Finland. Several talk like British students, others jabber in Greek so fast I can't even sense where one word ends and the next one begins. But it turns out they all love rap music. And they know this music, this American music, a lot better than I do.

This morning, four girls — slight, dark, bright eyed — come to class in black t-shirts with big glow-in-the-dark letters spelling out BITCH. It is their turn for a group presentation on Feminism. We've been talking for two weeks about Consciousness Raising in America in the 1960s (the subject of the course is America in the 60s), about the relationship between civil rights and feminism, about the difference between feminism and suffragism. We've read the stan-

Students ready for their presentation, and Thekla Constantinou, fiery secretary of the English Department

dards — Betty Friedan, Sarah Evans, and Sylvia Plath — and I've had the sense all along that these students are open-eyed, connected to the material in a way that they were not when we studied the Civil Rights Movement. I've asked them to reflect on their own cultural world and to see if the women's movement has had an effect here in Greek Cyprus.

The answer appears this morning in the guise of this spirited gang of four, decked out in their pink lettered T-shirts. They really take over the class and lead us through the early history of the women's movement in American, from Seneca Falls to the 19th Amendment, and then begin asking the rest of the class, where do contemporary Cypriots stand in relation to the American women's movement? But they do it via rap videos. They reach the class by playing music that they all hear and like but, apparently, don't listen to carefully. Some character named Fifty Cent who rap/sings about the "Candy Store," a booty-filled whore house where men get what they want, where they "melt in your mouth and not in your hand." I catch a reference to Eminem, and the M&M slogan, but still, who knew? What an elaborate and idealized male fantasy. And what works is that the students get it, that by not paying attention, by consuming American culture, they are only reinforcing these terrible images of women. I can feel this whole classroom of Greek-Cypriot women paying attention, having something important enter their consciousness. What I love is that this way of doing American Studies, of giving students control of the class content, actually works! Even better, they find a black female American female rap singer (why can't I use the word 'artist' here, I wonder?), Norah Jones, whose song, a take on The Revolution Will Not be Televised, that wonderful Gil Scott-Heron number, takes it to the male rapper, "I'm-such-a-big-man, let's-get-it-on" persona. "You ain't gonna make a revolution between these thighs," she sings. The students in the class are rapt now, they are listening, really listening. No rustle of papers, no whispering or shifting chairs. The song has their full attention. And with the fact that my four presenters look like Josie and the Pussycats, it's a bravura performance. I'm proud of them, of the work they've done, the pizzazz they have brought to the class.

When class is finished, the Pussycats follow me outside into the arched breezeways that circle both levels of the white colonial campus, accented in turquoise with terra cotta roof tile. I take their picture. I call out to them, "Maybe this will be your album cover." They hold each other and laugh.

A week later I get an email from another student in the class. Its one of those things that makes teaching real wherever I am.

ROZA PARKS

GOOD EVENING MR. RUTCOFF,

I WAS WATHCING THE NEWS ON TV YESTERDAY AND I HEARD ABOUT THE DEATH OF. WHEN I HEART HER NAME THE FIRST TIME I SAID TO MY FIANCEE I KNOW THIS NAME FROM SOME PLACE! AND THEN I REALISED THAT SHE WAS THE BLACK WOMAN IN THE BUS THAT DID NOT GET OFF.

I FELT SO SAD AS IF I KNEW HER FOR YEARS OR AS IF SHE WAS A HEROINE OF MY COUNTRY THAT ALL ADMIRE FOR HER CONTRIBUTION IN THE STRUGGLES FOR EQUAL RIGHTS.

I FELT THAT I NEEDED TO SHARE THESE THOUGHTS WITH YOU BY SENDING YOU THIS EMAIL. OUT OF NOWHERE I RECOGNISED THIS WOMAN'S NAME AND THIS EMAIL IS TO PAY A SMALL TRIBUTE TO HER MEMORY.

SINCERELY,

ANDRI MENICOU

STUDENT IN THE AMERICAN STUDIES COURSE

11 | 20 | 2005

I've been reading books on Cyprus history. The more I learn, the less I know. Each chapter of the past reveals an abundance of causes for any outcome, any number of reasons for understanding diametrically-opposed points of view. It does seem to me that Cyprus has simply, in large part because of its geographical place in the Mediterranean, been a small pawn in a vast strategic plan. No big insight there. But this lovely island and its warm and generous people has been torn between Greek/Turkish rivalry on the one hand and British/American Middle East power-politics interests on the other. That makes the so-called "Cyprus Question" into the Bermuda Triangle of historical and political comprehension. Once entering, there is apparently no way out. Bigger brains than mine have simply disappeared into that fog.

But this issue of transplant and rejection, of Andrea's recovery, won't go away. As the checkpoints open – there are now five of them, all but one for automobile traffic – change will surely come, not from without, but from within. One person, contact, exchange, date, bet, dinner, kiss, purchase, and even marriage at a time. One of my books talks about the ways in which Greek and Turkish Cypriot folk cultures share similar rituals and customs. Was it once a single culture with two ethnic and religious modes?

10 | 25 | 2005

We return to the far west of the Island, the Arkamas peninsula, north of Paphos, to the town of Ineia, twenty-five hundred feet above the sea. Down the narrow village streets we peer between the buildings, built so close to the road that we can almost reach in their front windows, and then see the far off sea coast through the rear ones. As if from a slowly-moving train, we see a repetition of the same image, one frame at a time, as we drive through the town — the ribbon of the Mediterranean stretched across the horizon, a strip of blue hovering between the even bluer sky and the green-brown earth. It is like looking at a Rothko painting, where the boundaries blur and shimmer in the sunlight.

Later, it takes about an hour in a jouncing four-wheel-drive pickup truck, the vehicle of choice in these parts, to spin our way eight kilometers to the shoreline below. A one-lane band of rough concrete, "much improved" our host Andreas tells us as he drives, shifts, and talks all at the same time, drops and cuts back and drops again. No guard rails and fortunately only one car, a British tourist we are sure because of the red license Z plates, going in the other direction. At the bottom, only dirt paths and tracks wind between scrub knee-level brush, Juniper probably, and the rocky outcropping that defines the shoreline. The sea is gentle here, and you can't hear it, only see and feel its movement, its presence, a liquid carpet.

We stand on the bluff overlooking the sea — the wine-dark sea, Homer called it. I can see why. The sun sets like an orange-red disk, rays reaching across the water from the horizon to the rocks at our feet. The sun drops so fast it feels as if we are watching it in slow motion, actually seeing its movement. In four minutes it disappears, leaving the indigo evening in its place, the water now dark, foaming and silent. The outcroppings we stand on look like Gargoyles — winter storms have lashed these rocks, penetrating them, carving figures and grotesque faces out of the bleached white limestone, leaving deposits of salt in mouths, and eyes, and ears over which we walk. Bending down, Andreas, who has been coming here to his wife's village for 40 years, finds tiny green

Woman outside the cafe in Ineia

Andreas with his wild capers

At the cafe, Ineia

shoots. He picks some and hands the delicate stem to us. "Taste it," he says. We savor the wild capers, fresh and salty, growing here in the cracks of the stone faces.

The next morning we awaken to roosters crowing from three directions, and a saw humming from a workshop in the distance. We marvel at the tranquility as we peek out, ears first, from beneath the mound of quilts we have built in shelter of the wonderful cold night air. After eight weeks in Nicosia, the cacophony of cars, motorcycles, trucks, scooters, and of course police and ambulances sirens bleating and honking and clanging beneath our windows has become almost tolerable. Now, we luxuriate in the deep quiet of the countryside. Curiously, it is like home, this rural solitude, this tidy life on the edge of a village. Rural Ohio lacks the drama of this land's end, but the charms are familiar.

We walk through the village later that morning under a cloudless high blue sky, the sun warming our backs. On the road we meet our ancient friend who still dresses in a single piece of black cloth, and follow him up the wood steps of an outdoor cafe. It is 10 am, and several old and then older men, caps and canes spread out across the seats of hand-made reed chairs, sip beer from well-worn, scarred KEO glasses. They offer to buy us a draft and when we shake our heads no thanks, two coffees and water appear instead. They toast us, and we them. Two brothers, each face more a map of time and place than the other. Features furrowed and dark, their deep eyes and smiles beam our way. Shepherds, we are told, they have been drinking in this place for a half century.

Andreas wants badly to show us his "lands." A patch, perhaps an acre, he carefully cultivates, his broad fingers and thick hands revealing his own village origins. It's been brewing in my mind for a day now, as we walk back though the village and down a narrow street toward the sea, which remains eight kilometers below to the west, that this whole island country of Cyprus is a big rock. Take the highway anywhere and it cuts through the same light limestone — stone, we are told, that is a million years old, thrust up by some primordial push that created what became Cyprus. It is the same limestone the British quarried to construct their imposing imperial buildings, and that forms the foundation of Old Nicosia's labyrinth city with its honeycomb of apartments, shops and workshops. Then we walk through the village's outlying streets, lined by the same stone piled waist-high in walls that define, enclose, and border the land as well as the buildings. Each piece is different, irregular, these chunks of stone gathered from the fields.

Andreas, perhaps in his early 70s, is suddenly towering over us. He has nimbly climbed up the rough uneven stone wall along some invisible set of footfalls. "You see this," he waves his hand, sweeping across the horizon of his land, "maybe ten truck-loads to clear it." Ten truck loads of rock, of white limestone, from just one acre. And he is standing above me, balancing on the top of the wall, his shoes wedged between the rocks. "Take this," he orders me and leans down to present a handful of almonds he has plucked from a tree that overhangs the wall, their outer shells soft as cotton. When D and I have filled all our pockets with nuts, Andreas reaches his hand down for my shoulder and hops, gingerly yet somehow gracefully, back to the road.

He teaches us how to put the almonds in the small notches, the v's formed by the natural cutouts in the rocks at the top of the wall about chest high. And then we crack open the shells with the hammer blow of another small rock, careful of our fingers, and pop the fresh nuts into our mouths. No need for roasting, toasting, salting, these are the real thing, sweet and savory. We open a few extra almonds and eat them slowly, tossing them back onto our tongues, as we stroll down to his field.

By the time we leave a half hour later our sweatshirts have been transformed into sacs overflowing with just-picked pomegranates, some already split and filled to the brim with their sweet-sour red juice, and figs, green and not yet soft but still fresh and tender. We will eat them for breakfast in Nicosia for the next week.

10 | 26 | 2005

I am asked, "Why do you think the Greeks hate the Turks so much on Cyprus?" We sit outside in the courtyard of a small villa, next to a mosaic-tiled swimming pool, beneath a grapefruit tree bent low with yellow fruit. The house is in a village about fifteen kilometers from Limassol, the port city of the South that is also the hub of one of the two British "sovereign" military bases on the island. I don't really know how to answer the question.

Our hosts have been living in the Middle East and India for 40 years as missionaries, both children of missionary families, and they are Arabists. And Americans. Lewis is a retired Dutch Reformed minister, and his wife Nancy is a Presbyterian who went to college in Wooster, Ohio. Wooster is where D., my wife teaches. She's Presbyterian too. They have already hit it off. Nancy works in a reconciliation project for Christians and Muslims and is one of the American members of the Cyprus Fulbright Commission. I really like her sense of humor. We talk about Amish clothing and she laughs out loud at the notion of hookless bras.

After postings in Istanbul and Beirut and Yemen, they have chosen to retire to Cyprus. I think I understand the choice. Somewhere between Europe and the Middle East, it keeps them in touch with both their cultural worlds. Lew wants to talk about baseball and peanut butter. But now, he's serious, looking at us, his glasses tilted down his nose, his white beard and moustache neat, his voice rumbling from a million cigarettes, as he asks me this question.

"Maybe because of religion," I say, even as I realize that his is a really rhetorical question. I've been here for two months. This man, his wife, and their family has lived and worked in the region for almost half a century.

He explains. I really like his candor and his humor and wonder if I can capture it with words. His eyes somehow reveal his interest/disinterest. They are clear, see deeply, and while what he says sounds far-fetched, his person gives his words credibility. Before the Ottoman period on Cyprus, he begins, before the 16th century, Cyprus was divided between Roman and Byzantine Catholics — a rivalry, he assures me, of considerable intensity. Following the Ottoman conquest of the island, while Greek Orthodox villagers and clergy received special protection by the Sultan, Roman Catholics did not. And many Roman Catholics, this is his first punch-line, converted to Islam to survive economically, socially, just to hold on to their livelihoods. It makes sense to me, because I've just read in an obscure history book that some Cypriots converted to Islam in the 17th Century as a strategy to avoid persecution but that they had continued to practice their own religion in secret, like the Jews of Spain. And then the clincher, proffered over a gin and tonic as the evening air becomes cooler, the sky darker. The clincher.

Go into some old Mosques, he says, and guess what you will find? This time I know it is a rhetorical question and I hold my tongue. But I like syncretism, it's my stock in trade as a student of African-American culture, so I wait. Their cat brushes against my legs and I pull my sweater closer over my shoulder.

The floor plan, he says. Not square, or symmetrical, but rectangular. Like a church. I have no idea if what he says is actually true, but it sounds so culturally rich and plausible. The Cypriot Muslims, the Turkish Cypriots, six hundred years ago, had been Catholics. The enmity between Greek and Turk today, an enmity whose intensity is remarkable and surprising when it appears in college students in my classes who have no memory of "before" before 1974, is nothing less than an expression of an ancient Christian religious rivalry.

On the way back to Nicosia that night D and I try to think of those things we have observed in common on both sides. Here is our list. Bacclava (sweeter than sweet, drenched in sugar syrup); beads (like Rosary beads, men hold them in their hands, twist them around their fingers, twirl them, keep them in their pockets for comfort); coffee (dark, boiled, rich); backgammon (men in cafes, on corners, playing, smoking, drinking coffee); and the blue, deep-blue, purple with a black center piece of glass — the evil eye. A good luck charm, but more than that — to keep bad spirits away. You see them everywhere — key chains, bracelets, beads — on walls, doorways, and dashboards. Makes me think of African-American bottle trees, trees with bottles hanging from branches to "catch" the bad spirits. Pepto-Bismol bottles, also deep blue-purple, work best in that syncretic adaptation of West African religion.

And one more thing, I add, as we spin our way though one of the half-dozen roundabouts on the way through Lemasol. Honking.

Drivers all over Cyprus must think their automobile horns are an appendage. (I repress my brain's reflex to make some kind of comment about blowing a horn.) On cue, the car behind me honks, for no reason that I can detect. It's a form of speech, isn't it? "Move over," "Go faster!" "Out of the Way," "How dare you," and simply "Hello, wassup." Whatever. They do it ALL the time, any time. So, add honking to the list. Maybe I'll have more by the time our stay is completed.

11 | 27 | 2005

It is 6pm in north Nicosia. Dusk. The shops are closing, and the normally teeming streets suddenly empty. Silence descends, but for an occasional car navigating the tiny streets, and, yes, honking at nothing in particular. A man with a shopping bag between his knees sits next to us on the park bench in the all-but-deserted town square. The wind blows the day's discarded newspapers against light-brown buildings, and umbrellas above empty cafe tables flutter in the breeze. The man's fingers play with well-worn yellow beads on a string held together by an engraved silver cap. And then it starts, just as the evening becomes dark, just as the sun sets below the Trodoos mountains to the west of Nicosia. The songs. The calls to prayer. First one, then another, perhaps a third behind both of them. Minor key, modal, soft, inviting — these chants from the loudspeakers atop the minarets announce the end, also, of the day-long fasting period that is part of Ramadan. It is said that Turkish Cypriots are very casual, secular, about their practice of Islam. But the empty streets, the closing of the shops, the scurrying home make it appear otherwise.

We have been invited to the home of Cem and Seray. "We eat at six-twenty," they told us the other day. It sounded very precise. And it is. When we arrive, the table is set to overflowing. Five chairs, although there are four of us, and another table for serving. Plates and dishes with yogurt soup, tahini, beets, carrots in yogurt, stuffed grape leaves, aubergine and zucchini, pancakes, cold potato pudding with mint, cauliflower coated with lemon juice and olive oil. Ah, we say to ourselves. A Turkish meze, a typical Cypriot-Greek meal of a dozen plates of any and everything. But this is all fresh, no meat or souvlaki and no alcohol.

Cem and Seray invited us to their shop for dinner. They sell Turkish rugs and jewelry not far from the checkpoint in Cedilla, the newer name for Nicosia in the north. It is Lefkosa in the South. It is Nicosia in both.

They are both lovely and photogenic. He's been all over the world, has photographs of himself as a younger man sitting with the President of Azerbaijan, leading a football team in a tour of the Cameroons, hiking in Tibet. His face, smooth and handsome and sweet, seems almost soulful, his eyes see deeply. There is something elegant about him. And Seray, alert, just this side of startled, with a smile that lights up the room, kisses us on both cheeks. (We need to add that to our list of north and South).

The table sits in the middle of their shop. Rugs are piled up all around, carpets of extraordinary rich color and texture, mostly Kilim. It's a kind of sanctuary, the room filled and covered in rich reds and purples, orange and yellows, blues and greens. We sit on the folded carpets high like benches and try to chat before we eat. But Cem, who last dined at midnight the night before, can't contain himself. He sits at the table and drains the yogurt soup in a single inhale. And looks up. Grins. "Bon appetite," Seray adds, inviting us to join in, and suddenly our plates are piled high.

Behind Cem the television broadcasts, first news from Ankara and then the daily odds for the hundreds of football matches all over Europe that day. Cem has bet on some kind of combo (like a Quinella, I guess) that could net him 16,000 Euros. We will find out next week if he has won. And so we dine slowly, talking, listening to the TV, Cem or Seray jumping up to check the computer at his desk for English to Turkish words that one or the other of us can't find. "Aubergine," which we know is French. They learn its English equivalent, eggplant.

She loves to tease him. She's in her late 20s and has an exuberance that won't let go. He's in his early 40s and has clearly lived a complicated worldly life, and breathes a gentle spirituality that is rare. He's well informed, knows history and has an opinion about almost anything.

I ask what they think of Pamuk, the new, almost Nobel-winning Turkish novelist whose autobiographical journal Istanbul I have just begun. I imagine I see both of them startle. "Dangerous," she says. "But I not read yet." She is very hesitant to speak English when her husband is around. He looks past the room, past the carpets hanging in the window, as if he's peering into the past.

Like Lew a few nights earlier, Cem has a kind of vision. This time I just listen. What he says goes against my root-for-the underdog instincts. But his indictment of Pamuk as a radical who seeks to undermine Turkish unity is not the ranting of a fanatic, is not the same as the calumny hurled against Salmon Rushdie. There are two sides to the story of the Armenian question (he will not use the word genocide). They, in concert with the Kurds and Georgians, had their own role to play in the events of the First World War — assassination, violence, and corruption. Hardly the ingredients of innocence. I have never heard this before, but find in it yet another example of my ignorance as well as a metaphor of my time here. Every story has as many sides as it has participants, and history becomes the forge on which politics is hammered into swords more often than plowshares.

Is it a coincidence that later, when we go to the English-speaking bookstore in South Nicosia called Moufflon, after a wild goat once nearly extinct now back home on the range, we ask about Pamuk? Ruth, who runs the store, is an erudite, gentle, soft-spoken, British-sounding woman. She seems to know and have read every book in the crowded shop. "I'm Armenian," she says quietly, not a hint of edge in her voice. "Look at my name." Ruth Keshishian. Her family has lived on Cyprus since the Armenian holocaust.

Pamuk, who wants Turkey to assume responsibility for the Armenian massacres, has been short-listed for the Nobel Prize in literature. He's a hero to these Armenians and Ruth seems disappointed when she tells me that Harold Pinter, the playwright, has just won the prize. In fact, the Armenians comprise, after the Greeks and Turks, the third ethnic group on the island. Just blocks from our apartment in New Nicosia, up from the headquarters of Zorba's bakery, is the Armenian Orthodox Church of Cyprus, relocated here from the Old City after 1974.

10 | 29 | 2005

It runs like a fault line, this year of 1974, through the whole society. Fault in geological and moral terms. We sit with Kleanthes, "You call me Glenn," the retired Cypriot Army Captain, at his favorite cafe in Lefkara. He has accepted our invitation to lunch in the center of this traditional lace-making Greek Cypriot town. "WATCH THE LADIES MAKE LACE" shout the huge yellow and black signs on the outskirts of Lefkara. At the cafe, we sit comfortably in the warm air and watch buses choked with English and German tourists descend on the town square for an allotted hour of shopping.

"Why?" he asks, this hardened military reservist who had recently led the annual OXI-Day parade though the narrow stone paved streets of his town. "Why I have to show my passport, pay for insurance, take a number to go and visit my town? I ask this for 31 years. Why!" He looks north, toward the mountains that shield Kryenia from our view. Kyrenia sits on the north coast of Cyprus, a

Colonel Glenn

city and region where he grew up. "I no go back. Not till they let me with no showing passport."

Later, when the souvlaki and a double brandy arrive, we engage in discussions about American policy. He understands a great deal, our Mr. Glenn, about monetary issues, the relationship between the Euro, the Dollar and the Cyprus Pound. And when D says something about "dollar hegemony" in relationship to the issues of development that she's keen on, Glenn looks up, grabs her hand and says something grandiose and completely authentic. "My dear lady, you have understood me perfectly." He grins.

"Now I want to ask you something," he continues as he cuts into the small piece of chicken, grilled on a wood spit to melt in your mouth, seasoned only with bitter lemon juice. "Which part do you think I want?" He toys with the tiny morsel and leaves the largest part of the chunk off to the side of his plate. "Why your Condeleesa Rice only leave us this small part? Not enough to eat. We small island. You not need big piece."

I don't mean to make him sound like Tonto. He's a very smart, savvy, sentimental Greek Cypriot. When he takes us through the town after lunch, walking down streets too narrow for a car to pass, taking us behind the tourist veil, he shows us his house, his church, his BMW, his dog and his fruit trees — the life he has made, and of which he is proud. In his mind, however — in his soul — he is still a refugee.

10 | 31 | 2005

In Old Lefkosa, the Turkish Cypriot side, we see an extraordinary puppet show, called Karagoz. Mehmet has been doing these shows for fifty years. They are part of an Ottoman folk tradition that is 600 years old, which became very popular on Cyprus in the 1930s and had practitioners in both communities. We sit on backless reed chairs in a small theater on the second level of the Birkuk, the local cultural arts center — six Americans, three Turkish Cypriots, and Mehmet, who explains his art to us in both languages — English and Turkish.

He is a one-man band. He keeps alive this wonderful tradition. He is its historian, producer, orchestra, puppeteer and voice. Small and nut-brown, bald, peering through spectacles, Mehmet turns down the lights and steps behind the screen, which is about the size of a large projection TV. It's draped by a

Mehmet – historian, producer, orchestra, puppeteer and voice

curtain of woolen carpet knots, which opens, and the show begins. The puppets are ten inches high, made of stretched and dyed camel skin in translucent vivid colors. They have articulated arms and legs whose rich hues — purples, reds, greens — make them shine like stained glass.

The show is of the Punch and Judy, Amos and Andy, Abbott and Costello, Vaudeville/Minstrel genre. Characters say one thing, mean another; they misunderstand language and meaning, wind up clobbering each other as a result. Maybe the conflict resolution folks here on Cyprus ought to catch one of Mehmet's shows. In a world where words like catharsis and hubris are native to many and known to all, the Shadow Puppets might have something to teach. The show we watch is about the adventures of Karagoz, a bumpkin who has been convinced by his city-slicker friend to sell his ideas in the metaphorical market place. He encounters a Greek, a Christian and a Jew — the stock characters, it seems, of the Ottoman world — and fails. Each time these characters don't buy his line, don't bite, he whacks them over the head in frustration. It is Ollie biting Kukla and the Three Stooges administering noogies. We laugh and laugh with and at them. The more we know what is coming, the funnier we find it.

Outside the Birkuk, groups of men sit playing backgammon, drinking tiny cups of dark coffee brought to them from small shops, Turkish-Cypriot style, by men carrying silver trays. Forget Turkish-Cypriot style: on both sides coffee is served with a glass of water. No matter where — poolside at the Hilton, that palace of imperial importance just down the street from our apartment, or on a tiny side street in the Old City. Someone tells us that "back in the day" a drop of water in a cup of coffee would bring any poison to the surface.

One man is cracking almonds. Pounding them with a stone, like we did only a week later. He is surrounded by two or three other men and they are all laughing. As I pass by he suddenly stands and lifts his arm over his head and rings a large brass bell that is loud and sharp. I guess he's announcing his wares. But for some reason I ask the group of men in my very bad German, "What is he saying?" Why German? I'm not exactly sure, but it seemed like a good idea to try not to be an American for a moment. One of the men answered, in equally poor German, "He says that America is imperialist." The other men laugh, and so do I. I answer in English, "I didn't vote for him." They laugh again — real, genuine men's laughter, barbershop laughter. Backgammon laughter.

Mehment — “America is imperialist!”

11 | 02 | 2005

It's hard to sense time passing so quickly here. What a luxury to have four months, and how ungrateful to even think — only six weeks before we leave. But, the experience has been so rich, and we both realize, D and I, how close we have become to some people here and how much more there is to learn, to know.

The weather has finally turned. It is fall. Early November, now, the sky pale, a bit of rain from time to time. The light soft and the evenings cold enough for blankets. The cat across the street, ever shrinking yet ever there, has been joined by a dead bird in the gutter. I considered calling the health department — the bird flu has so far passed us by here on Cyprus — but read in the paper that they've had thousands of calls about dead pigeons and now only want to be informed if a whole flock is down.

Roula calls down to us from upstairs and invites us to her son's house for coffee. We arrive at five and stay for dinner, til after nine. Souvlaki wins a quick vote over pizza, and we talk the whole time we are there. Georgiou, his wife Monica who is Colombian, Costas, Roula, an English woman named Loula who is married to the recent ambassador of Cyprus to Australia, and D and I talk politics. All evening. Except when D fences with plastic glow-in-the-dark swords with Constantinous, who has just turned three. They speak Spanish in the home, Greek outside, and the child has begun to take English lessons. He seems to understand D perfectly.

Our conversation, in deference to us, takes place in English, and no one misses a beat. We go round and round, talking about the Anan Plan of last spring (a UN-proposed 'road-map' for unification, one approved by the north and roundly defeated by the South). Only Costas voted for it. His adult children initially supported the proposal, then changed their minds over the small print. They felt the plan had been parachuted in by a team of experts who knew too little about the Cyprus Question.

If I start to write about this now I will never finish. But, it is clear that the small print — allowing British rights to off-shore oil; not guaranteeing the right to return to lost property in the north; and providing a non-Cypriot panel to end political stalemates — doomed the vote. What's not clear is whether these were actual provisions of the 3000-page plan or just fabrications, rumors, fan-

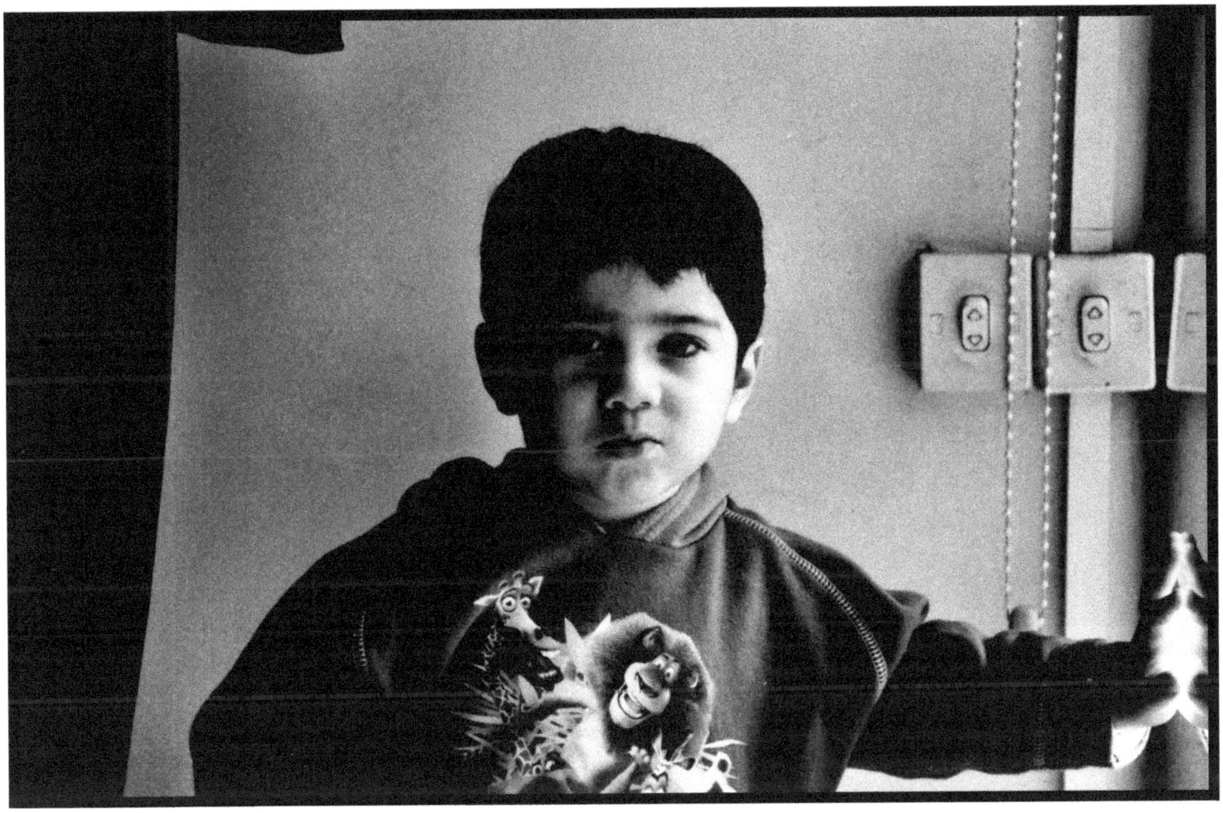

Constantinous — Power Ranger

tasies invented by newspapers, television and politicians to scare the Greek-Cypriot electorate. OXI spray-painted in black capital letters, NO in Greek, still mars every empty wall, sidewalk and construction site in Nicosia, scars of last year's bruising electoral battle.

Usually I sit and listen and ask a few questions during these discussions. But I've been reading lately and have formed some ideas. This night I can't resist. I try to talk about the difference between the idea and ideal of Greece — Platonic — that historically extended to Greeks living in the region: Anatolian Greeks, Cypriot Greeks, Dodeccanese Greeks, Cretian Greeks and the contrasting concept of Turkey. Turkey is a place administered politically by the state. It may have within it many populations — Jews, Christians, Arabs, even Greeks — but it is Turkey because the state is present. So, Turks in Cyprus can't really be Turks without the government of Turkey present. Careful! This idea pertains to Turkish history and nationalist ideology, not necessarily to Turkish Cypriots. On the other hand, Greek Cypriots can, finally, be Cypriots, and still participate in the business of being Greek. Yes?

On Cyprus, this played itself out in the wake of the battle for liberation from Britain in the 1950s. Then, Greek and Turkish Cypriots could agree that the British were the enemy. But some Greek Cypriots wanted enosis, unity, with Greece, while some Turkish Cypriots wanted separation of the two communities on Cyprus. How hard it must have been to maintain any solid ground between these two radical positions. The Invasion of 1974 created virtual separation at the cost of actual occupation. Today, with Cyprus proper in the EU, the enclave to the north must be clearly torn between business as usual, separation, and reconciliation. Unity means Europeanization a decade before Turkey enters the EU, and that means prosperity.

The round table spins that night. Some agree, some do not. No matter. I am participating in the discussion, not simply observing it. It feels much better. And they make me feel like I am a part of their family all over again.

I would like to come back here in a year or two. And I would like to learn to speak Greek beyond my "where is, how much is, please and thank you" current version. It still feels impolite not to even try to speak to my friends in their own language. And Turkish! Oh, my, too much for someone my age. I'll be glad to master in Turkish what I meagerly have already learned in Greek. It is such a difficult linguistic line for me to cross.

We've been back and forth over the Green Line about a dozen times now. What was once shocking along the strip of the Neutral Zone — barbed wire, stacked oil cans, sand bags, desolation — has become commonplace. We walk quietly now with streams of tourists, casino sightseers from the South, or day laborers from the north, and it's no different from a stroll down Broadway. The barrier has become invisible to us, the signs of hostility and enmity mute. But, in some ways this makes the actual division of the island even more powerful. When I talk to Greek Cypriot friends I really can understand the awfulness of that line, which, to most of them, is actually invisible. Look out the window, I ask myself, the window that overlooks the mountains, the spine of the Five Fingers that stretch east and west dividing the north Coast of Cyprus from the rest of the island, and think. There it is, close enough — the north — where the seaside treasure of Kyrenia sits but twenty-five minutes drive from Nicosia, and one cannot go there. It is a psychological contradiction — to have to imagine that this place that once belonged to Cyprus is no longer there. I think this is how they must feel, and in some small way it reminds me of the Twin Towers. Still present in my imagination and memory, but now vanished.

11 | 02 | 2005

We return to Irene's restaurant in Deftera twice this week. I want to see Andrea and photograph her before she leaves for the check-up in Houston. She is not there either night. But Irene, the aunt who runs the place in the evenings after closing her lunch room in Nicosia, sits down with us along with her mother and father. They beam when we ask about their granddaughter. She's at a football game, and they call her. We find it difficult to hear her over the noise of the crowd cheering, but she sounds great, excited about the trip.

In a few minutes Irene's youngest son, Panyioties, comes waltzing in. He's a fidgety twelve-year-old, sweet and looking for action or attention. I teach him three versions of "soul brother" hand shakes, and he loves it. "Gimme five!" he shouts at me, his braces filling his smile. Then he just sidles up and sits in my lap and plays with his cell phone, holding it to my ear, pressing buttons, injecting Greek football songs into my cortex.

Irene tells us that she will be going to Houston with Andrea. She has already visited the beauty parlor of a friend in Larnaca. Sporting a soft red-tint and a perm, she agrees to let me take her picture. She looks radiant. They will be gone for ten days. Irene says they will shop. I wonder. It must be frightening. It always is when I go for these checkups.

11 | 05 | 2005

Dinner in the Old City. Our whole Fulbright contingent crosses through Ledra Palace checkpoint. Seven of us altogether, we stop at the carpet shop to pick up Cem and walk through town. Ramadan is over and it is the three-day holiday, Bynam, that comes at the end. The city is deserted. And because the clocks have changed back to standard time, it is fully dark out. We cross Attatuck Square, normally filled with men playing backgammon, drinking beer, standing on line for the sole ATM machine in the district, or simply hanging out. It is empty, dark, silent. A car almost runs us down as we walk down one of the streets that would ordinarily be jammed with merchants selling halvah, Turkish Delight, blue jeans and belly dancing scarves. It feels like a cheap spy film, the way the headlights appear out of nowhere, white-bright, gleaming on the stone pavement, and streaking past us, the car's windshield tinted black, menacing and fast as we hug the cool wall.

In minutes we pass the Birkuk where a week earlier we attended the shadow puppet show. Then, the courtyard was filled with tourists, a small combo played traditional music, and the sun shone brightly. Now, like the rest of the Old City in the north, it too is deserted, blacked out, shuttered. An eerie quiet has blanketed this side of the city.

As we turn a corner, we come to a beautifully-lit urban plaza dominated by a mosque, with Turkish and north Cyprus Turkish Republic flags fluttering majestically in the soft spotlight. They hang between the twin towering minarets. The stone piazza, and the buildings that surround the Mosque, are clean and beautifully-restored sandstone, with a matte finish that less reflects the light than absorbs it. This is a stunningly beautiful place — luminous and peaceful, calm but not silent. Ahead, the restaurant we have been told to sample, El Sobor, turns out to serve Spanish-inspired continental food influenced by Turkish cuisine. We are not more than two hundred yards from the ghostly bazaar-market area of north Cyprus, and it feels like 2,000 miles. I can feel the logic, somehow, of the Spanish restaurant — tapas for meze, feta and olives, good and inexpensive wines in this space. Inside, affluent families, both Turkish and Turkish Cypriot, dine in elegance, the women in black evening dresses, even the children in bow ties and rhinestones.

Outside, it looks like a piazza — stone buildings and pavement dominated by a church. The Mosque turns out to be one of the many 14th Century French-inspired Gothic churches on Cyprus that the Ottomans transformed into Mosques. We have seen the one in Famagusta, whose minarets literally poke their way up from the center of the old church courtyard. In north Nicosia, this cathedral-mosque dates from 1356; the Ottomans refurbished it two centuries later. The guidebooks refer to it as both St. Sophia Cathedral and Sellmlye Camil. The talk we had two weeks ago with our retired American minister friend, Lew, haunts me anew after this visit. The period of Roman Catholic dominance, first French then Venetian, lasted about two hundred years, long enough to establish a powerful rivalry between Roman and Greek Christianity. His insight about the way in which the Roman tradition converted to Islam makes more sense now.

11 | 05 | 2005

Curiouser and curiouser — our conclusion after a day driving into the mountains. We head west out of Nicosia on a four-lane expressway that becomes an old state highway in less than ten kilometers. To our right, the north, the Five Fingers of the Kyrenia mountains still shield the coast, as well as the Turkish Republic, from our view. But ahead lies our destination, the Trodos, a range of mountains between the plain of Nicosia and the western coastline. This is where we will "climb" Mount Olympus, the highest spot on Cyprus. For the next thirty miles, however, Cyprus turns into southern New Jersey. Farmland with lots of tractor activity, just-turned soil, and food stands laden with gigantic gourds, fresh tomatoes and pomegranates. The farms are interspersed with light industry, wholesale outlets, used car lots and the usual array of quick-stop grocery stores and kiosks. When the roadway swerves slightly northward and we clear the easternmost extension of the Kyrenia hills, we can suddenly see the north coast of the island. The road signs point to towns on the Turkish side, between us and the sea, but they graphically display a representation of a road in white with a bright red bar slashed across them. No passage. Dead end. I wonder how the mirroring signs on the north roads look.

A new sign turns us left, to the South, and soon we climb into dark, tree-lined mountains. They look more like the Smokies or the Catskills than the Rockies. Ripples of mountain tops, some above the clouds, extend far into the distance. Here it's hard to imagine that we are on a mostly arid, desert-filled island. The higher we climb, along narrow horseshoe turns and hairpin switch backs, the more we feel we have slipped into another world. And it's a totally familiar one, visually. Outside, a touch of last evening's snow lingers in the shaded hollows of the hillsides, peering out from beneath fallen leaves, and from behind moss-covered branches. We are surrounded by tall pines, their cones dangling like ornaments; hemlock; and what looks like a variety of maple standing alongside the unmistakable gold of Aspens. The leaves are a riot of color — reds and oranges and yellows. The air is autumn-crisp, cold and clear. It feels like home, like a football afternoon, D says.

This wave of nostalgic memory for place and season lasts but a half hour. We snake our way up Mount Olympus, and close to the top, as the one-lane road turns to cinders, we pass a crew of young men running strongly down the hill, the muscles of their quadriceps flexing with each step. They are soldiers, and from their coloring — strong, lanky and pale — we think they must be British. When we reach the top we understand — there sits a large, white, c-shaped dome, behind chain-link fence. It occupies the very top of Mount Olympus, this electronic Zeus, collecting the electronic "chatter" of the entire region, from the Middle East, from Suez, from Constantinople. And that, folks, is one of the reasons, I suddenly realize, why this island is so contested. No mythology here, just very sophisticated eavesdropping equipment, staffed by the Brits, paid for by Uncle Sam I'd bet, and ceded to them by the government of Cyprus.

The dome spoils the beauty of the spot only for a moment — not like the oil rigs in the Gulf of Mexico, an hour's drive south of New Orleans. Out of sight, and as we drive back down the mountain, out of mind. Yes, the crest of Mount Olympus has been anti-climatic. But the rest of the day is not. We drive through a dozen mountain towns, each more picturesque than the next, all built into the mountains. The white and coral houses, with street-level entrances in front, drop off three or four stories down the sloping hillsides. Gold Byzantine flags flutter in front of their churches, and local stores flack blue, or green, or even clear glass bottles of home brew, Zivania, a fruit schnapps that seems to be the national drink, second only to KEO, the Cyprus-brewed beer.

If the British have occupied the very top of the island, and laid tourist claim to most of the coast, then this is where Cypriots come from. These villages, and hundreds more scattered all through the country. Before. Which means before 1974, when Greek and Turkish Cypriots had their own villages, but each village had a quarter that belonged to the other, and many Cypriots, they say, spoke each other's language, shared their cultures, and celebrated their special events. Cypriots lived next to each other in stone houses on narrow village streets, in these essentially agricultural communities where farmers tended fields and flocks beyond town. Before, when Nicosia was probably a quarter the size it is now, most Cypriots were peasant-farmers. The modern Republic of Cyprus we experience now is barely a generation old.

Walk our upscale neighborhood on a Sunday morning. It is virtually deserted, as empty as the north part of the Old City on a Friday night. Small groups of people with dark skin from Sri Lanka, the Philippines, Malaysia, and Bangladesh stroll the streets. It is their day off, these temporary five-year residents, and they take over the town. The people for whom they work as nannies, housemaids, and day-laborers have either gone home for the weekend, back to their villages, or to church.

Ledra Street on a Sunday morning and afternoon

Ledra Street on a Saturday afternoon

11 | 06 | 2005

Costas and Roula take us to their church today. It is our first visit to a Greek Orthodox service. D., who is occasionally Presbyterian and normally spiritual, and I, who am Jewish and hence only the latter, have asked to go with them. My only prior Orthodox experience consisted of taking college students to a Ukrainian Orthodox Church in Cleveland. There, a two-hundred-voice choir raised the roof, then all scattered homeward to watch the Browns on TV. Here, the service starts at eight but it isn't until nine-thirty that the church really fills up. That's when families arrive in anticipation of communion, of taking the bread and wine that is central to this celebration. Two hours of classical Greek in a tradition with which I am only slightly familiar proves strangely liberating. The chanting of two cantors and the priest provide a meditative experience that immerses me in the art and music of Greek Orthodoxy. Covered head to foot, stem to stern, top to bottom with paintings — the New Testament scenes that the Renaissance Quattrocento painters revolutionized alongside golden icons — the Church glows in deep color. Alcoves and ceilings, walls and columns are covered by frescos, and the screen behind the altar consists of a dozen gold and silver bas relief doors, behind which the priests and their assistants mastermind the ceremony.

But as we also discover at the remarkable Icon Museum in Nicosia — deep in the Old City, housing images that reach back to the Eighth Century — the Byzantine tradition has been systematically ignored by Western art historical understanding and interpretation. What I mean is this: As I listen to the chants in the service, surrounded by yards of frescos and icons, I experience an artistic culture that was not, is not, simple or flat or monophonic, or naïve. Rather, in the music I hear counterpoint, harmony and polyphony, and syncopation. In the art I see a wonderful blend of realism and symbolism, imagery combining perspective and shading alongside the gold-gilt halos and backgrounds that give the icons such a sumptuous feel. What this tells me is that the story I learned about western art — about its progressive reinvention during the Renaissance of Classical form — ignores the Byzantine. In slighting that culture, its art, music, and religion, we miss a point of great continuity, the mastery of complex and sometimes contradictory styles and meanings. The history of art, then, is not the movement away from flatness or plainness or one-dimensionality at all. That is only a story told from a Western European point of view. And perhaps that will be the beginning of a new understanding of what this place, Cyprus, is all about, too. It belongs to a history that owes much more to two millennia of Byzantine and Ottoman empires and cultures than it does to the British colonial overlay of the last one hundred and fifty years.

When we arrive home from church, Costas parks his Jag in the space right next to the desiccated cat. The rain has cleaned some of the dust off its fur. As the cat's body shrinks, the white boots of its feet get larger, more prominent, like an old man's nose. "Watch out," I call to Roula as she gets out of the car. "Don't step on the cat." She looks at me as if I am crazy.

11 | 09 | 2005

Turns out that Nicosia/Cyprus is not just divided by a Green Line. Rather, there is a neutral zone, a Buffer Zone, between the north and South. The Zone is sometimes as wide as several kilometers, containing whole farming villages in the east, and as narrow as a few meters in the middle of what was once Nicosia. Five thousand people live in this zone, a space carefully negotiated and policed by the United Nations. The Buffer Zone has within it the Green Line, the UN ceasefire line, and the lines that limit the territory of each side. In the city of Nicosia the Green Line-Buffer Zone runs through small streets, down back alleys, and even over a school roof. OP's, or observation posts, both Turkish and Greek, define either side of the Buffer Zone and are themselves supervised, policed, by United Nations Observation Posts that run right down the middle of the zone. In effect, then, there are three sets of OPs, wood sheds on stilts, some with peepholes and machine gun slits surrounded by sandbags, others with pairs of binoculars staring into the nests of their counterparts. Men, mostly boys really, in baggy camouflage uniforms tucked into shiny black paratrooper boots stand guard, some taking on cell phones, others pacing, their hands grasping matte-black machine guns against their chests.

We walk the zone through Nicosia, from one side of the Old City Wall to the other, in about two hours. Our guide, a British peacekeeping Lieutenant, is smart and savvy and witty the way British soldiers are. "Just having some fun," he says with a deadpan nod toward a razor-wire protected field overgrown with tall grass. It's one of almost one hundred not-yet-cleared minefields in the

The Buffer Zone — no photography

neutral zone. We wave to several Turkish soldiers who have come to check on our gaggle of political sightseers as we duck into an underground "car park," one left intact since 1974. Our guide tells us that one of his predecessors, a Canadian Master Sergeant, made ten thousand pounds a month selling parts from the hundreds of cars left in the garage. On the second floor of the garage we find six cars in absolutely mint condition and a room full of 1974 "artifacts," from olive oil cans to tins of sardines to a dozen television sets, burled-brown, plastic-cased Magnavox's, stacked in the corner of a dark concrete storage room. It is the only place we are allowed to take photographs.

The Buffer Zone is littered with the details of history. Walls pocked with bullet holes line once prosperous commercial streets; stone rubble shifts underfoot; and clever signs mark one's way through the zone. "Murray's Cafe," on the doorway of what had once been a coffee bar cafe where a British officer took his daily Nescafe before 1974; "Alice's," where an old woman lived and refused to leave; and, of course, the "Yellow Car." There, about half-way through the Old City, the concrete roadway reveals a thirty-two-year old crushed yellow Morris. It has remained parked along the side of the road since 1974. The Turks believe the Green Line runs from its front bumper to a drainpipe across the road. The Greeks believe otherwise. The line extends from the rear bumper to the drain pipe. This means that a triangular patch of crumbling pavement, its base the length of a Morris and its point a drain pipe across the street, is contested. The United Nations negotiated a settlement whereby the Turkish Army may stand sentry duty in the triangle for five minutes every hour and the Greeks may observe that sentry while he occupies that space. No detail is too small, then, to be disputed. A small sign marks the "Yellow Car" on the UN map of the Nicosia sector. Our guide Left-tenant Harry Wilson calls it more "shenanigans." Less humorous, however, is the shell of a house that leans right up against the path, its wall pushing out against the razor wire that reads "NOT GREEN LINE. UN CFL" — the United Nations Cease Fire Line. In this abandoned house, United Nations observers uncovered a cache of arms, machine gun emplacements, and even an artillery piece that one side had smuggled in by way of a secret tunnel. "It's all in good fun, really," Harry concludes. But no one believes him.

The more we walk, the more I think of the First World War, that horrid (and by all accounts putrid) nether world of trenches in which men lived side by side with death, rats, and mud for the four years that formed their eternity on the Western Front. The French, British, and Germans in this hell laced their survival with mordant humor, clever wit, and overblown, even elegant language. Ninety years later, this Neutral Zone in Nicosia runs like a trench, a scar that is still alive, through the heart of the city. It's impossible to imagine, as we look down from the roof of a bi-communal school, what it was like before. It must have been something when it was whole. Now the walled city is divided, inhabited by ghosts and boy soldiers.

11 | 15 | 2005

We go to Istanbul for a long weekend. Hard to leave Cyprus, but what a city is Istanbul! The extremes of poverty and wealth, of millions working at unbearably difficult tasks: men as human carts, bent double, their backs hoisting bales larger than their bodies as they mount the steep hills up to the covered bazaar; or reselling bus tickets from fragile wooden tables on street corners, their hands red and cold in the damp moist air; or shoeshine men, knees tucked up to their chins, applying polish with their fingers. And of course, the hustlers who are everywhere, holding menus, sesame bread rings, balloons, brooms, lottery tickets, flowers, newspapers and girlie show cards. "Old American couple," one calls trying to steer us to his carpet shop. He did not prove persuasive. "Let me help you spend your money," cries another outside St. Sophia, "I can help you understand."

This grand, cavernous Byzantine church, faded red and utterly fabulous, stood for almost a thousand years before its Ottoman conversion to a Mosque. Its glorious mosaics — icons high above archways and beneath the dome itself — have only recently been discovered and restored. When Turkey became a Republic, Attaturk transformed the structure into a museum. As such it teaches an important lesson — for Cyprus.

This tiny island, a mere dot in the Eastern Mediterranean, is a microcosm of the region. A thousand years of Greek Christianity and another five hundred of Ottoman Islam gave the people on Cyprus a dual heritage — religious, cultural, social, and political. Like two waves, these civilizations washed over Cyprus as they did over the entire region from the Danube to north Africa, and left their deposits in layers. As they do in both north and South Cyprus, men in Istanbul play backgammon, hold beads in their fingers, carry evil eye charms, drink dark thick coffee, and eat baklava. But as in St. Sophia, Turkish culture overlays an even more ancient Greek Byzantine, one that elegantly engineered cisterns and magnificent churches, plied the seas and painted icons, produced sweet honey and sharp feta. Yet unlike Istanbul, or even Athens, Cyprus also experienced Norman, French, Venetian (hence Roman) and British occupation, rule, and culture. But to simply see it as having emerged from British colonial dominance with its two ethnic populations at each other's throats misses the complex legacy of the Hellenistic and Ottoman Empires.

Today's Istanbul teems — the crowds walking at night, the cars choking the main streets, the buses collected by the dozen at central hubs, the spice vendors in the market, the police. I've never seen so many police. In several uniforms, some blue and some red, most armed with pistols and many with automatic weapons. They gather where the crowds are, in small clumps, chatting and watching. I feel their presence powerfully. I'm not sure what to make of it, but their menace makes me ill at ease.

Women walk arm and arm with men. Many are dressed in style. But some look like peasants just off the farm, skirts down to the ground, wearing heavy jackets and boots, their wrinkled faces shining out from beneath tightly wrapped polka-dot babushkas. Still others wear loose long wool coats, plain drab-colored wool, and cover their heads with silk scarves, which they pin carefully on one side. They accompany men in ski jackets and jeans, carrying bundles or young children. And then, at the Bazaar, or in front of the famous Topkapi dagger in the Sultan's palace, elegant women cover themselves head to foot in black, their chador's allowing only space for the eyes. But the fabric glistens. Silver threads shine, and black on black embroidery, elegant and fine, makes me realize that this is a complex social as well as religious costume. The ensemble tells me that there are many ways that Islam is voiced. And so, on Cyprus, where categories become reductive, the lesson of Istanbul is not lost on me.

When I emailed my sponsors, the Fulbright Commission, to inform them of my plans to travel to Turkey, they told me they don't want to know. Not officially, anyway. This is because I will fly from north Cyprus directly rather than from the South, which would require a connection in Athens. Previously, when I traveled to a Greek island and didn't inform them, they asked me to keep them up to date about my plans. Not this time, not this route.

When we depart Istanbul for the flight home we pass through customs and have our passports stamped on the temporary paper visas that one uses to go from south to north in Cyprus. We board an international flight and re-enter north Cyprus at their Nicosia/Lefkosa airport. We clear customs again and drive to a checkpoint in Nicosia that will allow us to pass into the Republic of Cyprus. We have gone from Turkey to the Turkish Republic of Northern Cyprus to the Republic of Cyprus. If the Cypriot police or guards at the checkpoint looked at our actual passports they could not tell we had been to the TRNC, even though we had just walked or driven past them on the only road from north Cyprus. The police and border guards as well as the armed forces in the TRNC are all Turkish. So are the telephone lines, the universities, and the mail system. But when we enter the TRNC from Turkey we are traveling to a foreign country, a state that no one else but Turkey recognizes, a place that is also under military occupation. This system of winks and feints maintains the appearance of sovereignty for all parties. But, like the Ptolemaic astrological system, it covers reality with confusion and confuses complexity with reason. I wonder how long Cyprus can tolerate the discrepancy between logic and necessity.

11 | 18 | 2005

My daughter Rebekah arrives from New York. It is Thanksgiving week. We spend two days taking her to "our" island, to both sides of the Old City, to Kyrenia, up through the spectacular mountain passes, to the sea, now churning and white-capped in the winter winds, and through the Buffer Zone. She has a thousand questions and I'm surprised how much I know. Maybe it's not the Bermuda Triangle after all, this place — maybe it's just complicated enough to resist simple understanding. Or, maybe I still just don't get it.

We want to take her to dinner, to Deftera. Andrea has been to Houston for her check-up at the Anderson Clinic, and I've been wondering about her, thinking about her, for the ten days they have been away. This time we know exactly how to get there — turn right just past the "Snatch" store on the road and look for the church steeple. Go slow, families are leaving the community center and strolling across the street. It's November and the sun has long set. Darkness coats the village, black and soft like a veil.

We walk right in. The restaurant has two spaces — on one side, the kitchen and grill room with a beer cooler in the corner. Irene's parents preside there, cooking, supervising, writing down phone orders ready for the cars that will come streaming by this Friday evening. We greet them, kiss them on both cheeks, and I see Paniyotes in the corner with a friend. "Yo!" I call, and hold out my palm. He pays me no attention, instead rolls his eyes and darts out the door with his pal.

But, Andrea? For a moment I fear the worse. She's not around, she's still in Houston, she's.... Right behind me, she smiles, her face still. And she greets us in perfect American English. I peer at her, as if I expect to see some sign, and blurt out, "How...?" She's fine, she appears fine, and she looks back at me as if I'm barely comprehensible. "Did you enjoy Houston?" I correct my course and feel myself relax.

We exchange stories as she darts in and out of the dining room, apron around her waist, setting out knives and folks, folding napkins, then serving us one course at a time.

She's our waitress again, alternating with her grandfather, who beams every time he sees us and sets a new dish on our table. He whispers conspiratorially, a pint of Famous Grouse whiskey sitting softly in his hand, "I'm the best." As soon as he ducks out, Andrea reappears. When we ask what the report was from the Doctors at the clinic she says, "Okay, I guess. I was asleep when it came through."

11 | 27 | 2005

We take my son and his fiance, who joined my daughter here, to Lefkara, the town where Glenn-Kleanthees presides, where the yellow signs still say "WATCH THE WOMEN MAKE LACE." It is a cold Wednesday afternoon, dark with the feel of snow in the air, and Glenn and Maria's shop is closed up tight. We wander into another place and the young sales person takes a look at my orange APOEL cap and says, "Don't wear that in Limassol."

I explain that we are going to the game there on Saturday night and she looks cross and tells us there is going to be trouble. Not only are the two cities competing urban centers, but the two teams have different political affiliations. APOEL is "linked with the right-wing DISY party" according to the British press here, while AEL is sponsored by a Communist Winery and presided over by a Deputy to the Cyprus legislature from the AKEL, or Cypriot Communist Party. Politics is everywhere here, even in the booze.

We drive to Limassol with Costas and Roula the afternoon before the game. They have an apartment just a half-block up from the sea. We plan to see the match and stay overnight. Costas says I may get to drive back to Nicosia. What he means is that I may get to drive his gigantic gray Jaguar, a prospect I find a bit intimidating. Still, it is our first time in the second city of Cyprus.

If Nicosia is a miniature version of Paris, compact and defined by inner core of the Old City, Limassol is Los Angeles. It is all sprawl. On the way from the highway we pass scores of new consumer shops, gleaming cars and appliances and home furnishings, new villas and condominiums, cineplexes and bowling alleys. The future is now, I guess. Further downtown, however, avenues of white hotels parallel the sea, their coffee shops, topless bars, t-shirt cities, and cafes home to British tourists still walking briskly in Bermuda shorts and Outback hats. The English seem to own most of the residential property that makes Limassol by the sea look like Santa Monica. But the Russian émigrés who have more recently settled there with their off-shore business accounts, make it into an international city. Where the local Cypriots live is not at all apparent to us as we drive up and down the shoreline gawking at the neon signs and increasingly fancy hotels. Costas tells us that he's not at all concerned about the game, "I don't worry about it," he says as his wife tells us to be careful.

We find his son, Michael, the treasurer and member of the board of APOEL, and drive in his SUV away from the seaside resort district back toward the motorway that joins the city with Nicosia to the northeast. Michael, or Michaelis, is a younger, dynamic, charming, and charismatic version of his father. An accountant who travels all over the world, he and his wife are passionate APOEL fans. But, as treasurer, he functions as something like the general manager, negotiating contracts and computerizing season ticket sales. We take the back streets, skirting the stadium to find the "right" side of the field to park near. We don't want to park where the fans of the other team will find us. It seems extreme to me, and I say to D "How could this be anymore vituperative than OSU-Michigan or Yankees-Red Sox?" She looks at me with that Ohio smile that has suffered with the Cleveland Indians for generations of losses and says, "Yeah, but the Yankees suck."

We find a place about three blocks from the stadium and arrive at the visiting team ticket entrance about an hour before game time. In the space of two minutes we are inspected, checked and then patted down, frisked actually, by middle-aged men who laugh at my abortive humor, wise-ass remarks about terrorists and flying. It seems hyperbolic to me, an overreaction reinforced at the last checkpoint. There, a Cyprus riot police officer in full battle gear lifts his Uzi just a spec, high enough for me to look right down the dark, blunt nose of its barrel. It makes me shiver, and speechless. I was at Yankee Stadium for a playoff game against Oakland about two weeks after 9/11. No one frisked me there.

But the crowd in our section, all from Nicosia and all for APOEL, is gay and cheerful. We pick our way up the steep concrete steps to the last row. It's a good place to watch football, to see the pattern of attack and defense, and we sit right at mid-field. Someone comes along and laughs at how one of the APOEL fans has just had a butane lighter found in the pouch of his undershorts. The men seem at a loss for words of explanation. It all seems in good humor. Michaelis and I stand in the aisle and schmooze. He explains about running the club and negotiating contracts and then turns around and looks down. It is fully dark outside now, little ambient light from this part of Limassol to penetrate the black night. He smiles and tells me that a dozen buses of "Ultras" ought to be arriving any minute. The Ultras are the young fans, mostly teenage boys, who stand, chant, clap, drum, and sing for their team the whole game.

Across the way from where we sit, the Limassol fanatics are gearing up for the ritual contest that will ensue between the two sections of Ultras, ours and theirs. Already the Limassol supporters, packed into the last section of stands just perpendicular to the goal line, have unfurled their banners, set off several bright red-pink flares and begun their chants. They stand and point their fingers across the field at us, like a Tomahawk Chop, their arms gesturing up and down, up and down.

It's a curious old stadium. Like the venerable, now lamented Polo Grounds or even Wrigley Field, massive steel girders rise before us to support the roof and block our view to either side. During the game we all look like spectators at a tennis match, heads moving side to side to keep the game in view. The concrete stands, filled with plastic bucket seats, extend along both sidelines but do not meet, do not join behind the goal lines. A chain link fence at least

18 feet high, topped with barbed wire, separates us from the seats the Ultras will occupy when they arrive. The field below is green-yellow, old faded grass, with the white lime markings barely visible. Compared with Nicosia's state-of-the-art facility, this is bare bones, constructed like a corrugated steel warehouse on the wrong side of the tracks.

Suddenly there is a stir. They are arriving, the buses. The Ultras. First the police car escort, a half-dozen blue lights strobing, headlights gleaming bright white. Then the buses emerging from the dark black night, snaking off the main Nicosia-Lemasol highway. We follow their headlamps as they barrel down the road toward us. When they pull in, the doors open and almost simultaneously platoons of riot police and tactical SWAT types, camouflaged, wearing dark green berets and shining black combat boots, come running up. But they are too few for the hundreds of young men, many with woolen head-gear pulled down over their eyes, scarves wrapped around their necks, who storm the stadium, running, chanting, and singing. The police form a double line, funneling the kids into the entrance that will put them below and to the left of where we are sitting. Michael and I lean over the outer wall, about fifty feet from the ground, and watch the scene. Out of nowhere a kid runs past a red car parked directly below us and flames burst from its hood. He's dropped some kind of flammable substance and is gone as fast as we see the fire jump into the air, puffs of black smoke behind the flame. It takes about a dozen police to quell the flames and push the charred car out of the parking lot. We wonder what the owner will think.

These five hundred kids fill the seats, or rather the steps of their section, since they will not sit down, and they begin the ritual calling out of the Limassol Ultras directly across the field from them. Our friends seem embarrassed to translate exactly what they are chanting, but it's something to do with treating the other team like the women they are. Still, we've heard this before at other games and we settle in to watch the match on the field.

As far as I tell, the game is very exciting. Two well-matched teams battle it out, some bad calls, lots of whistles from the referees and the stands, many exciting and balletic plays. APOEL scores first on a Bend It Like Beckham shot from about 35 yards, but AEL comes right back to bang in a header just before the half. I tell Michaelis that this is very exciting, and he looks around, and mutters something about not winning enough head-balls and losing momentum.

I barely watch the second half on the field. Each team surges against the other, but their defenses are too strong and I'm distracted. During the entire period, the APOEL Ultras begin setting fire to the plastic seats in their section. They must have brought in hundreds of butane lighters and cracked them open. When I think about it, I wonder why they frisked me and let the kids stampede right into the stadium. Each time they light a fire, and the red-black smoke fills our nostrils with the acrid smell of burnt plastic, a pint-sized fire truck appears. It backs slowly up to the stands and shoots a looping stream of water out onto the fires, like an old man at four am, and manages to extinguish the flames. But the kids light the next row and it starts again. Fire, flame, water, smell. And all this time the game on the field is moving toward a less than satisfying 1-1 tie. I can't tell what the other team's fanatics are yelling during this fire-water fight, but it sounds angry.

Still, we all file out in an orderly way, leaving the Ultras on the APOEL side to follow, and presumably to get right into the buses. A short walk down a very dark street, tinged with menace because of the possible presence of "thugs" from the other side, takes us back to the car, parked in a vacant lot filled with bricks and sundry building materials. We understand that the AEL fans have been detained in the stadium until all of us have left. We depart without incident.

What happens next is still unclear — but, we know this: As we walk to our car the AEL Ultras, their kids, protest, with increasing vehemence, the way the local police hold them in their section. Verbal abuse comes first, but physical attack follows, with fire bombs, bricks, and sticks hurled at the police. So much for careful searching. The violence leads to more than 30 arrests, six hospitalizations, and one death. A police officer, part of their SWAT team, carries a fellow officer out of the stadium on a stretcher and collapses with a heart attack. The man is 43 years old.

For the next three days the newspapers are filled with easy analysis — political blaming, regional hostility, condemnations of young men, of police passivity, and of the decadence that accompanies modern consumer culture. Cypriots profess shock, wring their hands at British-inspired "hooliganism" and call for reform, even for playing important matches in empty secure facilities.

I can't help but wonder — what is being acted out here? It felt like an extraordinary night — the fires, the passions, the antagonism, the chanting and shouting and jeering kids. But could it, as almost everything does here on

Cyprus, have more to do with the politics of division and of the way in which boundaries, from parking spaces to cafe chairs, become challenges? Ah. There is a boundary, a stop sign. Screw it — it's not for me. That other line, that bone that sticks in the throat, that brings tears to our eyes, the one we talk about always and deal with never, is the only one. The rest of these physical and psychological limits function like the stop signs that everyone runs. Ordinary boundaries have become merely suggestions about how to behave, but surely not rules that must be followed. Those one winks at. Normally, the match behavior of the Ultras functions according to shadow regulations, designed to allow a form of surrogate conflict as long as it doesn't get out of hand, a kind of ritualized confrontation. Sing, chant, scream obscenities — it's okay because everyone knows they won't actually get out of control. In fact, they are expected, even smiled at, surely tolerated, perhaps encouraged.

But at a time of the year, the end of the year in fact, when all of Cyrpus is talking about opening a new checkpoint, this time right down the gullet of the Old City, connecting Ledros Street in South Nicosia to Ataturk Square in north Nicosia, this football violence takes on a special dimension. Each side, north and South, wants to claim the right to open the new passage, and each accuses the other of bad faith in the planning. The United Nations stands between them in the Buffer Zone, fending off claims of subterfuge, of secret military planning by both Greek and Turkish Cypriot politicians. But everyone knows it's only political posturing, grandstanding, that it's only a matter of time before the new way will be open, and still more people from each community will experience the other, for better and for worse. Perhaps the Cyprus Football Federation needs to ask the United Nations to police the games. And perhaps, when some form of reconciliation is achieved, the psychic tensions released will no longer have to find a substitute match.

11 | 30 | 2005

Walking back and forth South to north, from Greek Cypriot to Turkish Cypriot Nicosia, remains routine. Each time on our right, just before we leave South Nicosia, we pass a public building, an old British colonial structure distinguished by its sandstone block and white wood trim. In large letters the sign outside proclaims in Greek, KYRENIA MUNICIPALITY. Kyrenia, of course, is in the north, a center of culture and tourism just on the other side of the mountains, invisible from the Greek side. Even the mountains, the Kyrenia Mountains, have a profound importance for Cyprus. They had been the source of the sandstone used for most of the classic buildings in the city. South Nicosia no longer has access to the quarries for its restoration projects.

The building sits like a question mark in my imagination until our trip to Limassol. D sees a similar building there, this time with a sign, FAMAGUSTA MUNICIPALITY, and she inquires. Turns out that Cyprus has six districts from its brief history as a single Republic (1960-1974) — Paphos, Larnaca, Limassol, Nicosia, Famagusta, and Kyrenia — and two of these, Famagusta and Kyrenia, lie on the "other" side. Since 1974, when Greek and Turkish Cypriot populations moved out of each other's jurisdictions, Greek Cypriot voters from those two "lost" districts, the Alsace-Lorraine of Greek Cyprus, have continued to vote for legislative representatives as if they continued to live in those areas. They remain on the voting rolls of Kyrenia and Famagusta, even though those districts are now Girne and Gasamagusta. From the Greek Cypriot point of view, these are two local governments in exile waiting to return.

This means that both Greek and Turkish Cypriots have serious moral and psychological claims toward their identity as oppressed minorities who fight against domination and even occupation. They are both Davids in a world of Goliaths.

That status is due in part, but only in part, to the British presence on Cyprus for almost a century. It "ended" in 1960, if you ignore the extraordinary Sovereign Territories of 99 square miles that they continue to occupy. The rebellion against British occupation began in earnest in 1955, with both Turkish and Greek Cypriot factions arming resistance heroes, freedom fighters, in that struggle. However, in the vacuum following independence, both Turkish and Greek Cypriots found themselves divided between elements, militant and armed, who favored different versions of the new Republic. Some Greek Cypriots sought enosis, unity (at least partial) with Greece, while some Turkish Cypriots favored taksim, separation of the island with a northern Cyprus aligned with Turkey. The new Republican government of Cyprus, the Mikarios regime, found itself caught between the moderates and radicals of each community and in a constitutional circumstance where, to their mind, fewer than twenty percent of the population, Turkish Cypriots, could veto any measure the government and legislature proposed.

It seems to me to come down to this: There are villains all around, more than enough. Between 1960 and 1974 militant supporters of enosis and taksim, radical/terrorist/militant groups called EOKA and TMT respectively, fought it out urban-guerilla-style against each other, the government, and against their own moderates. Bombings, assassinations, intimidation, and cruelty became daily occurrences. The British, who put up barbed wire as early as 1958 across Nicosia's shopping street, Ledra, then drew the first Green Line in 1963 to keep the two avenging sides of Nicosia apart. They, along with Turkey, Greece and the United States, especially under Kissinger and Nixon, continued to interfere in Cypriot affairs. Right wing, military Greek and Turkish governments worked openly to subvert the island's independence. And in 1974, when the Greek junta, the regime of the Colonels, failed in a plot to kill and depose Makarios (who fled), the Turkish army invaded the north, using their status as a guarantor power to protect Turkish Cypriot life and property. In a stroke enosis failed, taksim became a reality and the Republic found itself subverted and shattered. American connivance, in terms of prior knowledge and tacit approval of the coup, together with British tactical support that reportedly permitted Turkish planes to refuel at the Sovereign Bases, more than tilted the outcome.

Over the next two years, between 1974 and 1976, Turkish Cypriots who lived south of the cease-fire line and Greek Cypriots who lived north, something like 200,000 Cypriots in all, moved out of their homes. They relocated each to the other side, and transformed Cyprus into an Island of Refugees. In the Karpas Peninsula, the remote and beautiful Karpas of Golden Beach and Hassim's Turtles, 9,000 Greek Cypriots left their homes. No wonder it seems empty. It is.

12 | 01 | 2005

Cem and Seray invite us to dinner in north Nicosia. We stroll, the four of us, now old friends, through softly quiet residential streets. The mild December weather allows us to take our time, the breeze comforts. We walk through a neighborhood we didn't know existed, beyond the walls of the Old City on the Turkish Cypriot side. It is a kind of mirror image of our neighborhood in the South, but like so much of the rest of the north, it is poor and without the glitter of European economic prosperity. Yet we do find our way to a strip of upscale shops and a handful of restaurants where young men and women in their twenties mill around like extras in Saturday Night Fever. They wear tight clothes, sequins in their hair, and their cars play deep bass-pounding rap.

We dine on Turkish meze, about the same as Greek meze, only without the pork. The meats are grilled and succulent, the vegetables and cheeses fresh and savory, the beer light and cold. I no longer have any idea which culture is borrowing from the other. They both are.

We enjoy Cem and Seray. They are warm and interesting people. He, older and almost melancholy, has lived a full and complex life. You can see it in his deep brown eyes, and the way he reveals fragments of himself bit by bit. He is very gentle and open about his feelings and has a fine intuitive sense. He dreams of America, of opening a store in Alaska or buying a farm, or both. And she wants the adventure: to come to America to teach, to travel, to experience life. She is as mirthful as he is sad. Her life is before her and she knows it with the true spirit of youth. There is nothing to hide yet. Sitting next to her, I realize that she looks Russian, her complexion fair, and I think about how complex the ethnic composition of Turkey must be and must have been — with Greeks, Armenians, Jews, Azerbaijanis, Kurds, Persians, and Georgians, reminders of the Ottoman Empire.

D looks at Cem and asks what we've been hesitant to inquire about for the last week. Can you tell us about the Gray Wolves? Indeed. Militant nationalists we have read about, aligned with the military, committed to an idea of greater Turkey. Some call them fascist. Some acted as the military arm of the TMT, militant pro-taksim faction in north Cyprus 30 years ago. Cem looks up. "I am a Gray Wolf," he says.

And he tells us again about the younger generation who no longer love anything, country or god, and how he is sad at their ignorance. Gray Wolf, he reminds us, is an organization devoted to the rise of Turkey, but he means a secular Turkey in the image of Attaturk. It is a pan-movement, traditionally anti-communist, that is anti-Soviet, one that embraces one hundred million Turks to the east, Georgia, Azerbaijan, Turkistan, and to the west, on north Cyprus.

And as he talks, his eyes sad, I wonder about his presence on Cyprus. He says he is disillusioned with politics, that he wants no part of it. I recall that the man who tried to assassinate the Pope in the 1980s belonged to the Gray Wolf youth organization, and hope that this is part of what he's trying to leave behind.

Yes, some part of my brain, as much as I like him, thinks that he's been sent to Cyprus and is waiting. I have no idea for what, and I push it out of my mind. Cem rubs his temples. He looks at Seray, trying to bring himself back. Sorry, he tells us. I was thinking about my family, my mother, and what I missed. I can't help wonder about the linkage between his emotional and political needs. But Seray smiles bright enough to chase his melancholy away. She's ready to pack her bags and not look back.

12 | 2 | 2005

My students at the University of Cyprus spontaneously invite us out to a cafe. We drive back from the dinner with Cem and Seray and meet the kids at the closest thing to a campus joint in Nicosia. But it's a campus joint from Berkeley or Madison in 1966 — students sit around playing chess and backgammon, listening to American rock music, dressed in flannel shirts, sipping coffee and smoking. Where's the beer, the loud noise, the Hooters girls or BW3 wings? They are even talking about serious stuff — peace and reconciliation, American heavy-handedness in Iraq. It's remarkable. We join in and soon there are about twenty of us sitting around four tables pushed close together on the porch. December, and the temperature remains balmy. This is the life! These students, mostly female, who have chosen to remain on Cyprus rather than study abroad, who never come to office hours or want to chat after class, now behave like grownups, like people with whom I'd like to spend time.

And we do. The next evening, in fact. Four other students invite us to dinner at their apartment. They cook up a storm, a Greek Cypriot storm, the Full Monte of dinner with all the fixings, and they top it off with four desserts. What we both like, D and I, is how they talk naturally with us. They are all members of the student Communist party, and they work for peace and struggle with ideas of reconciliation. Their family past tugs at them. Most are from villages now in the Occupied north (their terminology) and they talk about parents and grandparents longing to return. Yet they believe that they and the Turkish Cypriots in the north are one people, that ethnicity has become poisonous to the future, driving them inward. I think about the Gray Wolf program and choose to remain silent. What is exactly communist about these liberal nationalists is hard to tell. They have no program, but they do confess something fascinating.

Anna, a sprite of a girl, with dark eyes and curls down to her shoulders, tells me — "We took your course, some of us," and she looks at Patrick, her co-host at this event, "because we wanted to keep an eye on the American." Turns out they expected me to give them the party line. "But when you told us what we thought we were going to tell you about America, well!" She laughs and tosses her hands up. We laugh too. When I taught them to sing We Shall Overcome on the third day of class, they must have realized I wasn't such a bad guy.

12 | 05 | 2005

I have asked Costas and Roula several times to take me with them to their old house in the north, in north Nicosia. They seem reluctant, but this day they agree. I want to see their world through their eyes, even though I know that this is unfair emotionally, even exploitive.

They have been back to the house twice before, on foot via the Ledra Palace Hotel checkpoint. This time we drive and we become the experienced travelers, they the neophytes. I can feel, each step of the way, the tightness in their throats, see the anxiety in their eyes. This voyage to north Nicosia, down a virtually empty highway with decaying housing projects off to the west, over the familiar speed bumps and past a vast Turkish military base surrounded by barbed wire, takes us back toward the heart of the Old City, to what is very nearly suburban. In fact, as we navigate down rutted streets I realize that we are blocks from the restaurant that Cem and Seray took us to only two days earlier.

We slow and crawl past an empty, boarded-up church. It is the one they all attended. They don't want to stop. Married since the mid-1960s, Costas and Roula lived in this neighborhood for a decade. It is where she was born, where her father owned a shoe shop, her "auntie" living next door. The low buildings are now gray and decaying, falling apart from neglect. Not the sandstone of the Old City, but a kind of concrete stucco structure one sees in small towns, built right up to the street. In South Nicosia and Lemasol many are now padlocked shut and held in trust. They once housed Turkish Cypriots. In north Nicosia, these connected but lopsided houses and abandoned storefronts all testify to the lack of prosperity, the overwhelming sense of poverty. These houses that belonged to Greek Cypriots are held in trust too, but in the meantime, are inhabited.

There. Roula points across the street. The number, 53, is still there, in blue, next to the door. And we walk up the path, through the front garden, tree stumps and cinder covering what had once been grass. A Turkish Cypriot woman appears in the doorway. Her name is Sevilla, and her face is weary, as if she has seen a lot of life and pain. She and Roula embrace and start to talk in Greek. Sevilla has lived in the house for more than 30 years. Her husband died during the war in 1974 and she had to move north from her home in South Nicosia the next year. She cut down the ancient lemon tree in the front yard that Roula still misses. We find their politeness, their warmth, remarkable and generous, yet also guarded. They do not know how to be friends, but they clearly want to try.

As the women talk, Costas sits on the front step of the house. He looks up at us. This is where I sat in my shorts and looked out at the neighborhood, he tells us. His smile is so sad. In August, 1974 a cousin called them from Kyrenia, on the north coast. He told them to leave. He could see the ships coming. But the Greek soldiers encamped across the street are playing football, they say to the cousin. Just go, he instructs them. Costas tells Roula to leave everything – pictures, silver, and jewelry – in the house, they will return the next day, surely. They simply bundle up their two children, jump in the car and, Costas still wearing shorts, drive to the South. They return thirty years later when the first checkpoint opens. They took nothing with them that day. Nothing.

It is like entering a museum. Or a time warp. This small and dark house, with high ceilings, just as they left it. The walls are a dull yellow, and there is little light in the parlor. A few black and white photographs of Sevilla's daughter – her wedding picture, her children – are tacked to the wall. Paper flowers fan out of a painted vase on the corner table, their stems are faded and bent. This is where two families have lived, reared children, dreamed and wept.

When Costas and Roula moved to the South after the war, to our neighborhood in Nicosia, they found a new apartment. It is a penthouse, bright and airy, with balconies overlooking the whole city. But they still talk of this place as home, even though they will never return. Here, he shows us as the women get coffee ready, here is our dining room set – a large table and half-dozen chairs pushed into an alcove. It is musty and ancient, an antique shop whose customers have long vanished.

We walk through the house. Roula's house, she tells us in English. And even

Roula and Sevilla at the peacock door; Costas sitting on the steps of his former home

as she continues to talk warmly to the woman who has been living here for more than 30 years, embracing her, we know how difficult this is for her. The front door, its wrought iron bent gracefully into the form of a peacock, has been painted white, its once bright colors no longer visible. The marble floor, real marble, is chipped and worn. And outside, where the laundry billows on the line, as if these threadbare shirts and faded pants are inhabited by phantoms, bullet holes pock the back wall. Later we drink coffee together, sharing a moment of friendship and hospitality. I don't know how to understand this — from my experience, from my senses, or theirs. I feel mostly sorrow for all of them. And I can't see any way out. Somehow I've become invested in a process of understanding, one that I secretly hope will yield actual concrete results. In this way Cyprus really is an emotional Bermuda Triangle, capturing all of us who enter, refusing to let us go.

I also feel guilty for asking Costas and Roula to take them with us, for forcing them to share their sorrow and vulnerability and memory. This is another idea that I force from my consciousness. If I do not, it will strangle me.

Roula enumerates the ghosts that inhabit the back yard, where long-gone trees one stood, or the swing where her children played, now covered in vines. She greets the Turkish Cypriot neighbor, a woman living in her Auntie's home, who came to Nicosia from Paphos. The woman wears the muted but multicolored skirts and sweaters of a farmer, her head covered by a kerchief. She offers, with her hands, the oranges from her tree. Roula looks upward with her eyes. "We have suffered too much," she says very quietly. But still she smiles back at the woman who understands neither English nor Greek. As we leave, we pick a dozen mandarin oranges from the limbs that hang over into Sevilla's back yard.

Later that afternoon, as the sun sets early and golden red, Costas asks us to drive him to the center of the Turkish side of the Old City, to Ataturk Square. It is a part of town with which we are very familiar now. We stroll through the shops normally crowded with trinkets and tourists. But it is Sunday and they are almost all closed. Only groups of young men, in threes and fours, walk the city this day. They are trim and fit and open-eyed. I realize they must be Turkish soldiers hanging out on a day off. The kids who stand along the Neutral Zone are now dressed in civvies.

This way, Costas urges us, I want to see the Post Office, the Courts of Law.

The Turkish Cypriot neighbor offering oranges

I know them very well, he tells us. And we follow him now, down the streets of his memory.

In the car he has been hesitant, not knowing exactly where to turn, feeling the disorientation of time and the distortion of memory. On foot he is sure. We walk past the entrance of the Central Post Office and down a side alley, then around to the back. The rear wall of the Post Office contains a thousand turquoise mailboxes with bright yellow numbers — against the old worn sandstone of this grand public building, lurid and vivid.

He remembers his old number. We stand there for a moment. He smiles, and tells us that this is what he's wanted to do for years. Now he feels satisfied. As we walk back to the car he says, "You know, without you, I would not have come here."

He relieves me of my guilt, but forces me to double back on my awareness. This is a neighborhood in which I feel comfortable, have even come to know two different fruit sellers, and nod easily at the nut and candy merchant in the Bazaar. It had first appeared as exotic to me, then simply another part of my Cyprus experience. And now through his eyes I see it as strange, intimidating, and hostile. The puzzle of understanding is profoundly complex.

As we pull out of our parking place a small boy appears just off to the side of our car. His deep black eyes peer into the window of the back seat, his hand close to Costas' face, on the other side of the glass. D tells me to watch out. I think she worries that I will hit the boy, and I pull away smoothly focusing on the road ahead. But, the kid has a gun in his hand and runs behind us. It has to be a toy gun, doesn't it? We turn the corner and pass through the Kyrenia Gate, out of the Old City, back to the main road.

Returning to the South, through the checkpoint, allows Costas and Roula to relax. I feel their bodies deflate, sag into the fatigue of the day as we drive back to our neighborhood. In the parking lot across the street from our building we peel one of the oranges and pass around the slices. It is fresh and juicy and bitter-sweet.

12 | 08 | 2005

When I first started teaching here, three and a half months ago, I couldn't tell the roomful of Elenas from the Nicolettas and Irenes. They all looked vaguely Greek, talked fast, wore lots of eye shadow, and seemed young and inexperienced. "Tell me what you don't understand," I would plead with them. And they didn't say a word the first few weeks. "It's a discussion class," I might plead to no avail. They were pleasant enough, but still, I was a strange, exotic newcomer just landed on their planet — a middle-aged guy from the 60s teaching about the 60s. Who did I think I was, anyway, with my "American Pie" and "Easy Rider" shtick?

But I kept it up. When they first started doing knock-out presentations, when those three girls put on black coats and hats, stuck yellow flowers in their lapels, and marched on President Wilson's White House, I knew something was up. They were starting to get it and I was starting to get them. And I told them that.

Today they bring their final journals to my office. Some just stick out their hands, proffering the notebook, saying so long. But others linger. I know them now, and not just by name. They have revealed themselves. Fragile or beaming, under the weather or full of their sense of the future, about to marry or getting brave about venturing out on their own, I know them and some of their stories. Stephanie, who is always freezing, a scarf wrapped around her neck even when it is 40 out, or Svletana, a Greek woman born in Russia who loves Angels in America"the very best." And Thanasis, who sits every day with a wool hat pulled down to his eyes and flirts with Caty on the porch outside our classroom. "He's engaged," she tells me one day as I come up the stairs. He shrugs.

They hug me, a few cry, tell me that I must return, that the course has changed the way they look at themselves, their society, and even America. Some leave me long letters, personal letters on the last page of their journals. "I think I speak for all when I say that you have managed to teach us something in a way that no other teacher has," writes one. "May you continue to teach what you teach 'American Style' for as long as you can, and continue to inspire your students as you have done with us."

Well. That's what it's all about, isn't it? I tell one of them, a lovely, soft spoken, doe-eyed Zoe, who has already lived a life and just returned to school, that her words mean a lot to me. She turns and grins, her eyes dance. It really makes my day. Some part of teaching is about this kind of exchange, isn't it? A basic do-you-like-me, I-like-you, gift-giving moment that pushes away doubt and sets the stage for affection, even friendship. Usually in the States it happens during

Ready to march on President Wilson's White House

their senior year. And these students are in their fourth year, even though I have known them for only four months. Come back, they tell me. We'll miss you.

I come back to my apartment, hug D and tell her we need to return somehow to this place. It's going to be very hard to leave.

Then we drive to Famagusta, on the Turkish side, where I do a lecture to first-year students on 1940s jazz, playing Charlie Parker and Dizzy Gillespie and Thelonious Monk for them on a boom-box. They have never heard of any of these giants, but they seem to understand what I'm trying to help them listen to. "It's a great revolution in music, you are in the presence of genius," I tell them. It's a good class, I nail it. I can tell by the way they stay focused and keep raising their hands as I throw out questions without answers. I don't tell them my energy comes from the kids back in Nicosia.

12 | 10 | 2005

The fields just beyond Nicosia have suddenly turned green. Its mid-December, the air is springtime warm, and the grass, and lettuce, flowers, and vegetables suddenly bloom and grow with abandon. Where three weeks ago the island was still dry, arid, and desert-like, now it flourishes. The earth, even that stone-filled gray dirt, looks rich. It is red-brown, and almost glistens with dew. The fields undulate softly here on the midwestern plains of Cyprus, sculpting odd shapes out of the gentle hillsides, breaking the horizon with their green-brown silhouettes.

Driving toward the Troodos Mountains, their peaks soft against the misty morning, we pass through a roundabout marked DEFTERA that guides us clearly left, south. When the road bends east, and then turns to gravel and we lose our way, we don't even mind. The landscape is so glorious, the villages Sunday-quiet, the green fields tinged with yellow like a painting in the sunlight.

We take coffee in Nicosia cafes these days, sitting in shirtsleeves in this December spring, as the city bustles around us. Nicosia is bright with Christmas lights. Cheerful shoppers parade up and down the avenues lined with boutiques, mostly women with children in tow, dressed in high black boots with pointy toes, sunglasses back on their heads. The municipal government has spent tons of money to string white snowflakes and red starbursts up over the streets leading from the modern city into the Old City. The decorations, anchored by a tall Christmas tree, lead pedestrians through the Gates, the wide openings through the Venetian walls that surround both halves of the Old City. On weekends, farmers from villages around Nicosia come to the walls and set up an extensive produce market. And when the Old City turns into an immigrant city, with workers from Sri Lanka, the Philippines, Palestine and West Africa crowding the streets, the market greets them with bargains.

As farmers drive into city, their four-wheel drive, four-door, diesel pickup trucks brimming with fresh goods, we poke our tiny Nissan through the countryside, in and out of tiny towns, eventually back to the misleading roundabout and on toward Deftera, Andrea's town. Aunt Irene has asked us to dinner. But what we don't know until we get there is that the whole family has shown up — grandparents, aunts and uncles, cousins.

And we, it seems, are the main course. That is, in addition to the chicken and lamb souvla, the grilled tuna and fresh-caught marlin, the pasticho, the roasted potatoes, the salads, tahini, olives, bread, grilled artichokes, wine, and fruit. We bring a woefully sweet and luxurious Profiterole cake — gilding the lily, to be sure, but everyone loves it.

Irene lives about a mile from her restaurant and her sister, Kiki, lives next door with her parents in a house in the rear. They have about two dozen mandarin orange trees lining the driveway, their limbs so laden with ripe fruit that they almost touch the ground. They cut several dozen oranges for us even before we hit the backyard. The bag is hardly in my hand before Irene's father calls us to his side. He is tending the charcoal cooker, its half-dozen spits turning slowly, the fat dripping into the fire. "You want whiskey," he asks, twinkling. Behind him large plastic crates filled with zucchini, tomatoes, and onions sit stacked against the garden wall. I think they must be for the restaurants, but after I see what he's cooking, I'm not so sure. His wife's flowers, pansies and carnations, spray their color from terracotta pots.

Clearly this is a family whose members work with their hands. In addition to their two small restaurants, they work in electrical and air conditioning installation, in a construction outfit, and in data processing at the Cyprus stock exchange. While they are not poor, this is not a professional family. Most have not gone to college, and they understand the value of what they do. The men drink whisky by the glass, the women hover and serve, heaping food on our plates, filling plates with more food and our glasses with wine as soon as either is empty. We offer toasts at regular intervals, "skinny yamas" someone calls out, and we reach across the table brimming with food and click our glasses and bottles, everyone standing, sitting, leaning to touch each other.

Elena and I talk quietly during dinner — she is Andrea's mother and Irene's oldest sister. When they discovered Andrea's rare form of leukemia she was just months old — one of only fourteen juvenile cases in the world. It takes eight years before they can bring her to the Anderson clinic for a bone marrow transplant. Elena tells me that she first thinks she has done something wrong — that this terrible ordeal is her fault. "But I did not drink or smoke, ever." She hopes that Andrea's condition has been contained — I note that she does not say cured — and I see worry etched around her eyes. When I tell her that we never stop worrying as parents, she looks relieved — as if this cliché is a revelation. Perhaps it is.

Andrea sits at the end of the table and babbles in Greek, in English and even a bit in French to everyone. Do you think I look like my mother, she asks me. She does not. Her older sister does, they have the same long face, the same light hair, the same almond eyes. But Andrea's round face resembles her father's, I tell her. She loves this. "He's my stepfather," she laughs and nods at the man at the end of the table. And I don't even feel stupid. She really does look like him. What a miracle that this young girl, all smiles and charm, is alive.

Turns out that the intervention of doctors at the Anderson Clinic in Houston made a huge difference to Andrea's case. Her condition had grown dire. Somehow the clinic became part of a process to discover a donor, a Turkish Cypriot man whose bone marrow could save her life as well as that of a critically-ill Turkish Cypriot boy. Both sides of the Cyprus divide engaged in identification of matching blood types, and the project became a beacon of hope for the process of reconciliation. The boy did not survive. Andrea lives to smile at us this afternoon at Irene's home. Andrea's story is well known in Cyprus, people immediately recognize her name or the outcome when I mention her to them. She tells us that she will be featured in a documentary made for French television on Christmas day. She says this with no affect, just matter of fact, like it's really no big deal.

And we just stumbled into her life. She has no idea how much richer we are for it.

Andrea

As we leave, we are dumbfounded by the family's warmth and affection. Most of the men depart to go hunting or watch football on TV and the girls scurry around getting ready for the first Christmas shopping Sunday of the season. Irene takes us upstairs to show us the rest of the house and the "stuff" she bought last month in Houston. Tucked away in her dresser drawer is a Guess watch, her Christmas present to herself that she obviously cherishes. She takes it carefully out of the leatherette box and holds it up in the light. "Polly-oreo" we both say, "very beautiful," showing off our expanded Greek vocabulary. When we come down to the kitchen, Andrea's grandmother, content to remain in the background washing dishes, rushes over to D She looks up at her and opens her arms to hug her. She is tiny, barely five feet tall, her face nestles against D.'s shirt. She has not spoken English to us at any time. "I love you," she says.

12 | 16 | 2005

Our last day on Cyprus. We've said a dozen goodbyes. Some twice. Leo and Soteria invite us for coffee again and again. Andros, D.'s bouzouki teacher, and Elena, his cabaret-singer wife, embrace us. Gem and Seray bring us back for a last dinner in their shop and dream about a life in America. And our dear Costas and Roula invite us for a last-moment breakfast.

I want a last swim, so we drive near the airport in Larnaca, approximately Texas on your Cyprus-American map, and go to the very first beach we visited in August. Only now there is no one there. Well, just a couple of English sun bathers, middle-aged, topless, red. It's chilly in the breeze — maybe 70°. To most Cypriots it is downright winter-cold. But the sea is actually warm, and I love the way the salt and texture of the water feels against my skin. I want to hold this in my memory as tightly as I can, to somehow press it indelibly into my brain. If I can do this, I will have saved and savored this entire experience.

When we drive back to the city and park in our place across the street, I look down. The cat has all but disappeared. But its rear paw remains, still formed, white fir boot and black leg. I suspect this is what will remain in my mind's-eye when all else fades.

Across the Green Line Again: 2007

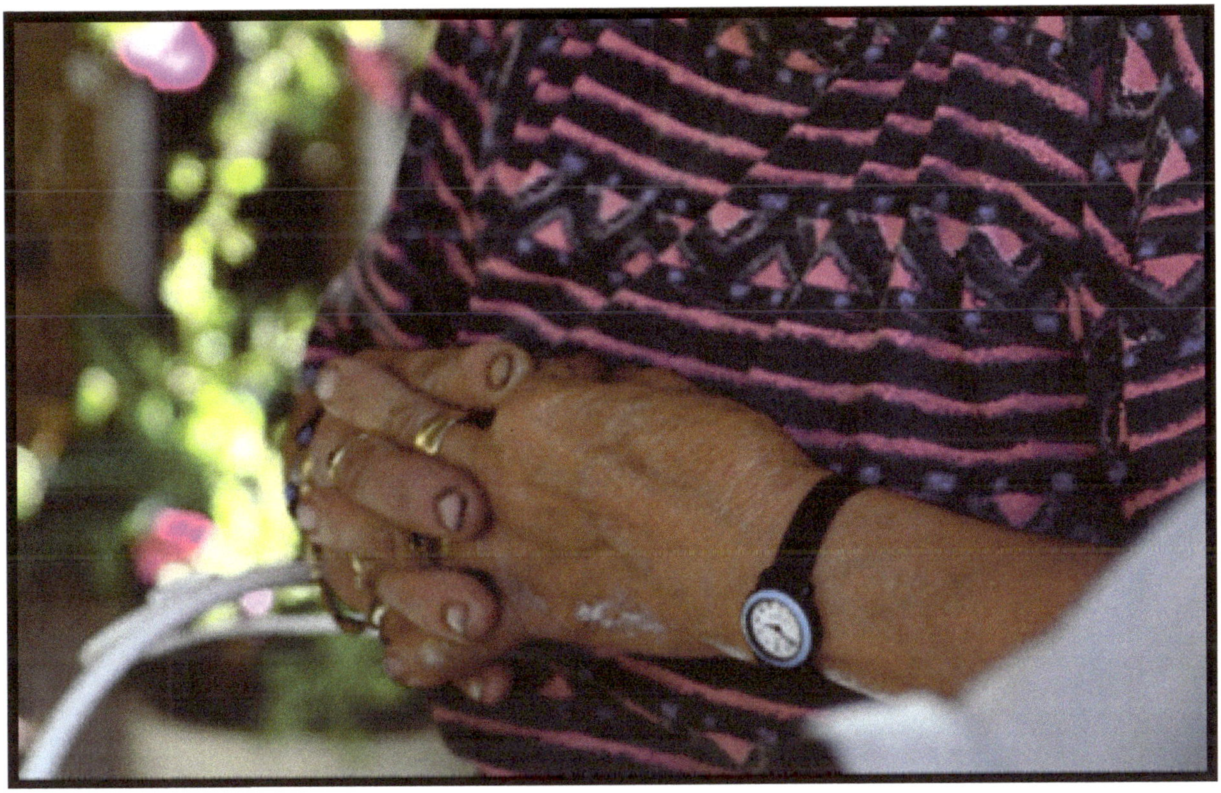

A grandmother's hands

09 | 11 | 2007

Obviously an auspicious starting point. I have only been back for six days. In some ways it is as if I have never left. Kennedy Avenue is too busy, drivers still honking. Costas and Roula upstairs remain exactly as before — warm, welcoming, funny, proud. Their children are prolific, two more grandchildren and one on the way. We even got our old apartment back. This time D is the Fulbright scholar, and I the spouse. She is even teaching in the same classroom at the University as I did.

But, of course, things do change. And even when they don't change, on Cyprus that is something to note. Cem seems older and more melancholy. We stopped at his shop and schmoozed for a couple of hours the other day. His face is drawn, weary. He kissed us both. Seray was not to be seen. Glenn in Lefkara was subdued, recovering from a broken leg and heat stroke. I can't tell if D and I seem older, too. I don't feel it. Irene had sold her tiny dine-in restaurant in Nicosia and has concentrated on the take-out place in Deftera. Andrea was at a concert. We didn't see her, but I'm very happy to hear she's well.

When we left 20 months ago they planned to open a new check-point downtown, on Ledra Street, where all the t-shirt shops and fast food places in the Old City vie for tourist money. The new Ledra Street, across and over the Green Line, would have joined South Nicosia with north right up the gut of the town. A boon for all the commerce on both sides. It never happened. Too complex to even tell why. Posturing from both governments. So, it is just as it was — the wall, armed soldiers at their posts, a dead end — and to us that seems depressing. Our friends express little hope that this situation will change. Even Leo, once irrepressible, has withdrawn. He's working on a film script, not showing any movies. "I've changed" he announces. No more chasing women. I think he means dreams. Soteria sits nearby, still lovely, quietly rolling her own cigarettes, smoking. The Weaving Mill now receives subsidies from the Cyprus Tourist Ministry, their small website proclaims.

For most of the last year I have been corresponding with someone named Chara. She has invited me to work with a small group of teachers from all levels and from both sides (!) who are committed to Historical Dialog. I had suggested a pilot oral history project to interview those on Cyprus from be-

Colonel Glenn, and Chara doing oral history

fore 1974. The US embassy liked, then didn't like, then sent me to the UN who liked but didn't fund, who sent me to Chara. She likes the idea a lot. But, she has no money. I've said I'd work with her "pro-bono." So.

We met for coffee on Monday downtown across from the Cyprus Museum. Chara is lovely. Dark-haired and open-faced, she is an elementary school teacher who commutes from Nicosia to Limassol. But she is also on the board of Directors of the group. We talk in the garden of a cafe, sprinklers seeding green on the dry rocky soil, a breeze soft behind us. She tells about what I hoped to find. A community of peace activists, Turkish and Greek Cypriot, who want better, who see "behind" the official verbiage and stories of both governments. They see History as revealing the truth, if only one could rewrite it correctly. I tell her this reminds me of our 1960s generation, of our quest for the "real" story, not the bullshit of Washington, the Pentagon, of President Johnson, General Westmoreland, and Dean Rusk. She seems to get that I get it. I don't try to introduce issues of subjectivity and all that modern epistemological talk — it doesn't have a place here. Instead, she invites me to give workshop on Oral History to a group of teachers in two weeks. She will invite thirty Turkish and Greek Cypriot teachers to learn from "Professor Rutkoff."

We walk half-way across the Neutral Zone and she shows me several newly-restored British Government buildings, colonial sandstone, that a local entrepreneur will turn into a restaurant cum condo development in anticipation of "reconciliation." Money talks, I hope. Then into the Ledra Palace, the once-stylish hotel that is now the UN Headquarters behind barbed wire and armed sentries. The Organization for Historical Dialog and Research has its headquarters there. Actually, it is a small room with a bunch of gray file cabinets, peace posters, and a small library surrounding a wood table large enough to seat ten. It is seedy and functional, plopped in the middle of a hallway of similar offices with rutted doorways that reflect into the faded stone floor. It makes me think of some ancient Bolshevik meeting room in Zurich filled with imagined cigarette smoke, samovars, and gesticulating rhetoric.

As we walk back to the south side of Nicosia we meet two men at a cafe. They are Chara's associates from the Historical Dialog group. One, a Greek Cypriot, is the first academic to teach Social Psychology at the University of Cyprus. The other is a Turkish Cypriot scholar who is writing about food and cultural identity. They are friends, speak English openly with each other, each explaining the subtle meanings of similar-yet-different Greek and Turkish terms of ethnic identity. They seem interested in my work about African-American culture. Meeting them is a sea change for me — they open up worlds.

What will our friendships be like four months from now, I wonder? But, for the first time this week, I have a sense of adventure. It is quite exciting. And humbling. I have dared to publish a small book about my stay here two years ago. And already I realize how little I knew. And now there is, at least, the opportunity to learn more. For example, in 1964 some Turkish Cypriots moved north in whole villages. I wonder what this story contains. I have not heard about it before.

There is, even now, a kind of experimental bi-communal village in the neutral zone, but Chara tells me that both groups are very intent on defining themselves culturally as opposed to the "other." I will have to visit.

9 | 15 | 2007

Cem emails us. "Come have dinner on Wednesday," he writes. We talked about going to the Spanish restaurant across from the mosque in the old city. When we visited him earlier in the week I gave him a copy of the book. He embraced me, and wouldn't let go of my arm. "You have understood me better than anyone," he writes at the end of the email. I wonder.

We cross the Buffer Zone early in the evening. Shadows play across the barbed wire and ghostly empty buildings. It is different from the sun and heat of the previous day, when Chara and I strolled up the entry to Ledra Palace. Far more eerie and even menacing at night. Turkish Cypriot workers jump down from the backs of pickup trucks driven by Greek Cypriot construction bosses, hoist their lunch pails to their shoulders, and walk exhaustedly next to us past Greek Cypriot police and though the chicane of oil barrels that funnel us up to the plastic Turkish customs kiosks.

My daughter Rebekah has joined us for the week. She and her brother, Josh, and his wife Lynn had visited two years ago during Thanksgiving. They have returned to experience a "new" season. It's hotter than ever, but this evening as the sun sets, a cool breeze seems to find its way through the labyrinth of the Old City and flutters awnings and flags as we stroll up the virtually deserted streets to Cem's shop.

As we walk, Rebekah asks what the restaurant will be like. Lovely I say — unless they are playing music, in which case it will be impossible to hear anyone talk. She shrugs. I lift my eyebrows. Cem has expanded his store to include three shops beside each other. One has the jewelry and clothing that Seray fashions, the other two the carpets that he sells. He grins as we enter, holds his hand out, palm out, like a courtier bidding us enter. There is a back room and he waves us in, past his computer, past the sink and bathroom, and motions to yet another door, this one to the courtyard behind the store.

The table, set to overflowing with a dozen salads, almost glows in the velvet of the night. We are stunned. It is the night before Ramadan, and they want to share this last "normal" dinner with us. Of course, there is nothing normal about it. Seray and another woman emerge from some invisible place behind the shop. We embrace. She looks older, not sad, but more worldly, her smile less open than I remembered, as if she has learned more than she will verbalize. But her English is so much better, she is no longer afraid to talk to us in front of Cem. Something has changed.

They introduce us to Cem's sister, Sebnam, fresh from Beverly Hills. She has her brother's coloring but not his face; it is broad where his is round, and she laughs. Her colloquial English allows both Cem and Seray to talk to us fully in Turkish which she quickly renders like a UN translator.

They cooked all day for this. And it is hard to remember that we dine in such a tortured and divided place.

Sebnam has only recently embraced the Suffism of Rumi and she is filled with the spiritual embrace of this new learning — as she expresses it, of love and pure energy. God is everywhere, she tells us, and we are all moved by her transcendental spirit. It also informs the ecstasy of the Dervishes, this form of Sufism. Outlawed by Ataturk in the 1920s, the "Whirling Dervishes" have survived as a cultural expression. We watched them two years ago at a museum in north Cyprus — mesmerizing and melismatic music sends the dancers into a trance, their capes whirling ever wider as they spin round and round. Now UNESCO has identified the movement as a cultural treasure and people are celebrating the 700th year of its origins.

Sebna's wonder informs the whole evening, even when we turn to Cem and Seray's dream of moving to America — he to work with his sister and she to become a teacher. "First," he tells us, "you know first, I must go Alaska." He is

Sebnam and Whirling Dervishes

real dreamer, Cem. Of vanished utopias (mythic places beneath the sea or in the national memory of the Turkic people, it hardly matters) and Alaska has become the newest version. We still cannot exactly imagine or understand his past, which remains as mysterious as his actual presence in north Cyprus.

But for this night, we are family.

9 | 15 | 2007

Our UN contact, Brian Kelly, tall and red, Irish-American and smart, overworked and congenial, has arranged for us to visit the "old" airport — the original Nicosia airport, now in the Buffer Zone — which has been virtually unused since 1974. "Sure," I say when the office asks if I know how to get there. "By the checkpoint, right?"

But the Irish peacekeeper informs us, "Not likely here. The airport is in a different sector." Ah. He scribbles directions, which tell us to take the round-about and carry on to the diversion. We get lost, and find ourselves talking to a Uzi-bearing Greek soldier at a very forlorn barricade that seems to lead to an equally abandoned road. The soldier takes my cell phone and calls Brian's office and waves us ahead.

We are nowhere. No other cars. Just a vista of abandoned farm fields, weeds growing between gaps in the macadam, and lots of barbed wire. It feels eerie at first, and then when we see a sign reading, "NO ENTRANCE LIVE MINES." My daughter says, "Oh shit," and I begin to sweat. Left or right? Who knows? We pass very close to a Turkish OP, a solder emerges, rifle cradled in his arms, following us with his eyes. I try to drive slowly, carefully, and Rebekah says "Oh shit," again.

We are alone as the road twists and turns past buildings with no entrances and no life. "Ancient empty streets too dead for dreaming," Bob Dylan's lines resonate in my brain as I steer up a steep hill, car engine pinging. "Evening's empire … vanished from my hand." The sun starts its slow descent before us, and the sky glows pink then purple off to the north, over the jagged Kyrenia Mountains.

Finally, a Slovakian MP offers to guide us. He's very nice and doesn't scold me for clearly driving through forbidden territory. One writer calls this the Dead Zone, a metaphysical and metaphoric place inhabited by abandoned cemeteries and abandoned tractors. And then, suddenly, we are in the world the UN has created for itself — soccer fields and golf courses, signs for the swimming pool, nicely decked-out houses, and a few renewed barracks now dot the landscape.

The MP hands us over to Brian, who hands us over to his "adjunct," another Slovakian officer, Michael Ivan (not Ivan as in Ruskie, but as in Lendel he tells us with great pride). "Follow me," he commands, hops into a UN Vehicle, very white and very official, and off we go.

No less eerie than the route in, but not frightening, is this airport. Like the Nicosia buildings along the Green Line, this shell of what once was is filled with silent voices. The main terminal, only in operation between 1968 and 1974, still reads NICOSIA INTERNATIONAL AIRPORT, except for the five-foot-high letters that are missing. The terminal is bad 60s International Style, the kind that Tom Wolfe would gladly blow up — a concrete, steel, and glass brick about the size of an American football field, perhaps five stories high. It is completely empty except for the signage, the 20-foot-high advertisements inside (banks and insurance companies) and the "Waiting" or "Departure" banners still fixed to the walls. Ribbons of barbed wire curl everywhere. We peek through the glass walls that define both ends of the building, laugh at the weeds turned into trees that sprout almost as high as the ceiling, and feel the sadness of this place.

The current Republic of Cyprus airport is much smaller than this relic. They are finally building a new one next to it in the salt marsh of Larnaca. This airport, intended as "temporary" when it was built in the 70s, was an expediency, a temporary solution until the "Cyprus Problem" could be solved. Now a new modern jetport will rise in the South to handle the tourists who pour into the island by the thousands each day. It is an admission that what was planned as temporary is now permanent.

"Do you want to see the plane?" Michael Ivan asks. "It is over here." It turns out the empty and gutted Cyprus Air jet has sat on the tarmac just to the north of the terminal for 34 years. Engines cannibalized, seats ripped out, tires flat, and the electronic nose and its gear amputated, like the terminal itself the plane is surrounded by razor wire. A local arts group poses a young woman in front of the open black snout, arms raised to the heavens for one of its posters. It is for a dance program designed to bring members of both communities together. Clearly a "safe" form of dialog.

NICOSIA INTERNATIONAL AIRPORT, the barbed shell and the last airplane

9 | 16 | 2007

For the past year and half I've been trying to obtain funding for an oral history project that would begin to collect stories of 1974 and before. I thought maybe, just maybe, this might become part of process of healing. And I had some encouragement – as well as some warnings – about the idea. About a year ago, a version of the proposal received initial support from the Embassy and Fulbright Commission. Then it evaporated, suddenly and overnight. I inquired with a handful of "peace" foundations around the world, Soros among them, and was received with indifference. But, as is my want, I persisted. One last proposal to the Embassy, scaled way down, requested a measly ten grand for the project. Yesterday came a two-line rejection letter.

It feels to me, confirmed by other small impressions, that people here are backing away from controversial projects. For instance, a British-Cypriot sociologist told me not to even try, and another friend said, also about year ago, "This will go nowhere if the government is in anyway involved." And then this.

The first sentence of my 2005 book about Cyprus refers to "our first visit to the Turkish Republic of north Cyprus." After I showed the rough copy to Leo and Soteria, just five days ago, Leo emailed me. "We must distance ourselves from the book," he wrote. It was too political. "We can't host a reception. It is forbidden in our by-laws."

I was floored. Yes, I had used the name TRNC rather than place it in quotes or "so called." Then I altered it to say, "we walked past the sign that read TRNC." But I had also, later in the book, written that only Turkey recognizes the "regime" in the north and had labeled photographs of friends there as coming from "north Nicosia." I was floored not just by the vehemence of what Leo wrote, but by the personal rejection. We exchanged more words electronically and he has now invited us to dinner so he can explain in person why this is so important to him.

Other writers have noted that using the words Turkish Republic of north Cyprus amounts to conferring on the "state" in the north a standing and status in International Law that Greek Cypriots deny. I have stepped right into the nest, haven't I? I wonder where it will lead. And I wonder who else I will offend.

A new book, "Echoes from the Dead Zone," written by a social anthropologist at the University of Cyprus, really digs into this complex of words, ideas, and identities. Yannis Papadakis, the first Greek Cypriot to live in the north in the 90s, learned Turkish and tried to fathom what has happened culturally and politically to this island. He does a much better job than I.

Each side, Greek and Turkish Cypriot, has created the image of the bloodthirsty, slovenly, war-like, over-sexed, violent, and oppressive "other." Each group accuses the "other" of exactly the same behaviors, the same omissions in historical story telling. Each has a museum of the other's atrocities, each a litany of families destroyed, property confiscated, and justice denied. And, equally remarkably, each group "remembers" that before 1960 or 1964 or 1974 (each important historical moments on the road to both independence and division) that they once got along well together, as Cypriots. They spoke each other's language, went to each other's weddings, and sang each other's songs, they recall. Now, it is as if the Golden Age of one Cyprus has become the era of the British Empire — a century that they simultaneously recall with great bitterness and against which they successfully united and rebelled.

As I've said earlier, it is the Bermuda Triangle of political misunderstandings perpetuated by historical mythology, self-interested individuals, and self-serving external governments. And now, more than 33 years after the two Cyprus were divided by the seismic fault of bitterness, fear runs down this fissure like molten lava.

9 | 21 | 2007

The Politics of Grammar, or rather the Grammar of Politics: what we learned during a four-hour discussion with Leo and Soteria last night — one that began at the Weaving Mill and ended at a restaurant right at the wall called Berlin 2/Checkpoint Charlie, was this: call the north the north, but not the North. Call it north Nicosia, not North Nicosia, and northern Cyprus, not North Cyprus. Capital letters to even these "progressive" Greek Cypriots spell recognition of a "place," a "regime" that they regard as illegal, without any international standing, a puppet of a foreign power, whose presence is due only to continuing military intervention and occupation.

You don't know history, Leo tells me, intermittently sipping a KEO or rolling and smoking a cigarette, his hair lank and beard trimmed to a long V. He looks Mephistophelean. "It is like a rape," he says passionately, "you can't commit a rape and then say I thought better of it."

I protest, rejecting the analogy. "It's really NOT the same thing." I hear my voice rising. "I wrote only about my own process of understanding, not a "history" of Cyprus." "No matter," they responded in chorus. To them, I had "sided" with the enemy. And this is like rape, apparently. They cannot support or accept my book. We point fingers at the text, finding words I used to name these places in the way they wanted it. "But not until page 113. Then it is too late."

"But this was a journal. That is when I began to understand." I'm pleading some version of ignorance and objectivity, an apolitical stance. I don't really believe in any of them, do I? But I am an outsider. Why not some slack here?

"No matter. You got it wrong on the very first page."

You cannot call the TRNC the "Turkish Republic of North Cyprus" without quotation marks. If you do, it amounts to recognition of a renegade state. I can't quite make them understand my "process" and I really try to understand their mindset. We stroll slowly down a few streets to an open air restaurant placed right at the Wall. A dozen tables are filled with locals and a few tourists, enjoying the cool evening, their plates filled with souvlaki, their glasses with beer. I look up to see an armed Greek Cypriot soldier standing sentry on the wall's ramparts. This makes a very powerful statement.

We go round and round with little resolution. Yet, somehow I think we remain friends. I really try to understand their point of view. I can see that my calling the Green Line a "border," something I regard as innocent, can appear very powerfully partisan to them. Sort of. I'm not sure who has learned what from whom.

Early the next morning, I write to my publisher and friend, Jerry Kelly in Ohio, suggesting that we make all Norths, Souths, Easts and Wests lowercase. I want to grant Leo and Soteria's ideas some validity without compromising whatever small understanding I have struggled so hard to achieve.

Finally, I am not surprised by their objections — I had rather anticipated them. I am surprised at their source and their volume. I send Leo and Soteria a very warm email thanking them for the evening and for working to uphold a friendship, and I explain my editorial changes. I wonder what they will say.

9 | 28 | 2007

Back across the Green Line to visit Cem and Seray and Sebnam. Maybe a Turkish carpet is in the offing, too. It is hot again, sweaty hot, despite the camouflage of a cool and comfortable evening. We walk very slowly across the Buffer Zone. We both say, interestingly, that maybe repetitions will allow us to focus on details that we can't see when the emotional impact of an experience is too powerful. Two years ago, at 2 am, walking back felt dangerous, even without the carpet we had enveloped in a black plastic garbage bag. Now, we stop in front of the building that the Historical Dialog group hopes to restore as a center of bi-communal learning and discussion. In the center of the ground floor, its shattered plate glass window jagged around the edges, is an old camera store. We had not seen it before. Inside, a New York Yellow Pages phone book from 1973, a bell-bottom jeans sewing pattern, a dozen bottles of beer in half-filled amber glass containers, and what looks like cardboard boxes of photographic chemicals.

Cem and his sister Sebnam are delighted to see us. We refuse their offer of a drink — it is Ramadan and they cannot join us. Cem looks crestfallen. "Either way we insult you," I say. "So get over it." He brightens at this colloquialism.

We sit on a pile of carpets and his face changes. He looks sad, yet is also very voluble. He begins what turns into an historical monologue. As he talks I think of Leo, on the "other" side. Same passions, same stubborn convictions. Cem tells us about "this government" being foolish, and he means the Turkish Cypriots, in trying to make "one country." This will never be one place, only two. "I admire Papadopulous," the Greek Cypriot President, "very much. He not want one Cyprus. He want two. That is his politic." So curiously, Cem sees past the rhetoric of the Greek Cypriot leadership for unification. "There," he motions toward the south, "there they say bad things about us here. They scare them people away." When I point out that both communities say the same things about the other, he just bulldozes me. "They stupid here." And I also think about the confused role of Turkish "settlers" in the Cyprus equations. They are, if Cem is at all representative, very mistrustful of the Turkish Cypriot "illusion" that they are still Cypriots. And Greek Cypriots, if Leo is at all representative, are very mistrustful of the mainland Turks for poisoning the politics and then the opinions of Turkish Cypriots. Without the presence of these Turks, their opinions and their weapons, the Turkish Cypriots would return to a peaceful coexistence with their Greek Cypriot brothers.

Suddenly then, Cem turns to the elephant in the room. We have wondered what to do and think about the Gray Wolves. Terrorists? Ultra-nationalists? Who were they and how could this gentle, cultured man — a man who sings a thousand Turkish art songs and can talk about the symbolic similarities of Peruvian, Iranian, and Turkish culture — have been part of this "neo-fascist" organization. And who are they?

And he tells us his story without asking — in retrospect, his story without him. After the 1980 coup in Turkey, the military imposed its will and tried to crush both the Grey Wolves and the Communists. The GW — and Cem makes them sound like Masons, secret and hidden — could not be destroyed. They were salted into the army and the civil service. The government had them scattered abroad, to north Cyprus, to Germany, to Azerbaijan — Cem has lived in all three places — where they became the unofficial arm of Turkish counterterrorism. These Jack Bauers, then, did the government's bidding unofficially, by striking back at the terrorist "enemies" of the state. They worked extralegally in the name of the Turkish Nation to support the very state that seemed to prosecute them as dangerous.

As Cem talks, I see how weary he is. I have wondered if he had been "sent" to northern Cyprus. But, he has still left himself out of this story. His eyes grow dim. It is mid-morning. He rose before 5 am to eat breakfast, and he will not eat again until sundown. If we were not there I imagine he would try to sleep.

But I ask, what is the alternative to fighting violence with violence? How does a society protect itself without perpetuating the cycle of human and moral destruction. Where does it end? I am thinking, of course, of Cyprus where an international army stands between two (or is it three!) sides, like the ancient Greek gods, watching their all-too-human brothers flex their muscles, strut, and pose to their lofty amusement. On the ground it is deadly serious, from afar both tragic and comic.

I am also thinking of Gandhi and Martin Luther King, of mass movements that resisted violence with non-violence. Of my own hatred of war and the marching I've done in the past. Is there someone here, on Cyprus, to bring these divided brothers together, as perhaps they once had been, with a real emphasis on the perhaps? And, while I'm at it. Who are the Cypriots? Were they once, back in the day, one people?

Sebnam offers the other alternative. We are all God's people, she says, her spirit glowing with real conviction, and if we find our way to him all this brutality will stop. It sounds beautiful when she says it. But, I feel worldly and skeptical on hearing it.

Cem has grown silent. Perhaps he is dreaming of Alaska.

10 | 1 | 2007

I talk to Costas and Roula for a few hours. I really like going up to their apartment. They live right above us. They have three balconies that circle their rooms, one set with a table and chairs where they take most of their meals and can watch TV through open glass doors that allow even the faintest breeze to cool the interior. The "business" with Leo has worked its way into my spirit. I am weary of this whole book process and of the way in which the minute offenses of Cypriot politics have suddenly collided with my own efforts. I can hardly call myself innocent in all this. After all, I did harbor, somewhere in my imagination, the possibility that I could make a contribution to this place. Remember, I tell myself one night when I can't sleep, remember what they told you two years ago, "Do not, ABSOLUTELY do not think that you can engage in reconciliation." I was just reporting, wasn't I?

Well, the same microcosm of annoyance and offense that we saw along the complexly-negotiated spaces of the Green Line have come crashing home. And now Leo is insisting that I give him carte blanche to go over the book manuscript to detect errors of "political correctness." Lacking this, he will insist on my eliminating any mention of him or his wife, Soteria, or his venture. I don't really know what to do and go round and round about it in my head.

I square my shoulders and say to Costas and Roula that I hope, really hope, that what I have written has not offended them. They trusted me and now I fear that I have betrayed that just by writing about them. Roula brings out a tray. "You want some fruits?" she invites rather than asks. The evening sky is black velvet; below, as far as our eyes can see, the whole city of Nicosia glimmers. It is wonderful to be in a place, in the middle of such an urban jumble, where we can still see the night sky. From here it is impossible to detect the boundary between the two. It is possible, however, to see the new version of the Turkish Cypriot flag now illuminated, blinking on the Kyrenia mountains in the distance.

And Roula looks at me. "My dear," her normal address, "you have made some mistakes, you know. We were not terrorists." And her eyes light up with a passion that I fear, because I am saying to myself, "Oh, man. Them too." But Costas tells me that he understands it is my book, that I am looking at their world from the outside and Roula agrees. "Of course, when you say the border" (and she really rolls her "d" into a trilled "r") "you must remember how we came with nothing after the invasion."

And I think how Leo insists that using the word "border" amounts to de facto recognition of the legitimacy of the other side, of north (not North) Cyprus. And here Roula — who lost all, who still dreams of her deracinated lemon tree in north Nicosia, who laments the war, the invasion, and their status as refugees — even Roula uses the word "border." And then I get it. There is no way that I can adjust what I write to please everyone. There are as many versions of the correct way to speak (and therefore to think) as there are Cypriots.

This kind of enforced or imagined orthodoxy just cuts discussion off at the knees. Well, not exactly discussion. For curiously (perhaps Alice in Wonderland might be an appropriate subtitle) virtually everyone we have met in Cyprus over the past two years has initiated a political discussion. Privately. But, put these ideas into printed words? No way. Omnipresent eggshells, bruised and delicate egos, a profound sense of unredeemable justice over lost and uncompensated property, and an enduring sense of inadequacy all make real open dialogue almost impossible. It feels like small-town America sometimes, where community opinion and approbation stifle expression like a wet wool blanket, smelly and irritating. And I'm still trying to figure out where to go with it all.

My new friends in the Association for Historical Research and Dialog seem to struggle with this as well. I attend their Friday night board meeting at the Ledra Palace Hotel. My wife tags along. She's having such a good experience here and wants to see if she can help. And she finds it as interesting as I had a week earlier to see "inside" this colonial-Moorish hotel, once clearly an outpost of British imperial high style. Indeed it is but six stories high — I remember thinking it much taller the first time I saw it two years earlier — and a thick rusted chain that winds around the posts of its wrought-iron gate is fastened by an old-fashioned padlock. I reach my hand inside the bushes that have over grown the left side of the gate, find a worn plastic button hidden behind the prickly branches, and push it. The Irish sentry — young, with blue beret and camouflage — admits us, and we act like we know where we are going as he smiles.

At the meeting room, a half-dozen young Cypriots, men and women, Greek and Turkish, sit around the non-descript conference table with plastic bottles of Agia Nicholae (Saint Nicholas) water irregularly placed and unevenly emptied around them. At the end sit two British UN soldiers. They are first on the agenda, and I am second.

Seems these two Brits have been working as liaison officers between the UN and this young group of teachers. They announce proudly that the UN has agreed to remove the spools and spools of barbed wire that surround and fill the building just down the street. This is the building that Charra showed me about two weeks earlier; they plan to turn it into a Conference Center for bi-communal discussions. Charra tells the British officers, proudly, that they have reached the final round of the competition with a Norwegian NGO that they hope will fund the project. The larger and blonder of the two men, legs crossed, hair cropped short, smiles and says he knows a thing or two about Norwegian philanthropy. But no one in the room seems to understand him — maybe his accent!-and so they smile politely.

Still, they leave with great promises for more cooperation and the meeting turns to me, to my plans to help them learn the ropes of oral history. We bat around ideas for a series of workshops with local teachers to take place in November and I suggest several strategies. For the most part, their nods indicate that my loosey-goosey form of learning-by-doing will meet their approval. But one woman, a Greek Cypriot teacher, wants more specificity. She wants to focus on one of the two key dates in recent Cypriot history, 1963 or 1974. I'm a bit taken aback. It is what I had first, in my most idealistic imagining, hoped for — the telling of stories about the invasion. But I had backed away, fearful that this would be too controversial. After all, if Leo could withdraw over the issue of a capital or lower case 'n' then how could we begin to train secondary teachers to work with oral history that centered on such a treacherous moment. Wouldn't we be walking through a political mine field?

Then an interesting counterpoint. I want to find an alternative to the Weaving Mill, and have asked them to consider hosting a reception for the launch of my 2005 Cyprus book. Here's what they say: "We are young and in a precarious place. It would be difficult." "Perhaps if we all read it first, twelve of us on the board." "Why didn't we do this with books some of us wrote." Clear enough. I gracefully withdraw. I don't exactly know what to do. Just let the book be published in the United States and not even worry about distribution here? Stay tuned, I say to myself.

10 | 1 | 2007

We attend the baptism ceremony of Lillia's third child, the sixth grandchild of Costas and Roula. It takes place on Independence Day – even though the actual date of their independence is in mid-summer. They have had trouble finding a priest precisely because it is a national holiday and everyone wants to be home with their family. It is a small affair in their terms – only about 40 adults and another 30 children. The immediate family. And us.

It is a real full-immersion dunking, this baptism. The two priests in attendance chant in counterpoint and as one of them holds the baby above the urn, naked as the day he was born, the rest of us crane our necks and cameras for a better view. The family has engaged a video and still photographer – it makes the ritual look like a cross between a wedding and a briss. They coat the child with oil, making the sign of the cross all over his body, and then swaddle him all in white. This event is sponsored by his godmother, who presides, clothes, and then fondles, while the actual parents sit off to the side, mere observers. The older priest has a short pony-tail and the massive body of a professional wrestler. His large hands envelope the baby, and we give no thought to the possibility of his being dropped.

In less than an hour, the service ends and we all drive off to a neighborhood restaurant for a massive spread. Dozens of dishes – salads, casseroles, pork loin, poached salmon, vegetables drenched in lemon juice – sit on long covered tables. In a matter of minutes, the men have shed their jackets and loosened their ties, and their wives circulate from table to table kissing the air, and pinching children on their cheeks. They are dressed to the nines, coiffed, bejeweled, and high-heeled. And, as the dinner evolves, each of the three groups – men, women, and children – have their own roles to play.

The children – whose dining takes at least three minutes, not counting an-

Roula at the baptism, and Candida

other thirty seconds for crepe-suzettes, ice cream, and dark chocolate cake — race up and down the cleared parquet dance-floor. Their mothers pop up like prairie gophers and pull them apart, before serious damage is inflicted. Even the presence of a magician — think the Ed Sullivan Show ca 1957 — fails to interrupt this pattern. The wooden cage where the magician holds his white and gray rabbits is particularly inviting and precarious. Children elbow each other out of the way to stand on tip-toe in order to pet the bunnies, mothers jump up to protect or intercept their loved ones, and the rest of us watch in awe. In the meantime, the men have left their dining tables. They are now gathered at a different table off to the side of the room, the sleeves of their French blue dress shirts folded up to their elbows, smoking cigars and exhaling puffs of gray smoke into the ceiling. Each group has clearly carved out its own space, given voice to its social and gender roles.

I think how much this feels like America in the 1950s: conventions of gender and age are choreographed with great precision. This middle-class ritual moment is a real reminder of how traditionally this Greek-Cypriot society actually behaves. Compared with two generations ago, they have achieved an unimagined degree of prosperity. But its newfound wealth has not really altered the primary and formative role of the family and religion. This is a village ceremony played out in the city.

10 | 3 | 2007

We drive to Deftera in the early evening. I call Irene and in Greek actually manage to make myself understood. We plan to come to the restaurant for dinner around 8 and hope she'll tell Andrea. I really want to see her. I want to actually see that Andrea remains in good health, to hear the lilt in her voice, to assure myself that all is right in her world.

The city planners of Nicosia have improved the roads since we last visited, widening a central artery that runs south from the city. The avenue passes first through the new suburbs and then towards nearby villages like Deftera. And remarkably, they have provided occasional lanes for parking. But we note, this early evening, that cars have jumped up on the sidewalks in front of already closed shops for the night. They huddle, dark and sad, at the feet of the glittering plate glass windows, waiting for the next day as if they were homeless, even hungry.

Along a parallel route, the main expressway out of town, the same planners have approved the construction of a spanking new Ikea and the island's very first shopping mall. The Mall of Cyprus, with a cineplex, shops, TGI Friday's and McDonalds, has opened since our arrival. But the accompanying ballyhoo has been dampened by the fact that the planners forgot to provide access roads and the rush-hour traffic backs up on the highway in sufficient volume to clog the only access to the equally brand-new municipal hospital nearby. And boy, has that created a stir. Postponed surgeries, snarled EMT runs, frazzled nurses, and angry letters to the newspapers.

So our avenue moves freely while a few kilometers to the east all hell breaks loose. They have also neglected to install signs informing drivers of the new road toward Deftera. But we persevere and find our landmark, the curiously-named "SNATCH" shop, then turn into the church plaza and park just beyond an awning that reads The Panic Room Café.

Irene, face flushed, brow coated with sweat, looks up and beams. She is standing in front of a waist-high charcoal fire-pit that extends across the width of the kitchen. She twirls the ends of the wood soulvaki skewers like a foos-ball player, chicken to the left, pork in the center, and crusty meatball sausages called sheftalia to the right, while she also answers the phone and tells her assistant what to do next. She's clearly in charge. We all embrace. "Come," she orders as she whips off her apron and takes us by the hand out into the cool night air. A cell phone appears in her hand. "Andrea," she explains as she calls her niece.

But it is not Andrea whom we see. A group of middle-aged men sit at several outdoor tables inspect us very carefully while inside this new coffee shop a dozen more play backgammon and watch football on a flat-screen TV.

"My father," she says proudly as Andreas emerges with a tray of espresso coffee cups, showing his grand smile, dancing eyes, and Erroll Flynn mustache. He greets us with equal warmth and invites us in, past the darting eyes of the men yelling at the small figures on the television. "Mama," he announces, and points to his wife, the woman who hugged D two years ago with such warmth. Ioanna bends over an ancient coffee maker, its top filled with tiny glass beads, fine like sand. She holds a long-handled Greek-Turkish copper coffee pot in her hand and runs it back and forth over the heated beads and the liquid in the pot turns, almost magically, into rich, thick, Cypriot coffee. She places filled

Irene

cups on Andreas' tray and turns to kiss us.

They have purchased this sprawling coffee shop just a block away from their daughter's restaurant, and the whole family shuttles back and forth between the two, tending soulvaki one moment, brewing coffee the other. It looks exhausting, yet clearly they are happy and fulfilled. "Boyfriend?" I ask Irene, who is the youngest grandmother I've seen this side of L'il Abner. "Not yet. No." She waves her hand as if to say not enough time for stuff like that. Turns out her sister and her husband, Andrea's parents, also run a Kleftiko restaurant a block in the other direction. They have Deftera covered, I think.

As we leave the coffee shop the men look up at us, this time approvingly, "Kale nichte," they call out to us cheerfully, "Good night." Clearly we have been accepted. Strolling back to Pan Rini's kitchen Andreas explains that this coffee shop is for the supporters of a local football team. They come to schmooze and to watch their team play on TV. It is entirely male but, Andreas assures us, they have "good character. No problem here. Good customer." I recognize the breakfast joints we love to go to in Ohio, all the grub you can down for a few dollars, and tables of men in Caterpillar hats chewing the morning fat.

We sit outside Irene's restaurant at a table set for six. Irene joins us, sharing the yogurt and salad but not the heaping dishes of chicken souvlaki and sheftalia. The patates are fried crisp and delicate, they really melt in our mouths. The KEO beer, light and ice-cold, goes down easily. A black BMW pulls up next to us. Andrea and her mother arrive and we embrace them both. Andrea looks virtually unchanged, even though almost two years have passed. But her English, D and I agree, has become more Greek inflected, which makes it even more charming. She hasn't been to the United States since her last check-up in 2005. She's clearly a teenager now, however — jeans, layered blouse and sweater, cell phone and a great passion for AMONIA, the other Nicosia football team.

She's been asleep. Her school is a grind. And already she feels the pressure to excel, to get good grades, to move into the flow of "normal" life in Cyprus. These cultural expectations, ones that she embraces, reinforce traditional gender roles. She will go to a local university, find a good young man, marry and have a family. And not too late, either. I try to tell her about college in the U.S., about a world out there, and she is adamant about what she hopes for. I completely understand.

Her mother seems relaxed, even happy. She loved what I wrote about all of them, she tells me, and when I ask if she can "now take a deep breath," she nods. "Yes. Finally." Still, there is something delicate and fragile about both of them. Where Irene is petite but solid and projects a sense of physical prowess, as if nothing can stop her, her sister and niece cry out silently for something more.

Andrea gladly shares our feast, bails us out of not finishing the too-much food with which Irene has graced us. In a matter of minutes she polishes off all that we cannot.

At that moment, as we push the plates slightly forward on the table, a man appears and embraces the family, particularly Andrea. He is her local doctor, the man who first took care of her, who engineered the process of finding the Turkish Cypriot donor, who helped her with treatment first in Israel, and then identified the Anderson clinic in Houston. He is truly happy to see her and we love the bond that clearly exists between all of them.

And then Andrea smiles faintly. "I have something to tell you," she announces. "Tomorrow is my seventh birthday." Seven years since her transplant.

We kiss them all goodbye. We will return to the cafe very soon. But as we drive away into the darkness of Deftera, headed back into the city, I experience what I can only call real joy. It has been the best moment of our visit. It renders all the other nonsense on Cyprus meaningless. Well, meaningless is too strong. Less overpowering, less dominant.

10 | 6 | 2007

I have represented my college, Kenyon, at several fairs for international students, including this one in my home base of Nicosia. The Fulbright Commission hosted the event at their center in the Green Zone. Just down the barbed-wired street from the Ledra Palace Hotel, the fair brought at least 400 Cypriots to us. And what surprised me was the large numbers of Turkish Cypriot students. They looked, most of them, very much like the Turkish kids I had met the week before in Istanbul. But then again, they didn't. It seems to me that these Turkish Cypriots are considerably less affluent than either their Greek or mainland Turkish counterparts. And whereas these other students come from, for the most part, high-powered English-speaking schools for internationals, the Turkish Cypriots present much more modest credentials — no IB programs, no preparation for A and O levels, no standardized exams like SAT's or TOFEL. And their English is less polished. Most of them seek technical educations; they have little idea of American traditions of liberal studies. But my heart went out to some of them. They sense something different, could make such interesting students, if only they had some encouragement and support in this direction.

In this way I think that the Turkish Cypriots comprise a double minority, demographically and socially. They are Cypriots, of course, but in north Cyprus they are a small number encased in a growing population of Turkish settlers who have been coming to the north for thirty years. And compared to Greek Cypriots, they are economically disadvantaged, less well-off. This adds another dimension to the "Cyprus Problem" which can no longer be understood as a conflict between the two communities, but among Greek Cypriots, Turkish Cypriots, and Turkish persons on Cyprus.

After the fair, the Fulbright folks hosted a dinner reception at the spanking new restaurant across the street, the one that has just opened in "spec" of a political settlement. It is lavish and elegant, complete with polished wood floors, outdoor dining verandas, antique carpets, and furnishings all set in the revitalized British colonial sandstone building that has been rescued from disintegration.

We dine outdoors, finally enjoying the breeze that only toyed with the heat of a late summer blast. This is Cyprus at its best. I walk over to the checkpoint to pick up D., who has been visiting with Cem and his sister Sebnam, and we stroll back to the restaurant through the dark night.

The presence of this upscale place completely changes the feel and the look of the Neutral Zone. It teases us to imagine something different, a landscape where bullet holes and barbed wire might no longer exist. Luxury cars parked on cobblestones, the lights of the restaurant itself, the sounds of laughter and wine being poured all give voice to a nocturnal fantasy.

We walk out onto the patio where a half-dozen round tables set to white-linen standards await us. Daniel Hadjittofi, the genial and engaging head of the Fulbright Commission, calls us over to his table. We join four couples, all Fulbright directors — some Greek Cypriot, some Turkish Cypriot, one American-Greek — and Daniel says, "You can say anything you want here." I understand

Daniel Hadjittofi

just what he means. He is very aware of my attempts to find a funding fulcrum for my dream of doing an oral history project on Cyprus, and the controversy this proposal has touched off. It is his way of telling me that he has understood me. It goes a long way to calming the waters of my spirit.

And like the restaurant itself, this group of well-meaning Cypriots, Greek and Turkish, sit comfortably and engage in discussion about almost everything, from the varieties of Halumi, the local cheese that everyone swears is best when it comes from their home village, to life "before." And, of course, "before" means prior to 1974. This collection of stylish and sophisticated colleagues who work together setting Fulbright policy and practice, attests equally to the possibility of reconciliation. Daniel, Cypriot-bred, a teen-ager during the war, a refugee from the north, American educated, truly stands for the kind of transcendence that the future of Cyprus so desperately needs.

As we stand in line waiting for our turn at the buffet, he tells me in precise terms what I've been sensing since our return to the island. "You know, we thought two years ago that we had to work hard to have Talat (the Turkish Cypriot political leader) involved. Now it turns out that it is this side that we must worry about." The President of the Republic of Cyprus has just declared for reelection in the spring and is once again playing the nationalist game that talks peace but walks a very hard line.

I can't recall how many Cypriots, Greek Cypriots in particular, have said, "If the politicians would leave us alone, we the people, we'd find a way to solve this." The table this evening, at least for a couple of hours, embodies this dream.

10 | 19 | 2007

These extensive travels are exhausting. Visit a city, interview some students, eat a bad cold dinner in a hotel room, catch an early morning plane and do it all over again.

After I return from Athens, Thesalonaki and Sofia, the weather turns. It is suddenly comfortable, shirt-sleeve temperatures during the day and refreshingly cool at night. We can even walk and not find ourselves drenched in sweat after a few meters.

Sofia is especially interesting. The layers of recent history — Ottoman Empire, monarchy, Soviet client, and aspiring European democracy — have all left their architectural marks. Neo-classical public buildings, pastel and charming, sit next to monstrous concrete "blocks" that make the Taylor homes in Chicago look almost welcoming. And traffic. Well, all these cities in this region — Turkish/Greek/Bulgarian mixtures of sweet-smelling spices, honey pastry, and grilled chicken — are stuck in a thick pudding of automobiles, buses, trucks, and cabs that congeals at every intersection. Bulgarian cabbies work with special effort to speak only their native tongue, drive too fast, get pissed off at almost anything, and really lean on their horns. "Traffic," they each say, shrugging their shoulders and raising their palms to the sky while the meter ticks and ticks and ticks. I'm sure it is the only word they know in English.

Sofia looks lovely downtown, but within three kilometers the city appears poor and unkempt, where no one cuts the grass or picks up the garbage, or feeds the dozens of stray dogs that lie curled up against curbs and trash-bins. Tiny shops in plastic kiosks replace flashy downtown boutiques. Men huddle in plastic-leather coats smoking cigarettes, their pale blue eyes following passers-by.

This is a poor country by EU standards. And I think, as the plane lifts off from a virtually brand new and virtually empty international airport, that the people in Cyprus don't know how good they have it. At least the people in the south, in the Greek-speaking Republic of Cyprus.

In Cyprus the new cold front greets me, deep blue sky, no humidity, a breeze brushing across my face as I descend from the plane down to the tarmac. The almost-crisp air renders the outlines of buildings and mountains with remarkable clarity, especially the five knuckles that look down on the giant Turkish flags that are now illuminated each night. It feels good to be "home," I say it to myself. Back on the wrong side of the road, back in a place where the souvlaki tastes ever-so-sweet.

For the first time since we have been back on Cyprus, the store shelves are filled to overflowing with pomegranates. They blush with red-yellow-gold, as if, like autumn in Ohio, they have donned the colors of the season. We add them to our breakfast table, alongside the Greek yogurt that has the dense velvet consistency of sour cream combined with the tang of real cream. We add local honey, made in a monastery up in the Trodos, and cardamom. Cut in quarters, the pomegranates yield their ruby-red seeds like tiny babies-teeth, deep-red on top, almost white at the root. They glisten and shine as we break them loose from the web of their ecru membranes. Breakfast is normally a time to talk about the day ahead, but the seeds compel our full attention, as if raising our heads will break the spell of their sweet-sour hold on us. They will be here for the rest of our stay, the next two months, and that brings us great pleasure. This is the Cyprus that British writers in the halcyon days of the Empire adored from their verandas.

A counterpoint of disquiet, however, adds a dissonant note. During the ride home from the airport we pass a convoy of tanks, hatches open, machine guns at the ready. The commanders sport tiny microphones that wrap from ear to cheek, ones that I first saw Madonna wear in concert almost 20 years ago. My driver, a laconic English-Cypriot named Paul who loves to talk about American television, tells me "Ah. The Greek army." When I state, oh, they must be on maneuvers, he tells me no, they have, all 15,000 of them, been stationed in the south since 1974. "To protect us," he says proudly. So, there it is. The Greek Cypriot army is supported by the Greek army while in north Cyprus the Turkish army remains a force of some 40,000. I wonder if there are Turkish Cypriots in the Turkish army. I expect they are the only people on the island who are unarmed. I will have to inquire of Cem.

10 | 21 | 2007

I decide to go and visit Mehmet, the Karagoz shadow puppet-master, and Mustafa, the shoe-store owner in north Nicosia. They are each warm and welcoming to us, greeting us like old friends, offering coffee and tea in tiny hourglass-shaped cups. Tiny spoons with filigreed handles adorn the silver and make these ritual formalities evermore unique. We are struck ever more powerfully by the difference between the north and south versions of the city — how much they have grown apart economically and culturally. north Nicosia is a catacomb of tiny shops and tumble-down stone buildings with off-duty Turkish soldiers roaming the narrow streets, in stark contrast to the ever expanding consumer capitalist economy of the south. I show these two Turkish Cypriots their photographs in the copies of my book, and they are very pleased. No effort to censor, or change, or critique here. Just a broad smile. When we return through the Greek Cypriot portion of the checkpoint a police officer with a shock of curly white hair approaches us. "What is your nationality he asks." It is the forth time in two weeks this same policeman has asked us the identical question.

The next day we cross back over the Green Line to see Cem, Seray and Sebnam. "Just a short visit," I state *sotto vocce* as we clear the Turkish police-border guards who scrutinize our passports, examine our faces, look back down at our passports, say something unintelligible to each other and wave us through. D nods. She knows just what I mean. Short visits have a way of turning into marathons.

Just a cup of tea (one learns) and a chat. We have brought a box of profiteroles, the most gooey chocolaty concoction made on the Greek Cypriot side at Pralina, where we enjoy coffee across the street from Costas' office from time to time. Seray and Sebnam adore chocolate. We put it in the fridge up in the loft that sits over the carpet shop. We know they will find it soon enough. We pass the time with the "girls," who giggle and laugh at almost everything we say.

As we make motions to leave, Cem leans in and says, "In just ten minutes we prepare brunch." He is smiling broadly, his pointy shoes shined to perfection, his silky shirt loose and unbuttoned at the neck. Impossible to say no, and D and I both know it. We don't even bother to go through the usual phony consultations that married couples indulge in to get off the hook. "Sure!" we say. And since we know they will absolutely not allow us to help, we sit on the pile of carpets in the main room and start talking with Cem's newest business partner.

He wears a Georgia Tech sweatshirt, is tall, pale and wears a stylish short beard. His blue eyes are alive. He is Iranian. "Bush is good," he announces proudly. "He is strong. Life is better now." Well, it doesn't leave too much room for my usual "don't blame me, I didn't vote for him" line. This young man, surely this side of 30, loves America, loves our current president, and thinks that Iraq and Iran are better off for American military intervention. We can't begin to fathom what he is suggesting, except for the "my enemy's enemy is my friend" logic that lurks beneath his statement. Fortunately, we are saved by the dinner bell.

Up in the loft the table is set for eight. So much for a spontaneous, improvised meal. Cem and Sebnam's father, recently arrived from Ismir, lounge glued to the mid-day news on the TV that sits, like Elija, just off the head of the table. Sebnam's father is of indeterminate age, handsome like his children, and speaks only Turkish and French — something D and I can manage some of the time.

He loves showing pictures on his cell phone of the 1930s when he was a young man. Next to him, one of Cem's high-school friends, a burley mustachioed fellow with long black curly hair, flattens himself into a soft easy chair. He has materialized out of nowhere, literally arriving unannounced in north Cyprus from his home on the mainland. It is just after the end of Ramadan, and he knocks on the door, opens his arms, and falls into Cem's warm embrace.

As the dust of his arrival settles a new face appears at the table. "Dervish," he announces proudly, intently peering through rimless Ralph Lauren eyeglasses. A Turkish Cypriot, mild-mannered and trim, Dervish engages my wife next to him as I try to listen in between mouthfuls of fragrant brown bread, a Turkish frittata of eggs and cheese, fresh tomatoes and cucumbers, and coffee.

Dervish tells of his involvement in the events of the early 1970s. A teen-ager then, he was recruited — but it is not clear by whom-into a Turkish Cypriot militia and armed. He describes the home-made Thompson machine gun that he carried and used, with mechanisms imported from England, stock and assembly home grown in Cyprus. One night, following the invasion, close to the Green Line, he stopped a Greek Cypriot staff car, and....

Then abruptly, he looks over at me. "You have shopped for Turkish Delight?" Yes. Of course, at the bazaar. "I have sold it to you, from my shop." And we both, instantaneously, remember the other. Now he is a city councilman for north Nicosia, and is carrying out plans to build a sport field on the empty, dusty lot between Cem's shop and the old Venetian Walls a hundred meters away.

This is our brunch, then. A Gray Wolf and one of his closest friends, likely another Wolf from Ismir; an Iranian carpet and jewelry dealer; a Turkish-Cypriot militia fighter turned city councilman; a Turkish-American carpet expert (Seray); Cem's father, still glued to the TV; and two "pink" Americans. Three hours of talk and food built on a twenty-minute visit. Hardly unusual, but so different.

We begin to shift in our seats, preparing for the usual "you didn't eat enough," and "what, you are leaving so soon" when Dervish again turns to my wife, D. He asks if she has seen the Turkish flag on the mountains. He means the giant Turkish and TRNC flags that are now illuminated every night, strobing on and then off, a "look at me now" message white-bright against the black Kyrenia Monuntains.

Indeed we have. From two windows of our apartment. Daily, I can feel D thinking. To us the flag appears a provocation. You can see it from as far as 40 kilometers south of Nicosia. She pauses. "I think it incites hostile feelings." Bravo, I say to myself. I'm not sure what I would have answered. He looks sad for a moment, the same eyes as Cem, deep and mournful. But that was not my intent at all, he says softly. We only want to tell the world that we are here.

10 | 22 | 2007

Our first football game this season. We're back in our old seats with the APOEL regulars. This game is at their home field in Nicosia. They play the team from Limassol that we watched two years ago, when a near-riot caused the death of a local policeman. This time, the consequences of that sad moment are evident — the riot police are in full gear, with Plexiglas shields and bright yellow jackets. They sit in double rows up and down the stairs in the four corners of the stadium. Normal fans sit across from each other from goal line to goal line, while the young kids, the "fanatics," fill each end. The cops fill in the seams between all of us.

And then they begin — the game and the chants. Banners fly as if it were a battle, waiving in the night wind as the kids sing each other deaf and mute. Flares appear, laying down wispy smoke that drifts up and hovers over the playing field. The flares burn bright iridescent red, and the crowd sways to the rhythm of the chants. As the game begins, however, the fans quiet down and pay attention. We relax up above in our perch at the home team's forty yard line and appreciate the way the new players move the ball, passing it with precise authority, making football the wonderful combination of individual skill and teamwork that it is.

We score twice in the last twenty minutes of the first period. Each time a forward steals the ball from the other team's defense within striking distance of the goal and each time they put it, as they say, "into the back of the net." Our neighbors high-five each other, light up huge cigars and beam. They are happy to be ahead. Time winds down.

And then, from the far end of the field, a flare spits its way out from the seats and onto the field. And another. They land behind the APOEL goal-keeper, who turns and gestures to the crowd. He is pissed, they have gotten to him.

Then a long white piece of metal or wood soars out, like a spear, and finds the grass, bounding lazily until it settles near the net. The Limassol "kids" are in a frenzy and the rest of us stand to see what is happening.

The referee says something to the coaches, the announcer says something in Greek that gets the Limassol fans even more involved, and then the whistle blows signaling the end of the first half. I stroll up the stairs to the restroom, located strategically behind the KEO beer garden in the upper deck, and as I return to our seats I note that many fans are simply leaving. I think to myself, just like at baseball games at home, they are leaving early to avoid dealing with the parking lot grid-lock at the end of the game. But by the time I return to our seats something else has clearly happened.

D is smiling. "It's over," she tells me. "The referee called off the game." I grasp this immediately. "Oh, they forfeited." Not exactly. The other team will be punished, the referee felt his own safety was in jeopardy and the stadium announcer had appealed for calm at least twice in the waning minutes. It seems a shame. The APOEL team had played very well, and now as we walk to our car, all the home team fans are subdued, even quiet.

On the way home Yiorgos, Costa's son who brought us to the game and who had once played on the Cypriot national team, joins us in discussion. A few bad apples, he says. Just send in the cops and drag a few out and it will be over. I advance my own political/anthropology view that this is about boundaries and confrontation of authority in the face of the inability to deal with the real ones "out there." Nonsense, says another fellow, a government official who works with sustainable energy; it is just teenagers acting out. Well, that's kind of what I meant, I add.

The next day the newspaper points out that two men have been arrested for throwing dangerous materials on the field. They have been nabbed thanks to a surveillance camera system that now operates in the stadium. One man was 22, the other 29. So much for teenaged hooliganism, I think to myself. And I wonder.

10 | 25 | 2007

We meet my student, Anna, from two years ago at a local cafe — the one that feels like Berkeley in the 1960s, American rock on the sound system, scruffy flannel-shirted college students from the University of Cyprus, dark tables, the whole bit. She has returned to Cyprus for a few months between earning her MA in Birmingham, England in Latin American Studies, and moving to Vienna to be with her new boyfriend. This is our second meeting since my return to Cyprus and I find that I really like and admire Anna's outspoken directness, even more than I had two years ago when she invited us to dinner at her house.

The conversation starts slowly, about old school friends, classes, plans for the future. But since it is OXI-Day weekend the discussion turns, as it almost always does here, to Cyprus. OXI-Day is a Greek national holiday that celebrates a military decision to deny, say "no," to a 1930's German request to send troops through Greece. It has become the second biggest celebration in the Republic of Cyprus. This year the government, with presidential elections on tap for February, has instructed schools to make sure that the children who take part in the marching band parades do not appear scruffy and disorderly as they have in the past.

We talk about the right-wing obsession in Cyprus with Greek nationalist symbols. Even the fence at the football stadium proclaims that "APOEL IS GREEK" on a blue and white banner. How powerful these symbols and emotions are, and how inhibiting they are to the process of reconciliation that everyone says they want but seem unwilling to act on.

We tell Anna that we have met Dervish, the man who constructed the Turkish flag on the side of the mountains. And her eyes, already deep and intense, positively glow with anger. This humane young woman, committed to peace and to a version of social and ethnic equality, stares right through us. "I hate that flag," she says. "I hate it because of what it represents and because of what it did to my parents."

She breathes deeply, as if stunned by her own fervor. "And they are using our fucking electricity."

And there it is. The division of the island of Cyprus into two unequal entities has left a scar just a fraction of an inch beneath the surface of even the most progressive Greek Cypriot's skin. And I feel myself react to Anna's emotion.

The contradictory whip-saw that exists between the now-released nationalist fervor of Anna's response and my own reaction to it, at once appalled and humanely sympathetic, moves me. And yet, I think, how can I even imagine the

Anna

depth of pain and suffering that so many Cypriots — Turkish and Greek — have endured for the past thirty-five years. It makes the fault line of 1974 bottomless.

10 | 28 | 2007

The group that I met at Ledra Palace Hotel a few weeks ago invites me to conduct a workshop on oral history. Chara, the leader and her closest colleagues, a lovely woman named Rena and a deeply intense intellectual social psychologist named Harris, greet me early on a Saturday morning. We have arranged to use the Fulbright office in the Green Zone — my friend Daniel offers it at no charge, one of the many ways that he supports, unacknowledged, what I shall call "the movement."

The Association for Historical Dialog and Research is a bi-communal association of history teachers, primary and secondary, in Greek- and Turkish-Cypriot public schools. They are, as I tell them in my introduction, the real heroes. Both as teachers (and I feel exactly the same way about the dozens of urban public school teachers I work with in the U.S.) and as women and men courageous enough to work together for historical understanding. They so much remind me of my better self from 40 years ago, and I am proud to be part of their group… hence my sense of The Movement.

I have them for three hours. And they are like so many teacher groups, a bit shy at first and then remarkably adept, intelligent and open. Most of them have been working in this group for awhile and they know each other. It is a real pleasure, after encountering so much cultural/ethnic/religious hostility, to see these Greek and Turkish Cypriots greeting each other with kisses on both cheeks. They have, some of them, worked to learn each other's languages, and become clearly affectionate colleagues and friends engaged in common enterprise.

It is clear that the common commitment to some version of historical truth and understanding underlies the solidarity I feel from the workshop participants. They believe that their received truths are merely versions of political ideology, and have come together to find common ground in something that they can see is true and real. Of course, that is what is complicated, isn't it?

I lead them in a discussion that many have probably had before, that the revelation of multiple narratives subverts received knowledge and at the same time nurtures critical thinking. The implications of this, the light on the elephant in the room — they like this turn of phrase — means that the anis horiblis of 1974 can be addressed. It is what they want to talk about anyway, and like a three card monte dealer, I've concealed and revealed it all morning.

Not a person in the room flinches when I ask them to complete a homework assignment. I hand out inexpensive disposable cameras and ask them to shoot a roll of photographs on "anything about 1974." And I refuse to qualify either "anything" or 1974. I want them to pick images and use them as prompts to write oral histories. They'll bring them all to the next workshop, and with some luck, we'll have 60 or so pictorial/narrative stories about 1974. But, who knows — I guess I'll find out in three weeks how this experiment works.

10 | 29 | 2007

Two old, dear friends — Alice and Richard — are visiting. I've known them for more than 50 years. Richard and I went to elementary school together and Alice and I to camp. So I've known them longer than they've known each other. They arrive with good medical news and we want to celebrate by taking them to a taverna for meze and song. But, the place we like, Minori, is closed this week. What to do?

Elena, who sings so beautifully, and her husband Andros, a gleeful bouzouki player, agree to go along with our improvised plot. As the house singer at Minori and also as our friend she will sing two songs for us at her house.

Hers is a home we have visited many times. Andros taught my wife, D to play the bouzouki two years ago. Elena and I would drink tea and talk about family as D and Andros practiced scales and tremolos in another room.

A cross between a banjo and a mandolin, the eight double strings on the bouzouki lend themselves to a style that combines melody and rhythm. This makes it just right for the intense and often sad traditional Greek songs that accompany equally intense and often joyous dance. It is Greek soul music I think, roiling the emotions with the same passion as the blues.

Of course, our American friends know nothing of our plan — only that we are introducing them to two of our Greek Cypriot friends and that we are picking up some take-out souvlaki to bring with us.

We arrive and spread out the wrapped pitas on the table. Their fillings, fresh and warm chunks of grilled chicken and crispy charcoaled meat-balls, spill out onto the plates. Elena and Andros bring over armfuls of beer, wine, water and zivaniah. We share introductions. Elena and Andros include Elena's mother, a wise and witty 90-year old woman dressed in traditional black. She makes fun of my Greek and answers in loud English. "Kale nichte," I say meaning "good night." "Kale Spera," she corrects, "is good evening, not nichte, not night." We sit elbow to elbow, she and I. And next to her, across from D., is Xenofon, Elena's older but not eldest brother, who has only recently returned to Cyprus from twenty years in Greece. He speaks excellent English, loves to gently tease his mother, and not so gently tease his sister. He is a singer as well.

As we clear the dishes, something not normally allowed to a male in this household, I softly ask Elena if "it is ok." She smiles softly, "I don't know. I'm embarrassed." Then she looks back into the dining room and grins. "Yes. Sure." And she opens the bouzouki case and hands the instrument to Andreas.

They sing two songs. He plays with such verve but remains behind the loving intensity of Elena's rich soprano voice. We are completely silent, entranced, as she sings two traditional Greek love songs, ones we have heard many times at the club. I watch D's eyes close, for she has tried them herself on the bouzouki. And then I see Richard and Alice. They are entranced. It is a gift and I'm so pleased to have been able to help present it. I'm grateful beyond words to Elena.

She stops, takes a sip of water and looks over at her brother. "Do you want to join me?" It is an unofficial and impromptu encore. His baritone, he tells us later, doesn't always fit with her range, but this time they match like twins and sing a song that really dips and glides around the room, enveloping us in its sonority and beauty.

Elena and Xenofon spend most of their time goofing on each other. Not now. They tell each other that they love and respect their human person and talent. And we all understand that we are privileged to witness this exchange. My friends have tears in their eyes. They need no Greek to comprehend the magic.

11 | 1 | 2007

It is officially the start of winter. The Hilton drains its outdoor pool, women start strolling down Micharois Avenue, the Fifth Avenue of Nicosia, lined with upscale shops and outdoor cafes. They wear brand new knee-high leather boots, huddle in cashmere sweaters, wrap wool scarves around their necks. It is 82 today.

But, it does get dark at 6 pm, and daylight savings ended almost week ago. Outlines of Christmas decorations now hang overhead, between buildings, at the entrance gates to the Old City. With neither Halloween (save for ex-pats) nor Thanksgiving (save for us) to distract them, the Greek Cypriots have a straight uninterrupted shot of virtually two months of holiday shopping before them. Just up the street from our flat a small but modern glass-fronted gift shop has boxed up its contents — ruby-red blown glass and filigreed silver knick-knacks, and replaced them with an ever-expanding landscape of faux evergreen, even fauxer popcorn necklaces, and countless red, green, and yellow plastic birds perched on the evergreens' branches as if to dine from the ropes of popcorn that drape over the limbs of this forest fantasy.

We walk downtown to the Old City to visit the fabulous Icon Museum at the Makarious Foundation. We've seen them before, these gold-leaf and ruby red images from as early as the 11th Century. The faces of Jesus are dark, some of them, and they look real. As if these anonymous painters, or schools of painters, worked from life, crafted volume and depth into a supposedly two-dimensional flat picture plane.

But what strikes me more than the truly beautiful icons are the flags that fly outside. This is a central complex of buildings in the old city — an orthodox church of magnificent, sumptuous decoration, a museum, and a gallery — and the only flags flying are those of Greece. A friend here talks about an immature political culture and how the showing of Greek national flags, either instead of, or in addition to, the flag of Cyprus speaks volumes. Of course the blue and white colors of Greece attest to the "we are Greek" sentiment of southern Cypriot national identity just as the Turkish flag on the hills to the north attest to their national identity. But, how is this "nationalist?" A single people of multiple ethnic, linguistic and religious backgrounds each call themselves Cypriot, yet many on each side see that identity not in American hyphenated terms, but in pan-national ones.

Even the garbage bags that line the median on the main highway to Limassol and Paphos have been decorated with the Greek flag this last week in honor of OXI-Day. Are there no yellow and green Cypriot plastic garbage bags to be had anywhere? Perhaps this is yet one more sign of the heightened disappointment that I've been sensing this time.

Two years ago, the spirit of expectation, of hope for a "solution," seemed much higher, even given the defeat of the unification referendum in the south. Now there seems to be a widespread acceptance of the moment, an embrace of the new material prosperity, and an abandonment of idealism. As another of our friends argues, the younger, post-1974 generation never knew a united Cyprus, so this divided one, this country in the south, is their only political reality.

We learn the word for civil war today in the Greek conversation class we take with a lively Cypriot-English woman down the street. And I look up and ask, "Does anyone ever refer to events here between 1963 and 1974 as a Civil War rather than a conflict between two communities? Erika looks at me over her half-glasses, a glance I have often deployed to convey skepticism (another good Greek work for knowledge). I can see it is beyond her cultural experience to consider this redefinition. And that seems to give me a kind of intellectual courage or permission to think a bit more about the "Cyprus" problem.

People here, Greek Cypriots and Turkish Cypriots, have imagined a prior "golden" age where Greek and Turks lived together, respected one another, went to each others' weddings and funerals, and bought each others' goods. "Leave us alone," they say, "and we'll find a way to live together the way we once did." But call the era between Independence and the Turkish Invasion one of civil war and they shake their heads no, "we were two communities." Can't be both, can it? Two communities in conflict or a single one engaged in peaceful cooperation?

And then, candidly, some will admit that "before" 1974 Greek Cypriots held the upper economic hand, and that some (many? all?) exploited, even extended their dominance. In this respect, Turkish Cypriots had been an oppressed minority for a long time — hardly one peaceful happy world. The combinations make my head spin.

Still, the young here, and that extends to men and women in their 30s and even in their early 40s, have no first-hand experience with "before." Their only reality is the current one. And integral to this moment they seem suspended in amber — beautiful yet frozen. Many like my friend and student from two years ago, Helena, rail and struggle against this culturally-imposed paralysis. They feel like they are trapped in an iron lung, still breathing but pinned down, helpless. The bright ones, like Helena, finish at the top of their class, do a Master's (as they call it) in England and then come back to Cyprus to teach. In many cases they teach English to immigrants in after-hours government language programs. Working from 3 pm to 9 in the evening, living at home, the only real alternative is marriage and a family.

And so we are back to Betty Friedan all over again.

But also back to understanding the village underpinning of Cypriot life. Everyone still refers to the village they or their families come from, even when those villages have become suburban towns along a highway like so many beads, worn and matted, on a restrung necklace. Old shops and coffee houses next to chain bakeries and shoe stores, venerable Orthodox churches side by side with neon-lit taverna. And families ensconced in houses they have lived in for generations (unless they are refugees), next door to brothers and sisters, uncles and aunts, Yayas and Papus. And doting grandmothers who cook for everyone, who baby-sit grandchildren, or later like good suburban American housewives, drive them to football practice, English and swimming lessons, and buy them sweets.

11 | 7 | 2007

We are officially a week into winter here. But no rain — except for the six drops three weeks ago, and the city is bone dry. Dust accumulates overnight on everything. It coats our floors and settles on the kitchen counters. It reminds us that we are living, in fact, in the desert.

And it gets dark much earlier now. We are at about the same latitude as Rome or Madrid, but the dark (no less than the sand and dust) cloaks us by five thirty. Streams of red and white car lights mark the overcrowded roadways and horn bleats feel ever more intrusive with evening's blackened imposition. So it seems especially eerie this late afternoon, a Wednesday, to stroll down Ledra Street in the Old City.

In winter the shops close, for the most part, at 2 pm on Wednesdays. With the early evening and the first cold snap of the fall — all the way down to 70 — this bustling, tourist-filled street is virtually empty. In late summer you have to walk close to the ancient buildings that line Ledra Street just to find relief from the blinding heat. We usually stroll carefully in the shadows seeking dark, cool corridors that barely seem to escape the gravity of the sandstone walls. Sharing that space that files past t-shirt, ice-cream, icon, clothing and trinket shops for at least a half-mile requires a certain tolerance. German and Swedish and Danish and of course English tourists are everywhere. They dress in shorts and sandals and hold their tiny digital cameras a foot in front of their noses. As summer moves to fall they get older (school does tend to triage them by generation) but otherwise they look identical — healthy, ruddy, fair, and decidedly pink.

But now in early November, the street is deserted. Only a handful of local residents, immigrants mostly, Palestinians, Africans, Sri Lankans and Filipinos, sit at vacant cafes or lean against worn doorways. It is a different city altogether.

We meet one of my new teacher friends for a chat and she takes us to a cafe to listen to jazz. We'd been there two years ago, but now it feels like a Greenwich Village coffee house pulled out of time and place, and like Dorothy's farmstead, dropped into a different dimension. It is long and narrow with two levels, tables inside and out, waitress in black, a proprietor in geri-curls wearing a cross that dangles down his chest. He is stylishly unshaven, has granny glasses, and speaks beautifully accented Cypriot-English. Groups of men and women, all in their 20s, tilt the backs of their chairs up against the cafe's stone walls. They all smoke, prying unfiltered cigarettes out of crumpled packets.

Rena teaches elementary school history in all grades. She is the mother of five-month old twins and seems remarkably energetic and self-possessed. She shares harrowing tales of the world of "official" text books in Cyprus. Until recently the public schools here used Greek text books, written and published in Greece. Like old American Basal readers they were filled with legends, or as she calls them, "myths." As she talks I think last decade's U.S. culture wars over the appropriateness of including minorities in state-adopted history text books in places like California. In Cyprus, one legend has maintained that the Orthodox Church played a critical role in preserving traditional education in Cyprus — that is, Greek culture and language, which the Church nurtured in secret against the wishes of their Ottoman and English oppressors.

As Rena tells it, about three years ago a Greek historian re-wrote the history of Cyprus text book for use in primary schools, eliminating these stories and working from solid academic sources. All hell broke loose. Public meetings – imagine local school boards in the American mid-west debating Evolution. There were ministerial crises; counter-arguments and rebuttals evolved into such a brouhaha that the publisher withdrew the book. As a result, now there is no textbook at all, and teachers like Rena are on their own.

This is one of the many reasons that the group she works with, the Association for Historical Research and Dialogue, is so important. Even thirty or forty public teachers from both communities committed to liberating history from the iron cast of politics (not that this is ever entirely possible) marks an important step. I wonder how they and I will react to my second workshop in two weeks.

We stroll, Rena, D and I, through the Old City back to our cars. It is only 7 pm but it is night time. Old faces in ground floor windows peer out at us, barely visible, tracking us with silent eyes. I realize that we've never been inside on of these small inner sanctum houses. Some are boarded up – did they belong once to Turkish Cypriots? – and others are falling down. But many have scaffolding and dumpsters in front. Gentrification is coming to the Old City. It will surely follow in the wake of a new bunch of upscale furniture shops and artisan workshops that are fanning out from the art center at Famagusta Gate. What will that mean to the traditional residents? What will it mean to the migrants as well?

Later we walk through quiet streets, cobble-stone, shuttered, silent except for the sound of our footfall. It is somewhere between eerie and holy. We whisper. The moon hangs white and bright overhead, peeking down between the jagged spaces of buildings, some as old as the city itself – maybe a thousand years. It is a small world, and we meet another couple we know, a man, Brian, who works as the Public Information Officer for the UN and a Polish journalist, Agnieszka, who writes for the British newspaper here. It is very late, but when they offer to show us Brian's place we can't resist.

It is like being admitted to a private club, seeing behind a veil, peeking into an inner sanctum. Behind the scarred wood door secured by a wrought-iron clasp, behind very plain and equally scarred stone walls, we find light. It is a courtyard inside which connects to a courtyard outside as well. The apartment is modern and spacious, tiles covered by Turkish-Iranian carpets meandering through rooms that extend in an L around a luscious, planted garden. Pink and purple flowering trees bend over pebbled walkways that make this simply elegant residence both beautiful and welcoming. And Brian has accepted reassignment to Darfur.

11 | 11 | 2007

It is Armistice Day. No meaning here. The Turks celebrate their victory at Gallipoli against an invasion that seemed a neo-crusade to them, the British Empire hemorrhaging gallons of blood on a spit of land south of Istanbul. The Greeks remember a war that lead to terrible population transfers in the early 1920s. Armistice Day is another reminder that our perspective, from the mind's eye of Western Europe, is only that. November 11 is also Roula's birthday.

The next night we take Cem and Sarai out to the new place around the corner from them. It is a brand new restaurant, Fine Meze, with the refined small dishes of pepper and almond and tahini that we have come to treasure. The restaurant, placed on the newly restored brick walkway that leads from the Turkish control point back into the northern part of the Old City, has a great strategic position, like Cem's newly-expanded carpet shop. Anyone crossing over from the south on foot — virtually everyone except a few diplomats who gun their menacing black Mercedes and BMWs as they fly past the rest of us — must walk right by the restaurant front door.

Inside we are greeted by a small group of musicians tucked into the back corner. They are playing traditional Turkish music on several instruments: the kanun, the 74-stringed zither that Cem knows how to play; a violin; and a small hand-held drum. It is mesmerizing, this rhythmically complex, soulful, layered music that seems to float in the air. Cem closes his eyes for a moment and sings silently in accompaniment.

They continue their strange dance, Cem and Seray. It has taken us two years to realize that they are not married. In fact, it is central to their two-step. Stay together or maybe not, come to America or maybe not. It is sad to watch them try to negotiate all the differences that manifest themselves in affectionate hugs and needling teases. Her skirts are too short, his hairline receding too quickly. Her optimism a sure sign of innocence, his melancholy reflecting a life lived.

Cem reveals even more hard-core traditional views. We talk about music as the kanun sings lyrically behind us. "This rap is shit," he says, holding an imaginary boom box up to his shoulder. Then he leans his head back, eyes closed, and hums along with the traditional Turkish folk song. "We have lost our character, all of us," he sweeps his hand around the room filled with Turkish, English, Cypriot, and American patrons. "I hate democracy." I've heard this before. From the woe-is-me brand of neo-conservatives who teach political science; from the anti-black liberals who bemoan the social crisis in the breakup of the family; and from people like me who still can't understand much of the angry, anti-feminine bravado that informs contemporary Hip Hop. No matter how hard I try it, the music as much as the lyrics, lay beyond my tastes. But still I refuse to draw the (too) obvious social conclusions.

11 | 14 | 2007

We watch a film on our DVD player, bought two years ago and left in the care of Costas and Roula. It is called "Attila 1974: The Rape of Cyprus." It is a documentary about the invasion and its sorrowful aftermath. Created by a Greek-Cypriot director, the film is rich with evocative portrayals of local events. The old saturated-color Kodak stock renders the story even more lurid, and as we view the film it reminds us of its own political engagement.

Using the Turkish name for the line that marked the division between north and south, The Attila Line, and not the Green Line, the film's subtitle works against any sense of balance. And this is what makes the film so deeply flawed and so remarkably interesting. As an inquiry into the terrible events of 1974, the film squarely places initial responsibility upon the intervention of the Greek military dictatorship of the early 1970s in Cypriot affairs. Interviews with Archbishop Makarios, president of Cyprus a year after the invasion, reveal a strong and even charismatic man. So strong that the Greek Junta in collaboration with the Greek Cypriot EOKA-B (the most militant and armed wing of pro-Enosis — unity) desperately but unsuccessfully tried to depose and assassinate him in July, 1974.

Even after the Turkish invasion a few weeks later — to protect the "rights" of Turkish Cypriots in the wake of the coup — EOKA-B maintained a campaign of violence against supporters of Makarios. So, the film is clear — Greek

Cypriot "nationalist" militants in cahoots with the Greek junta left the country open to a Turkish "riposte." How I love that polite French word culled from 19th-century diplomacy.

But the film is equally clear that Cyprus was raped, and in these terms, the rapist was surely Turkish. So on the one hand, the director establishes his credentials as a liberal, even progressive, Greek Cypriot. On the other, the story is not about all of Cyprus, but about the suffering of Greek Cypriots — in detention centers, in refugee tent-cities — fending off treachery from all quarters. And the film doesn't spare American policy. The only difference between Cyprus and Chile, says one of the men on camera, is that "Makarios survived, Allende did not."

The director interviewed dozens of participants, but with the exception of Rauf Dentash, a Rod Steiger-looking Turkish Cypriot leader who speaks like the English barrister he trained to be, no Turkish Cypriots appear. The Cyprus that was raped was Greek Cyprus.

This allows me to understand Leo's melodramatic pose a bit more. I can see how he straddles the divide between progressive and patriot, just like the filmmaker. Admit to mistakes, condemn the right, the ultra-nationalist, but go no further. This is the voice of a film from 1975. The shock is in still hearing it so clearly and uncritically forty years later.

Sometimes a film opens windows of tiny yet penetrating insight. This one did so with the Nicosia buses. We often make fun of the public transportation system in Nicosia. Old buses, few and far between, ply the main arteries carrying the working people (mostly non-European), the immigrants, to and fro. One shot in the film shows the return of Cypriot prisoners of war in the winter of 1974. They are on exactly the same buses. No less than in some arenas of public opinion, the public transportation system still runs on fumes left over from the war.

Yet of course, change is everywhere. Early in the film, the director has footage of the pre-1974 conflict, which shows the Greek word for unification ENOSIS clearly marked in huge bock letters on the slopes of the Kyrenia Mountains. The word glared down at the city, and must have aggravated no small segment of the Cypriot population, both Greek and Turkish. No wonder that the Turkish Cypriots who first marked their flag with painted stones and now illuminate it with strobe lights choose the exact same spot. Take that, it says.

What I didn't expect was the amazing reception that Makarios received when he returned to a newly-democratic Greece in the winter of 1974. A vast throng of Cypriots. It reminded me of the great film Z, the political thriller made by Costa-Gavras in 1969. Set in Greece at the dawn of that fascist experience, Z, like Atilla 1974, demonstrates the passions of the region and the era. Z is the character representing "he lives," which they also said about Makarios. To see Makarios standing before a river of cheering, banner waiving, delirious supporters is to gain a measure of his political standing. Makarios had it in spades.

11 | 15 | 2007

It is a sunny day, so I walk about the Old City. The tourists have returned. The streets teem with returning tourists and the ticklers are plying their trade. It is as if the night landscape — deserted, lonely, yet beautiful — is but a dream.

I decide to find the two men who restored old cars, just down the street from the NO BOARDER clothing store and around the corner from the Weaving Mill. They are all there, these men who look like brothers, and they remember me, smiling broadly when I hand them the photographs I took. "Oh," they say, "you were the one who helped us push that old Jaguar."

This time I remember to ask them their names. Izete and Ihan, they tell me. Izete is Turkish Cypriot and Ihan is Turkish. But Ihan has married a Turkish Cypriot woman and earned the kind of identification card that allows him to cross through the Dead Zone and work in the south. Our other Turkish friends, Cem and Seray, can only come into the Republic of Cyprus from the international port of entry in Larnaca — which means, for them, to travel 200 yards they will have to first fly to Athens, then change planes, and fly to Cyprus — about seven hours and 500 dollars. It takes Ihan 15 minutes to walk from the same place in the north, through the Ledra Palace checkpoint and into the southern part of the Old City.

There is a third man working on an beautiful old Mercedes. He tells me that his name is Kimon, that he is a Greek Cypriot and owns the shop. Kimon is tall and dark, and like Izete and Ihan his clothes are splotchy with oil stains. He stands up from his crouch beneath the brake-linings he is replacing and shakes my hand. I ask how unusual it is for a Greek Cypriot to employ two men from "the other side." And he tells me something that I realize I have heard a dozen

Izete and Ihan

times, maybe more. "We are friends, Turkish and Greek Cypriots. This is all the politicians doing. Leave us alone and we will find a solution."

What was it really like before? Depends on before when. 1974? 1960? (The founding of the Republic.) 1925? Well, let's say before the troubles. What were Turkish-Greek Cypriot relations actually like. Who kissed? Who married? Who worked with, and for, whom? Had I another lifetime, I believe I would try to answer some part of this question.

11 | 15 | 2007

We talk with Xenofon during a late night car ride through a deserted Nicosia, driving him home after a lovely evening with Elena and Andros. Hard to believe that in a few hours cars will choke these empty streets, bellowing exhaust, screams of rush-hour frustration, and accompanying hand gestures that we've just found out are VERY insulting. We take him to his new neighborhood, off to the east of the city, not far south of the place the Green Line wiggles its way toward Famagusta. The neighborhood holds block after block of low-rise apartment buildings, sturdy concrete construction, simple and stark, on new streets without many amenities. We are in a government housing project, Xenofon tells us, refugee housing for which he recently qualified.

In the late 1970s, those who moved south in Cyprus became eligible for government housing, compensation for lost property, and since Xenofon's family came from the north, he even now could request refugee housing. Another long story of loss and displacement.

But he invites us to come to taverna where he is the house performer. Next weekend he will bring about thirty Turkish and Greek singers, a bi-communal choir, to the taverna. "They are going to really dance," he tells us proudly. He means, of course, get down.

11 | 17 | 2007

I do my second oral history workshop with the bi-communal group of Turkish and Greek teachers. I had asked them to take photographs of anything from 1974 and choose two to write about. This was an idea called Photo Story that a friend told me about; I thought it had real promise both for andragogy and content. I imagined a whole portfolio of images and words that together could add up to something meaningful — incorporating yet transcending individual, subjective points of view.

They knocked me out. I guided them through a discussion of the uses of oral history first, asking them not to discuss the "Cyprus Question." They found this almost impossible. Greek or Turkish Cypriot, they all came back again and again to this ache in their hearts. It is what is actually on their minds, isn't it. And as teachers committed to forging a new community based on love and respect and cooperation, they are faced with a monumental task. Where did I fit in?

We sat on worn metal chairs in the middle of a virtually empty ballroom in the old Ledra Palace Hotel, the barbed wire, chain-link, and blue berets of UN peace keepers equally omnipresent. I was disappointed with the small turnout. Twenty-five had signed up, perhaps eighteen appeared. But that, as my mother used to say, that is my mishigas. As we formed ourselves into a circle — physically conveying unity, I really thought–we talked, and I listened and pondered the rich irony in our gathering.

At the very same moment my wife, D., was attending a conference at the main campus of the University of Cyprus. I had visited the meetings the previous day when she delivered what turned out to be a wonderful paper about women and sustainable development. We all sat there, in a glorious lecture hall outfitted with high-speed internet and simultaneous translators; but the two languages, Greek and English, gave the conference away. No Turkish presence and no mention of the island-wide issue of environmental sustainability the conference was addressing.

There, in a cavernous bare room deep inside the Ledra Palace Hotel, yet no further from the Green Line than the University of Cyprus five kilometers to the east, we couldn't stop talking about the very subject that our well-financed counterparts never mentioned. This too is the Cyprus problem.

For an hour or more they read from the photographs and paragraphs they have assembled. It is a good teaching experience. I say virtually nothing, as they tell their own stories — personal stories, individual and real stories. As we round the circle and come to the last person, I feel some relief. This has been three-and-a-half hours of intense discussion. But I believe the chance I took in having them work on 1974 subject matter is working. I'd worried that it was my arrogance, that choice. But I took a chance and these people took it in great directions.

Rena, a good-hearted and intellectually serious woman, shows us a photograph of a letter her mother wrote about 1974. It is an image of a letter, Rena explains, because all the family photographs had been lost. The letter tells her daughter what life had been like before, yet ends with the phrase, "I do not hate them." Rena looks up and says, perhaps that is why I work so hard for peace.

Ionis, a Turkish Cypriot, brings us two photographs of huge concrete shelters, one from the north and one from the south. In 1974, civilians hid there from invading armies and the squads of EOKA B who wreaked havoc and vengeance on both Greek and Turkish Cypriots. He tells his own story, that of a seventeen-year-old kid from Paphos forced with his family into one of these shelters and then discovered and sent north.

I intrude. I note that so many of their images are of "home," of houses, shelters, hotels, of places they hid, or lost, or moved to. I invite them to think about this larger theme, one we discovered amongst ourselves in this exercise, one that actually does transcend the particular. They all nod in quiet acknowledgement.

The last to report is Fezile. She is a Turkish-Cypriot woman who works for the Education Ministry. She is lovely, vivacious and beautiful. But there is something more. She exudes a remarkable generosity of spirit. I mentioned to her the day before at a short meeting three of us held in north Nicosia that I loved the round Turkish sesame-seed "pretzels" they sell everywhere in Istanbul. Today she appears bearing a plate of hard-boiled eggs for Rena, a dish of olives and cheese for everyone else, and a bag of fresh sesame breads for me.

She passes around her two photographs. One is of a display from the years 1960 to 1963, the very short moment when the Republic of Cyprus lived in relative peace as one country. The other shows refugee women fleeing from an off-camera horror. It looks to be from a newspaper that reported on the terrible events surrounding the invasion of July, 1974.

And then she speaks. This striking and athletic woman – who speaks very little in our gatherings because she is unsure of her English – she speaks from the heart. She tells us of the many Greek friends she has, and of the pain of her family and the Turkish Cypriot civilians who are in flight in the photograph.

Fezile

Her exact words matter less than the feelings she expresses. Sitting next to her, I see the mascara slide down the side of her nose inside a tear. The room is silent as Fezile speaks of her hopes to not forget, yet also to embrace us all. Although not a member of their communities, I feel this no less powerfully.

I think we are all stunned yet not surprised at all. This complex of emotions and feelings has been sensate just below the surface all day, and we all know it. We began the workshop by reintroducing ourselves, not by professional affiliation but by some other form of identification — "I love to sing," says one. This final cathartic moment arrives at the end a day in which the political has yielded to the personal. I believe we are all exhausted, and as I try to wrap up, I feel the inadequacy of academic words, so I simply stop trying.

11 | 21 | 2007

It is the day before Thanksgiving. We have a turkey on order from the local market, sweet potatoes in the cupboard next to the bag of multicolored marshmallows and the spanking new container of sage. I asked for "patates zacharie" literally potatoes sweet, and it worked. And to top it off, it poured last night. Felt like home, a comforting light rain for hours, and then at dawn a rousing chorus of thunder and lightning accompanied by triggered car alarms and the zapping sounds of electricity hotfooting it from here to there. Traffic was a mess, our Greek teacher reports. The storm caught everyone unprepared. But we know that tomorrow all the dry grey-brown soil will come to life. It will be like spring.

This disassociation of seasons is disorienting. Similar in ways to what I feel as I deal with the book I've written about Cyprus, to which some have so curiously reacted.

I feel like a bull in a china shop here. I have no idea where the shelves are until after I sweep my hand in some spontaneous gesture. By then it is too late, the shattered pieces lay scattered across the floor. I hear this too often: "we need to be careful. These are sensitive issues. The funding will be in jeopardy." And I've heard it from at least three very different sources.

Last night Rena called. She just read the book and she told me, "It's more like a travel book than a political one." Bingo — Rena gets it. But, of course, what isn't political? I'm coming to a sad conclusion about this place, one I hope will change with a more experience. But, I'm not sure that it will.

Right now Cyprus feels like what I've imagined Czechoslovakia must have felt like. Before. A remarkable lack of freedom of expression, a remarkable absence of dissent, and a remarkable current of fear grinds this society into silence. It is not only attitudes that are, comparatively speaking, a generation behind progressive ideas and practices; but the people are genuinely afraid of real expression, real public expression. It can backfire here in the form of either disapproval or loss of money and position. As a very intelligent academic told me during my workshop last weekend, "We need to be careful about the epistemological implications of what we say about oral history. Someone can easily accuse us of relativism."

11 | 23 | 2007

Once again the personal trumps the political — Thanksgiving is a triumph of improvisation and of laughter.

We work all day, just like at "home." Only here, the local market, called Golden Star, roasts some delicious chicken breasts for us and throws in a few baked sweet potatoes and a Pyrex dish. The owner, like so many Greek Cypriots, has lived in Astoria, Queens and knows the Thanksgiving routine by heart. D whips up a tasty sweet potato pie/pita (do I sense a common theme here) and we manage to duplicate my son's famous SP casserole — from a recipe he brought home from school in second grade. I've cooked it ever since. The only downer is the absence of fresh cranberries. I love the sweet-tangy taste of real cranberries ground together with oranges. We settle for some British canned blend that tastes like cranberry jam, sticky and sweet, that neither entices nor delights. You can't have everything.

Costas and Roula come through big time, lending everything we don't have available — and that's a whole lot of kitchen gear, from a table cloth to a serving utensils. With a touch of bravado, Costas announces, "For your Thanksgiving you will not need to buy wine." He brings down two reds and two whites (kokkino kai aspiro in your Greek-American lexicon) and sets them on our kitchen table.

We invite their whole family — two more generations — and our friends Andreas and Maroula. Only Michael and his wife Vangelou can't come — she has given birth, by Caesarean, just the day before. Everyone else is present, and I mean present. Yiorgos and his brother-in-law Demos are a great pair, engaging and funny. They egg each other on, singing APOEL songs to the delight of their father, doing a wave to salute D's sweet potato pie, telling hysterically funny stories about malapropisms in English. "You told me not to bring my husband," a woman said to Yiorgos, who had actually told her not to bring her handbag to a company dinner in Vienna. The Yiorgos and Demos show rolls on — Demos specializes in making goofy-funny faces at his youngest child. We are in an uproar most of the evening. D and I even try out some of our Greek, to their delight.

Maroula, who speaks virtually no English, but who channels a Jewish Grandmother perfectly — "eat more, eat," sits quietly next to her husband. I catch his eye and tell him in very halting Greek, "Andreas tell Maroula that I don't think she's had enough to eat." The whole house applauds. At least I think that is what I say. And if it isn't, then they all think it uproariously funny anyway. Yiorgos and his sister Lilia both attended college and graduate school in America. They are fluent, idiomatic, and completely at home in both languages. Lilia takes her son from Demo's shoulder and puts her finger in his mouth. Vasilly is six months old, and even he seems to laugh at everything. Must be his father, Demos, who continues to make goofy faces at him.

And of course, Constantinous. He delights with hugs and "gimme fives" and singing "Hotel California." He goes to an English-speaking school and while English is his third language, it is the first one he has learned to read. He comes down from his grandparents' apartment about once a week to "study" with D. They play hide the clothes pin, and then she teaches him to write his name in Roman letters or to read from the flash cards his teacher sends home with him. He's five now, a bigger version of himself as a three year old, and we feel very close to him. He is affectionate and considerate and wildly doe-eyed.

11 | 25 | 2007

The taverna where Xenofon sings is decked out for the holidays. Red and white flowered tablecloths (not checkered), carnations in small pitchers, and folded napkins all made the place festive and welcoming. By 9am the room has filled with close to fifty people, some dressed to the nines — shiny white

Maroula

high-heeled boots and dramatic eye-makeup for the women, dress-shirts and even an occasional tie for the men. And Xenofon up on the tiny stage, his playback system blinking, microphone in hand, covering a wide swath of pop standards — Paul Simon, the Beatles, even Elvis ("Fools Rush In"). It is bustling as the wait-staff, trays held high, negotiate the narrow aisles between long tables, laying down small plates of salad, hummus, olives and warm pita — the start of a standard meze.

The late arrivals dive into the buzz and make the rounds kissing those already there on both cheeks, greeting each other as dear friends. There is no way that my wife or I can at first distinguish between the Turkish and Greek Cypriots in the restaurant — except for the more extreme fashion statements of the younger Turkish-Cypriot women who favor wide, and I mean wide, belts and a wild spectrum of hair color, and those white Nancy Sinatra boots.

Xenofon introduces us to Annia, the Greek-Cypriot choir director who sports a wild mane of henna-red hair and a loose orange blouse. She is Melina Mercouri vivacious, with a broad smile and a personality that brightens a room instantly. I see that she and her husband place themselves at a table where the woman with a tight-black dress, long blonde hair and Sinatra boots is seated.

Xenofon has carefully crafted this evening. For the first hour he sticks to the soft, mostly American music, his voice clear and sweet above the din. And as he sings, his friends — who have clearly come here to applaud him — dine and toast each other with shots of zivaniah or beer or red wine. This bi-communal choir, aged from 22 to at least 75, eats quickly as if they want to get on with it. Then predictably, Xenofon changes the pace and the style. In place of Neil Diamond he sings several up-tempo Greek songs, the kind that pulls first a few and then more than a few Greek-Cypriot dancers into the narrow space between the long tables. At first only women dance, in long tight black pants over high-heeled black shoes with the pointiest toes I can imagine. Well, except for the oldest guy in the room, a short and stout fellow dressed like a banker, who sheds his suit-coat and dances with arms at his side, suspenders loose on his shoulders, as a way of warming everyone up.

We all begin to clap in unison as the tempo of the music quickens and more women command the tiny space. They hold each other's hands high, one waves a red napkin.

Annia makes it her business to get as many people as she can entice into the flow. She shimmies up next to me, takes my hand, motions upward with her eyes. Shy, I resist, smile back politely. Not so the man with Eugene Levy long curly hair behind me. He has placed a carnation Billie Holiday style behind his ear and despite his bulk is remarkably light on his feet.

They move some tables out of the way now and make a larger space. Women hold hands in a circle and the men — and it is clearly their time to show off — enter and dance alone as the women boogie around them. The men slide and stop, hands held dramatically high, heads tilted to the side, as the music becomes more intense. People sitting at the tables clap and cheer, raising their glasses, beaming at each other. This is clearly what they have come for. Xenofon tells us that the Greek-Cypriot members of the choir have driven over to the Green Line to pick up their Turkish-Cypriot friends at the checkpoint. They are bringing them to the restaurant.

During Xenofon's break, two of the Turkish-Cypriot women, one very blonde, the other deep red, sit on the stage and sing unaccompanied into the mike. Their song pulses with energy, yet it is soft and sweet like the night air. No one dances, everyone listens. It is their turn.

Then the floor fills again, the sound system comes to life, and Xenofon finds the mike. First the women sing with him, then Annie steps forward, her voice soaring, and more men dance, arms waiving, kneeling, slapping their shoes, the floor, anything. Someone floats white napkins and red flowers on to the floor. Xenofon sings his heart out.

We sit, D and I, about five feet from the dance space. Twice in the space of a few minutes two women stop at our table — first a Greek-Cypriot woman, then a Turkish-Cypriot — one of the singers. They first ask where we have come from, then say virtually the same thing. "We are Cypriots here. All of us. They divided us. Now they should leave us alone."

When we get home I say with some irony that I propose a three-state solution to the Cyprus problem. One for the die-hard Greek-nationalist Cypriots, another for the die-hard Turkish Cypriots, and in the middle, an ever-expanding state for these people. I wish my history friends could meet this choir. They all need each other. It raises our spirits, this better part of the generosity of the human spirit on Cyprus, and we are privileged that they shared it with us. Once again we feel the ache of sadness at the prospect of leaving.

United in song

11 | 25 | 2007

A short excursion to the north. To Nicosia/Lefkosia, a brief stop at Cem and Seray's and then I wander down to the center of town, to Attaturk Square, past the Post Office where we took Costas two years ago, past the courts of law, up the narrow, busy streets that lead to the covered bazaar. I want to stop and talk to Mustafa at his shoe store. He always invites me for coffee and I always find that I am in too much of a hurry.

He smiles so very sweetly when I enter. He makes me feel that he is glad to see me. I see the copy of my book, the one I presented to him a month ago, on top of his cash register. When I ask after him he shrugs. I am healthy he tells me. But, nothing else works here. And he means northern Cyprus. Look, he gestures toward the boxes of new shoes and sneakers stacked floor to ceiling that circle the shop. Look. I work here all day, I'm on my feet all day. You know how many shoes I sell in that day? Four. Maybe I make 8 lira, and then I stop for bread and I have only 4 lira left.

By this time I am eyeing a pair of black Nike's with gold swooshes gleaming on their sides. They feel soft. You want to know how I am, he says. He stops for the few small seconds it takes me to affirm. I am not as good today as I was yesterday. And tomorrow I will not be as good as today. The shoes are a bit tight, but I know surely I will buy them.

You look around, he says. How many shoe shops do you see? It is another rhetorical question. They all sell same thing. We all sell same thing, he affirms. It not always like this. And I remember that Mustafa had been educated in Istanbul as a civil engineer. So, I look again at the black and gold shoes, smile inwardly, and tell him "I'll take these." I hand him 20 Cyprus pounds, about double the price and tell him please keep the change, "for your wife." He is embarrassed and so am I, but he nods and then says after a moment's hesitation, "Thank you very much." When I come back to say goodbye in a week or so we will have coffee together.

Just around the corner from Mustafa is the Han, the lovely renovated Cavaransarie that the municipal government of north Nicosia has transformed into a craft center. On the outside of the building, constructed of soft-gold sandstone, are a number of small shops that face the street. Here two years ago I stopped and a man called out, "America is Imperialist," as I snapped his photograph. Today I enter a small spice shop and there he is. I realize that he is the owner, and I hand him a copy of my book. His eyes light up and as I flip to his image at the bottom of a page, he says, "Yes. I remember."

He invites me inside and we sit in the back of his store. He is proud as can be and tells me about himself. Like the puppet master upstairs his name is Mehmet and he is from Turkey but has lived in Cyprus for more than twenty years and is married to a Turkish Cypriot woman. This allows him the kind of identity card that will take him to the south — unlike other Turkish nationals who can only enter south Cyprus through Larnaca.

As customers enter the shop he rises quickly from one of our two small chairs and greets them, in Turkish, holding the book out, showing them his picture, and saying something like "this American" as he nods in my direction. It pleases me that he feels so proud. And, as is the custom, always, he invites me to have a coffee.

He points to a CD first. He's going to play it for me.

You like Bossuki, he inquires. This is very special. It is, the music of a master from Crete who lives deep in the Trodos mountains and who plays the hell out of the instrument. None of that Zorba the Greek melismatic arpeggio stuff, no, this is rhythmic and melodic, more ancient, probably in modal scales, and "deep." Mehmet smiles and asks "You like." Indeed. Then he stoops down and pulls a blue butane tank out from behind a curtain, screws on a burner, lights a match, and presto. Long spoon in his teeth, he takes some coffee, measures it, and slides it into the already boiling water. Turkish/Cypriot/Greek coffee is dark and heavy, strong without any bitterness, and it flows though my body like a magic potion, setting me on fire with its warmth. We sit together, listening to the music, sipping our coffee and smiling.

11 | 27 | 2007

Evening comes earlier and earlier these days. Dusk at 5 and dark, really dark, by 6 pm. Just in time for rush hour. These days the traffic on Kennedy Avenue backs up for more than a mile. The traffic lights that control access to the main highway to the south, just beyond the Hilton Hotel, are the source of the congestion. But what scares me is this — as local drivers slalom ever more dangerously and aggressively in their attempts to best an unbeatable system they

Working among but apart in South Nicosia

dart in and out of traffic like gnats.

At least they have — usually — their lights on. But they will never see the increasingly numbers of bicyclists filling the streets, mostly non-European immigrants — Pakistani, Sri-Lankan, Filipino, Thai, West African, and Chinese. Many ride old throw-away bikes without any illumination, peddling down the side of the street, virtually invisible. They are an accident waiting to happen, I fear.

Their invisibility extends far beyond the issue of traffic safety. They are the people who, as one of our friends put it, "do the work that Cypriots won't." They sweep the steps of the shops in the morning, carry out the trash, cook the food behind closed kitchen doors, pump gas, hoist wheel-barrows at construction sites, clean homes, and above all, take care of children. They are everywhere, as I can finally see through my camera-eye on Sunday in the Old City, and their invisibility becomes more troubling the harder I look.

Like the Turkish, the mainland Turkish "settlers" in the north, these dark-skinned people in the south constitute a class apart. Because they live in the Republic of Cyprus on temporary visas, up to five years, they are not discriminated against in ways that would seem familiar to Americans. But their very invisibility, their taken-for-granted presence, their lack of access to the commerce and institutions of middle-class Cyprus make this a benignly segregated world. Everyone is polite, so there is little overt hostility, but behind the facade of good behavior there exists a category of the second-class to which all the immigrants of color belong.

There exists as well another class, a group of people who are slowly disappearing. They are Greek and Turkish Cypriots in both halves of the Old City who are the remnants of a skilled artisan class— among them carpenters, masons, mechanics, tailors, instrument makers, potters and jewelers. You see them bent over tables and docks, the doors to their workshops open, sawdust and tire-rims stacked outside. Occasionally a busy artesian will sit behind a window open to the street, blowtorch in hand, soldering a piece that will appear in their vitrine a few hours later. This must be the truly old Nicosia, the heirs of the skilled trades people of an earlier age. Now they have few children by their sides, and their craft, like the lace-makers of Lefkara, are under siege from a barrage of goods made in China.

11 | 28 | 2007

Each side in Nicosia has a museum devoted to the history of their role in the creation of modern Cyprus. I expected them to be mirror images of each other and The Other. In fact they tell very different stories.

North Nicosia, the urban part, is only about one block deep — traffic-choked and bustling in the near neighborhood to the west of the wall, perhaps a mile from the Lidra Palace crossing. Turn off the main drag, away from the Puma and Levis shops, and you find shaded streets, modest private homes in quiet repose. Enter these streets just ten meters and the hum of all engines disappears, and it is peaceful.

Down one street, at number 2 Ifran Bey, in the Kumsal neighborhood, is their Museum of Barbarism. It is an actual house that belonged to a Turkish Cypriot doctor then serving as an officer in the "Cyprus Turkish Army Contingent." At a moment when perhaps 200 or 300 Turkish Cypriots were "slaughtered" by a "mob" of Greek Cypriots, the Officer's wife and three children had been shot to death in the bathroom. The house has been "preserved" as it existed in December, 1963. It reminds me of the Lorraine motel in Memphis where Martin Luther King was shot. Both remain relatively undisturbed. In King's case, the simplicity of the setting makes it more powerful. Here in north Cyprus, this museum underestimates the complexity of the story and instead presents a single example of victimization.

Greek Cypriots appeared and shot up the house, killed most of the family, and left. There is virtually no context provided for the breakdown of political and social communication in the fall of 1963. It feels like a tableaux depicting a gangster mob hit — bullet holes in the walls, bathroom tiles shattered, an automobile sprayed by an automatic weapon. Three small rooms filled with old photographs show the carnage in the house, the refugee housing that the Turkish Cypriots created for themselves in the wake of the mass violence directed against them that year. There is one especially moving image of a stricken woman fleeing an unseen horror. This is the same image that Fezile brought to our workshop last month, which one of the other teachers informed us had been identified as a Cypriot woman running away from war. Of course, the fact that the woman could be either Greek or Turkish Cypriot is the most telling of all.

And it is a point that neither museum is capable of making. For the corresponding museum in Nicosia, just adjacent to the Archbishop's palace in the center of the old city, is devoted to the history of Greek Cypriot martyrs. But the theme of this museum of "Liberation" is quite different. It is devoted to the "heroic" and "epic" struggle of the Cypriot people against the English on the one hand and for "enosis" on the other. It voices the struggle in anti-colonial terms, with images of the "brave" Greek Cypriot freedom fighters who lost their lives in the struggle with British imperial "subjugation and slavery." In a sense it is a museum devoted to the E.O.K.A. organization of Archbishop Makarios and his military partner Dhigenis (Grivas). And it tells the story of a great and successful movement of liberation that unfolded between 1955 (the year of the founding of E.O.K.A.) and 1960. And it is a story of Greek (not Greek Cypriot) triumph, echoed in the Greek flags that still fly over the palace to this day.

In the case of the Museum of Barbarism, the inherent message is the overwhelming need for Turkish Cypriot protection against the blood-thirsty Greeks. And in the case of the Liberation Museum, the message is teleological inevitability of Greek unification. In other words, each museum conveys exactly the political and ideological position of its sponsoring "community." Taxim or separation for Turkish Cypriots, and Enosis or unity for the Greek Cypriots. Neither represents the range of opinions on both side of the Green Line that seek alternatives.

11 | 29 | 2007

Cem and Seray telephone — not an easy thing to do from north to south here on Cyprus. The call requires special cell phone codes and zones where the signal from one side may be heard on the other. It is a miniaturized version of the porous, mostly random way in which people and information cross though and now over the Dead Zone. Interesting to note, it seems that the British cell phone company Vodaphone has a significant interest in both Turkcell, the mobile provider in the north, and CETA, the Greek Cypriot phone company in the south. Maybe like the sewage that runs beneath the city, the buzz in the air above will run both ways as well. We all struggle for metaphors in this town.

They invite us to diner. Cem's sister, Sebnam, has returned from a visit to their family home in Ismir (Smyrna of old) and she has brought her Sufi Sheik along with her.

This will be a special evening, he promises.

Indeed. In the space of about ten days their two Iranian "boys," the new business partners who have imported truck-loads of different carpets, tent hangings, and glorious hand-painted glass fixtures, have transformed Cem's shop. It is filled with a kind of middle-eastern array of color, carpets hang from the walls, clothing and jewelry in pastels and silver overflow from glass cabinets,and a whole shelf of hookas. Only a Mussolini-like photograph of Rauf Denktash, the now-deposed TRNC leader, spoils the aesthetic vision they have crafted.

Upstairs in the rafters where Cem and Seray cook and wash, the family is praying. We join them and sit in a small room covered wall to ceiling with Turkish, Iranian, Caucasian carpets. It is like entering a tent, awash in reds and purples, browns and golds. In the middle sits a man, forty-something, wearing a Moslem prayer cap, a "O'Neill World Tour: 1962" t-shirt, and a sheep-skin vest.

His wife who sits to his left, her eyes deep and her hair covered with a silk turban. They have come to Cyprus from Los Angeles. He is Sebnam's Sheik. But he talks to us first about his work as a middle-school history teacher in Los Angeles. Most popular, he tell us, among his almost 100 percent Hispanic students. And it is easy to tell why. He is remarkably fluent not just in English but in American vernacular. Just the slightest hint of an accent and an engaging smile. He cares about his students, it is clear, and they love him in return.

But quickly, the conversation transposes into an extended monologue, one that we find as exhausting as it is fascinating. This holy man, Turkish by birth and education, American by citizenship and language, belongs to the Sufi branch of Islam, one that traces its lineage to the ninth century and then to the poetry of Rumi. They, and he, speak of the One, of eternal love, of overcoming the ego, of transcendence. Sufi Dervishes, once outlawed by Ataturk, now celebrate the 700th Anniversary of Rumi's poetry, marked this year officially by UNESCO. The "whirling" dance of the Melevi Dervish is intended to block out the illusion of the material world, produce a state of spiritual ecstasy, and lead the faithful into the "portal" of consciousness of the One.

This man is as well versed in the texts of world religion as anyone I have

The Sheik from L.A.

ever met. He speaks with fervor about the Hassidic mystics and Cabalists (for my benefit?) of the Illuminati and the Free Masons, of the Third Eye and the Chosen people. For more than an hour his free-form sermon unravels its multiple threads and he takes his awareness from one strand to the next without ever missing a stitch. We wonder, as we listen, toward what end? His message, like Sebnam's a month earlier, is remarkably simple. Free oneself from the prison of the ego and the world will be transformed into a good place.

But he also talks of codes and conspiracies, of secret plans to control the universe, of the meanings of the grand quests for the Ring, the Grail, for Truth. And finally, this engaging man of peace sounds remarkably like his host, Cem.

For he also speaks of the great Turk empires of the past, of Genghis Kahn, that render Alexander's power miniature by comparison. He praises the tradition of cultural tolerance practiced by the Ottomans and the wisdom of their rule. He, in a word, echoes Cem's paean to the idea of a Greater Turkish empire and people.

And then he takes a breath and speaks again of love, of universal, transcendent love.

We clear away the dishes, for this extraordinary monologue has taken fully three hours, during which we have walked the empty streets of north Nicosia, and dined at Cem and Seray's new apartment, our legs crossed before us on the floor. Cem has whispered to me that this night he will be received, initiated as a Dervish. The Sheik has interpreted a dream of Cem's as evidence of his preparation, as the end process of "seeking" that will allow him to receive the Sheik's formal blessing.

They motion us, my wife D and I, away from the center of the now-cleared room. They draw the shutters, and the lights grow dim, barely reflecting off the tapestries that hang from the walls. It feels now like a sanctuary.

The ceremony takes perhaps five minutes, mostly with Cem holding the hands of the Sheik, their minds and spirits intimately intertwined. Kneeling face to face, they chant prayer after prayer until the Sheik raises Cem up with his hands and then it is over.

Cem moves about the room silently, bowing, never turning his back on the Sheik. Red and white packages of Marlboro 100's sit at every corner of every table of the room, a curious benediction. The Sheik and his wife smoke virtually non-stop, but not at all during the initiation ceremony.

We wonder aloud as we walk back across the Green Line that evening if this is the moment of transformation Cem has been waiting for. Is this the occasion of the emergence of his better self? Will he now leave this shadow past, the military, gray-wolf past behind. Only two days earlier he told us about a conflict with the Turkish Cypriot who owns a Donner Shish-kebab place in the next store. They have squabbled over a parking spot. Cem says, you know, I can call someone and have this taken care of. There is no ambiguity about what he means. But this new man, reborn as a Dervish, a Sufi, will he banish this other version of himself? Or at least send it to the rubbish bin.

11 | 30 | 2007

A very eventful and satisfying day. We were invited to the local English radio program on Cyprus public station, RIC, for an interview with someone named Rosie. She has asked me to talk about my book, finally published and arrived here in Cyprus. It is dark early now, and we drive across town craning our necks in search of the broadcast tower, the only "address" they gave us. Probably it is just as useful as the normal "go down there past the traffic lights and turn" routine that Cypriots practice. We do find the station, of course — it looks like a miniature Eiffel Tower, a constructivist concoction of steel-girders, cell-phone parabolas and blinking red lights.

And Rosie turns out to be charming. She's English, with short grey-white hair, blue eyes peeking out from gold-framed glasses. She's actually read most of the book and actually seems interested in it and in me. She asks good questions about the difference between fiction and non-fiction, about how the mood on Cyprus has changed over the past two years, and about how the book came to be written.

The quarter hour speeds by. I've only done a live interview once before, and I have no expectations, only a vague sense of anxiety that accompanies public performance.

But it speeds by. I look up and Rosie is segueing from our "chat" to a number that sounds like a cross between the Eagles and Fleetwood Mac. Rosie looks over her glasses at me, as she has for the entire interview, and in one slurp thanks me, sips a soft drink, cues up a new disc, and dials the phone number for her next guest. "See you," she says as I hear the handset ringing next to her ear.

And we are off. Now toward the Old City to a coffee house/bookstore called Oktana. The English Department at the University has decided to host a reception for my book, inviting faculty and students, and we are already late. But, not really late, only American late. The reception is scheduled for 7:30, which means no one will arrive before 8:15 and it is just 7:40. But still, our pace quickens along the dark and deserted streets of Old Nicosia. Like in the Third Man, footfalls and fog make it feel eerie and vaguely thrilling at this time of night.

Oktana has glass doors atop a set of concrete steps. There are no streetlamps so the light that glows from the doorway seems to have been painted there by Edward Hopper. Everything else is very dark, almost black. The light seems pale yellow, yet still bright. The center hall of this coffeehouse-bookstore is filled with copies of Across the Green Line. It feels good to see them all spread out. But, like so many parties, I begin the skein of anxious inner questions. What if no one comes? What if no one wants a copy? And, camera at the ready, what will I do about the student who has promised to "picket" the event. This last issue is of the rumored-to-have-been-heard kind, but I say to myself that I really don't like this kind of threat.

A young waiter dressed head to toe in black motions us into one of the rooms off to the side of the center hall, away from the books awaiting adoption on the library tables. "This way. Book reception," he announces proudly and reaches around us to push one of the two black double doors open. I convince myself that if six people are present at least we'll have a good time, drink a beer or two and get home early. It's already been a long day.

The room is packed. I recognize a group of my students — and I even remember their names — from two years ago. And a few faculty colleagues, and a bunch of D's students. They sit at long-tables, coats draped over the backs of their chairs, smoking and drinking beer and wine and coffee. And then I look over at the far corner. Costas and Roula have come! What a wonderful treat. Of course I had invited them. But I never expected them to make it down-town so late in the evening. Normally by 8 pm Costas sits in a very comfortable chair upstairs, feet up, watching football on TV and, if D is around, sipping Zivaniah. But here they are, all dressed up and beaming. They have already engaged Anastasia, our colleague in English, and Costas is talking conspiratorially — though I cannot make out the words — in hushed tones with gentle gestures. I'm so glad and surprised to see them. It is a genuine act of friendship on their part.

The book reception

The students welcome me and D and I toast them back and talk for a moment about how this is the way that intellectual communities sustain themselves — through celebration. It is a genuine feel-good moment to me. And I had worried about the Neo-Leo that rumor had it would picket the party. That's why I brought my camera, isn't it?

But it never happened. Instead, like the old American TV show "I've Got A Secret" (more on this later) a surprise guest arrives.

Well, she more than arrives. She makes an entrance. Fizele, mauve pants-suit, matching pointed-toed boots, and wild hair, strides in, arm and arm with another, likely older, but no less attractive woman. She turns out to be an Egyptian-Cypriot and together the two of them bring something very different to the table. I'm quietly pleased that Fizele came to support me and politically even more pleased that a Turkish Cypriot felt brave enough, or is it strong enough to just walk right in. This is how it is supposed to be. Fizele and I have been working together on plans to bring some Cypriot teachers to the United States for a summer project at Kenyon College in Ohio, where I teach. She's going to be a big hit.

Then plates of food arrive. Hot hors d'oeuvres, salsa, skewered meats, which allows us to talk about religious food rules and whence they come and why. And with the food, lots of cold Cypriot beer. Keo. The students around us all seem intent, talking about life at the University, what's ahead, what they dream of. As I remembered from two years ago this is such a more adult and relaxing way of talking with kids than goes on at American colleges.

They ask me to read a bit from the book, and I do — a section about teaching them. Then Maria, the chair of the English department, invites the students to ask questions, and they do. Very much on the order of the ones Rosie pitched my way only two hours earlier — why did you write this book? Who did you imagine the audience to be? What's different in Cyprus today?

The last comes from Patrick. He is the student who invited me to dinner two years ago, who has remained in touch, who has just finished a whirl-wind year as student-president at the University, and who organized the reception. He's a young man with whom I have a special bond and he asks a wonderful question, or rather makes a remarkably insightful statement. You have orientalized us and made us exotic, he says, but that is all right. Because you have shown us ourselves from the outside, and even when you don't understand us perfectly, you also show us as students that you know to take chances and to even make mistakes.

It takes a bit longer that that, but he hits so close to home. He is incisive, insightful, dare I say a natural teacher. For the criticism he offers is right on the mark, yet delivered with a humanist's, rather than an egoist's, eye. I'm pleased as can be that this young man was once my student.

12 | 5 | 2007

We drive down to a small town, just to the east of Larnaca, called Pyla. It sits atop the boundary of the smaller of the two British "sovereign" air-bases and just below the southern dip of the Green Line. It has been a place of open commerce and communication between Turkish and Greek Cypriots ever since 1974 because of its location. That location makes it the only town in Cyprus that exists as "before." With a population estimated at 60% Greek Cypriot and 40% Turkish Cypriot, Pyla has earned a reputation as a model village.

We drive from the highway about 10 minutes north past the hard-packed and ever-so-dry desert ground past clusters of concrete and stucco villas. Even in the late fall, it is dusty and a bit desolate. Someone must find this locale attractive — perhaps exiled Lebanese, for the many signs are in Arabic. It seems barren and desolate to us, lacking only Eastwood's smoldering cheroot to make it the landscape of a spaghetti western.

The signs at the southern edge of town warn against taking photographs by order of the United Nations. We pass through a meager outlying commercial area with shops selling "Turkish Gold" and dry goods. I wrap my camera in my jacket, allowing the winter sun just enough angle to warm my arm and hand. The sunrays are bright white and I squint to make out the outlines of the village.

There are two of everything. Peripteros, cafes, churches and mosques, second-hand stores, but they are all in sight of the other, scattered around an irregular town square itself anchored by the building that harbors the United Nations police force. The UN patrols the town itself. But, as we climb a tower left over from French Crusaders' conquest, we see a Turkish flag flying high above a ridge to the north. It looks as if the town has been carved out of these hills, and the ridge looms over us, silhouetted against the bright sky. There, next to the flag, is a standard lookout post, a lifeguard tower on stilts, and next to the post two small and one very large soldier, Turkish, armed. But, as I look through my telephoto lens, it is clear that the larger of the figures is a cut-out, like one of the thousands of shadow people, themselves two-dimensional black silhouettes, that dot the rural Ohio landscape where we live — second only in lawn-ornament popularity to the concrete geese that have replaced lawn jockeys of late. The giant border guard is, I realize, a Potemkin villager.

A pickup truck breezes past and stops a few yards ahead in the middle of the Turkish Cypriot quadrant of the town square, just behind the mosque. We walk over and the driver emerges and lifts up the sides of the pickup cap to reveal baskets of fresh fruits and vegetables on cantilevered shelves. This bounty rings a bell of memory for me — thirty years ago, people sold fresh produce, dairy, and even delivered garments from the cleaners in vehicles like these, back in New York City.

Within minutes we are surrounded by a half-dozen local townspeople — impossible to know if they are Turkish or Greek Cypriot. They come to us out of curiosity, and we purchase a bag of mandarins, local oranges that taste like honey at this time of the year. I try to say that I'd love to take this man, his wife who is the driver, and his entire truck back to the States. But he looks at me blankly and smiles. His wife reaches down and puts two more mandarins into our bag and waves away our gesture to pay a bit more.

"He say you speak too fast." A boy is at my side, a teenager, holding a sprig of broccoli to his face and inhaling its fragrance. He offers to help. Translation complete, the vegetable man grins and waves his hand in an arc before him as if to say, this is where I belong. "You like broccoli?" the boy asks. "Yes, and aubergine," says my wife pointing at the shiny and tender eggplant.

"Then why you not come my shop for some coffee." This is from a third player, another young man who has joined us, smiling, as we stand in the bright sunlight. He looks like the actor Billy Baldwin, with a Cheshire-cat smile, eyes that twinkle, and a head of shiny black hair. "You come. You like shish-kabob?" He tells us his name, Ali, and says he is the town barber — as far as we can tell, the only barber in town.

If there is a more charming young man in Cyprus I will be very surprised. After some initial wariness — I mean, what does this guy really want? — we settle in. He gives a hair-cut to a two-year-old Irish boy, the son of a UN police officer, and tells us about himself. From a small island south of Anatolia, he

Ali the barber in Pyla, and nearby, no pictures

came by boat to Cyprus a decade ago and has been barbering in Pyla ever since. He's now 27. At his side is his nephew Murat, a general gopher for his uncle; a bright voluble kid, in love with American films, "You know Spider Man?" They make a team. Ali sits on the coach with D., beaming as he chit-chats about the world, as Murat stands off to the side rattling off names of American films and actors.

They proffer coffee, chocolates, and Turkish Delight (also known as Delight Cypriot). After an hour of genial eating and talking, our conversation takes us to a tiny globe on Ali's marble counter to locate Ohio, and Venezuela, and Mexico. Ali grins ear to ear and says again, "You like shish-kabob."

We do, but not this day. And we take another turn around the town and snap a few more pictures before being warned by an Argentinean peace-keeping soldier who wags his finger at us and smiles at the same time. "No pictures." Just like the sign reads as we drive back to the highway.

12 | 12 | 2007

Such interesting contrasts. One evening I attend a talk at Ledra Palace Hotel — a place I've become well acquainted with — a mishmash of Imperial-oriental architecture, a skin of sandstone and Moorish arches encasing a deserted interior. UN soldiers inhabit most of the long and barren hallways, sixty watt bulbs dangling from towering ceilings, and only a few "civilians" like Chara's group have any regular access to the Palace.

Blue-bereted Malaysian peace keepers dutifully unlock the rusty padlock on the chain link that secures the entrance and usher me inside. It is the same room where I did my first oral history workshop, but this time the chairs are in precise rows and the cold and damp early winter weather forces us to keep our coats on as we fold arms across our chests for warmth.

At the table toward the front of the room is a slight man, distinguished by white hair and a trimmed mustache. Chara introduces Ahmet Djavit An, a Turkish Cypriot physician who is also an amateur historian. Well, he has written or edited nine books in his spare time, perhaps amateur is not the right word, is it. In tones as dry and spare as the man, almost without affect, he speaks for an hour. But he is hardly boring. In fact, I can't get over how careful he is and how committed to the historical record as far as he can see it. He provides a perfect example of what the Historical Dialog group stands for.

History that transcends political ideology, at least in part.

The gist of his talk is clear. Divisions in Turkish-Cypriot politics have determined the narrative, as my friends at home would say, the "discourse." The truth as he sees it lies in the unspoken, the unsaid. Since the early 1970's when Doctor An was a medical student in Istanbul, Turkish Cypriots have been divided between the ultra nationalist "ranting" of the right and the peaceful internationalist position of the left. These correspond, in his mind, to class divisions. When the Nationalists succeeded in purging Turkish Cypriot trade unions and intimidating voices of reconciliation, they also set the stamp on the politics of the north in Cyprus.

We talk a bit about the Annan Plan, the 2004 UN-sponsored proposal that the Turkish-Cypriot public supported and the Greek-Cypriot opposed. An believes that there was enough to start with, imperfectly, but that Greek Cypriots had good reason to be mistrustful. Even here, in his interpretation of what he might have taken to be a devastating defeat for unity, for a "solution" to the Cyprus Problem, even here his position is one of understanding and transcendence.

Later that evening D and I walk across the Green Line and meet Sebnam. Someone has given her tickets to a Sufi-Dervish performance at the large comprehensive university on the outskirts of north Nicosia. We have seen this once before and it is not to be missed, so we brave a dreary and rainy evening, fight off the fatigue of too much to do and not enough time to do it, and go across the Green Line again.

Cem greets us looking even more melancholy than usual. Seray he tells us is "indisposed." We don't know quite what that means, only that they continue to struggle with their partnership. It has just dawned on us that they are not married and now they seem close to going their own ways. Cem, now a Sufi-Dervish, Seray not, have different paths before them. "A-Shala," as they say, "God's will."

In Cem's place appears the man we had met a few weeks earlier, the man who proudly announced that it was he who had designed and executed the Turkish-Turkish Cypriot flag that straddles the Kyrenia mountains. This Dervish, now a Vice-Mayor of north Nicosia, sports a beautifully pressed suit and drives a Mercedes with left-hand steering.

The evening is much as we had expected: a half-dozen young men all in white turning, turning, turning — for almost an hour it seemed — in their attempt to reach ecstasy, to be at one with the universe. They demonstrate their whirling on a broad stage and they dance to music performed by a dozen musicians, some of whom also sing a mournful prayer-like chant. What we have not expected is a crowd filled to overflowing with young university women in head-scarves. Turkish Cyprus has a reputation for a secular and laissez-faire attitude about religious observance and both are in evidence this evening. Later, someone shares the opinion that the head scarves are as much a fashion statement as they are a sign of religious observance.

Our host, who turned up these much-sought-after tickets, brings us back to his cavernous automobile. The five minute ride back to Cem's turns into a half-hour as he glides us through the dark slick streets and offers a running commentary on the political geography of division and separation. For every new building site that he proudly shows — and clearly north Nicosia has gained prosperity in just two short years-there is a former battleground, a wall or a cellar where he fought in 1974. The car seems to move silently through the night now, on empty and foreboding streets where faint moonlight casts shadows across his memories. It is chilling to listen to him proclaim the virtues of the AK-47. But not as chilling as the bullet holes in his neck, scalp, and shoulder that he also bares later that evening.

We walk back across the Green Line in silence that evening. The street lamps are out and only a small fluorescent light hangs over the still-chained Ledra Palace Hotel gate. The old building that the Historical Dialog group has purchased is to our left. We can still feel the presence of the coils of barbed wire, even though we know they have been removed. And now that it is past midnight, the stars shine just bright enough overhead to force their light down through the fog that cloaks this "dead zone."

12 | 13 | 2007

This is the time we have dreaded since our arrival. We leave in a few days. It is time to take our leave as we did two years ago. Dinners and lunches with our friends here, and tears and hugs. One last meze with Elena and Andros and Xenofon, a quick drive to Deftera to see Irene and Andrea, and a long Sunday brunch with Costas and Roula and the whole family. They have really taken us in, and we toast them this day, telling them how much their friendship means to us. Constantinous jumps up, arms around my neck, and kisses me. We copy recipes and share email addresses and wonder how and when we might see each other again.

As we sit, the winter sun is warm through the glass that encloses the corner of Costa's and Roula's terrace. It is perched high above Nicosia with its constant view of the flag-draped Kyrenia mountains. Costas tells us of his most recent trip to Romania, and quite suddenly this gentle grandfatherly man is transformed into a tough-minded business executive. He has been forced to deal with pilfering in some of his stores and he will not shirk the confrontation that it requires. As he talks, I get a different vision of him — Don Costas. Sitting the midst of his adoring and rambunctious family, he speaks of "business," of taking care of the "problem." And he leaves no doubt that he means business as well.

We also spend a delightful few hours later that same day with Andreas and his wife Maroula at the outdoor cafe just across the street from Costas' Timberland store. It is called Prailina and they serve the best pastries in Cyprus. Over sweets and coffee we sit and talk about the future. Our Greek is better now; we make stabs at full sentences and Maroula beams her approval on us, especially toward D., whose vocabulary and sense of grammar has left me in the dust. It feels very good to be in their company.

Andreas, from a village in the north, expresses something that I find both compelling and a bit sad. I've been wondering about the generational divide in the south, among Greek Cypriots. People like Andreas and Costas, like Maroula and Roula, have evolved a kind of wisdom about the Cyprus "problem." They, and many others, seem determined not to forget even as they leave the pain of 1974 behind. As Andreas puts it eloquently, we who are old enough remember the time when we all worked together and that is what gives me hope for the future. "You see, my dear Peter, my dear Mrs. D, we all knew each other then. The young people know only today and this is their only reality. No wonder they can't imagine unification."

Our conversation turns briefly to another issue in our building. It seems that an apartment on the second floor has been let to two Chinese women (whom we have never seen) and suddenly the hallways and stairwells are filled with men smoking cigarettes who seem to be waiting their turn. As I say to Andreas,

A wind-blown Costas

in Greek, "their door is always open."

This is, in fact, a serious problem that has two meanings for Cyprus. First, the women in the apartment embody the most significant social phenomenon that is transforming Cyprus from a homogenous to a heterogeneous society. The larger problem, however, is that most middle-class Greek Cypriots refuse to see it as a problem. It has become the norm that middle class families rely on colored, non-white service — domestic and unskilled — to maintain a high and prosperous standard of living.

The second issue facing Cyprus then, is this: Cypriots on both sides of the Green Line have come to attribute social change (and hence social pathology) to the presence of The Other. Greek Cypriots hold occupying Turks responsible for a rise in crime and prostitution in the north, and Turkish Cypriots hold the immigrants in the south responsible for that society's increases in crime and prostitution. This is, of course, all anecdotal. I have never seen any data, any evidence, of this so-called crime wave, only the assertion of its existence.

Where Andreas and Costas are generous in their vision of the past and hope for the future, many younger Cypriots hold neither. This is what makes the group of teachers engaged in the work of the Association for Historical Dialog so remarkable. They are bucking the system as it is manifest in the politics of education, in the official ideologies of both north and south, and in the spheres of class and generation.

In the evening we cross the Green Line one last time. We will have a traditional Turkish dinner with Cem and Seray at their new apartment, about a ten minute walk from the carpet shop. I say jokingly to Seray and Sebnam, "we'll only come to dinner if you cook for at least two days before." I think they get the joke, but I'm not sure.

We meet at the shop and out of the blue in saunters Fezile, whom we have introduced to Seray. Both sides of the Green Line remain, clearly, small towns where people know each other, honk at each other's cars, and cross the street to avoid face-to-face contact. Because they are both interested in improving their English, Fezile also becomes part of the evening, in his magenta corduroy pants suit.

But so does the Vice-Major, whom it seems is also courting Sebnam. He is waiting for us at the apartment. As Seray and Sebnam put the finishing touches on the feast-to-be behind closed doors, the rest of us sit on pillows and pass the time. The meal is worth the wait, as we knew it would be — yogurt soup, delicate homemade raviolis, zucchini pancakes, fresh and crusty bread, lemon-drenched hummus, pungent stuffed grape-leaves — each dish a visual delight. This cuisine is remarkable for its subtlety. Where Greek cooking is direct and straight ahead, the same dishes done in a Turkish style reveal a range of aromas and spices that range from the sharp and piquant to the pungent and fragrant. It is like entering a very sophisticated culinary world, one where the variety of smells and tastes and textures and designs contribute to the art of each dish.

We dine, as we have in the past, sitting on the floor — and since one of my knees doesn't bend, I suffer a great deal of ribbing for my pretzel-like posture. We pass plates round and round, and for some wonderful reason, the television remains on but with the sound muted.

Dervish and Cem remain with me as the women wash the dishes and then out of the blue Cem asks, "Peter — do you work for Israel? Or for the United States?" It is one of those questions that makes me see red. After I explain about the Protocols of the Elders of Zion and the lies that sustain anti-semitism, I look up and say, "If you continue to ask these kinds of questions I'm going to have to rethink our friendship." I'm stunned by the query, by the underlying premises, by Cem's even asking. I've tried to "show" them my Jewish background because I don't want them to be uncomfortable, and because in this part of the world to be Jewish (rather than Israeli) is very unusual. So, I am floored, almost as floored as I was by Leo three months ago.

A few minutes later as I walk to the washroom Cem gets up to show me the lights. "I ask you these questions because of Dervish," he tells me. "You know I love you."

I accept this at face value. But, not really. Why would he do the bidding of someone else in this matter? It makes sense and I remain puzzled although no longer as put-off as I had been. My enmity switches to his friend. I tell myself I was right all along to be uncomfortable with him. But, I don't really know that either. In any case, it is a downer for me and I find myself withdrawing from the emotional aura that surrounds this last time together.

Even as we ready ourselves to say good-bye, as D and Seray hold each other and cry tears of farewell, each knowing that much will be different the next time we meet, even then I can't bring myself back. It makes the sadness even more heavy, and as dark as the night air across the Green Line.

12 | 14 | 2007

Our last day on the island. It is still cold and rainy, gray and unyielding as we drive downtown to the Fulbright office. D wants to say good-bye to our friends there, to Daniel, the Head of the Office, and Ioli, the Administrator who makes the Fulbright Fellows program work like an old Timex. They have been very supportive to us during our tenure here. As we stand in the vestibule, next to the twinkling Christmas tree, the whole staff saunters in — Anna, who helps with Education programs; Voulla, Daniel's secretary; Kyproula, who keeps the books and her good humor at the same time; Revy, who speaks English like she's from Pittsburgh; and Maria, who speaks no English at all but always communicates her good will. It is the photo-op of the season, the whole staff and the tree, and as we hug each other, Daniel looks up and asks Anna, "Did you tell him?"

My heart skips a beat. "Tell me what?" I hope it means that a small grant I had written to the Fulbright Commission has been approved. "Your grant," Daniel says, "the Embassy is sending it to Washington for the final approval."

WOW! (I say this to myself.) WOW. What a lovely farewell gift. Rena and Fezile and I had dreamed up a project that would bring 10 of the Historical Dialog teachers to my Ohio college this summer for two weeks. The idea was for them to join a history teacher education project that I co-direct for the Cleveland public schools. I had asked for funds to pay for transportation and room and board and books for ten teachers and the Fulbright Board liked the idea and forwarded the proposal to the Embassy. And now they like it and I'm so proud I could burst. Of course, I should hold my enthusiasm in wait for final State Department approval. But, hey, it's in the bag. Isn't it?

We drive back to our neighborhood late that afternoon, with just enough time to return the old Nissan war-horse we've been renting for next to nothing. It is not quite rush hour and so, even in downtown Nicosia, the traffic flows steadily. Off to the east the sky has cleared and shafts of sunlight stab earthward even as the rain continues to drizzle. We stop at a very busy intersection, where Makarios and Digini cross, and we both look up. There, just to the northeast, a grand rainbow unfurls, deep-deep purple and pale yellow with all the colors in between. It is lovely. And as romantics, we think it is fitting too. Good news and a rainbow!

12 | 15 | 2007

Not sure if this counts as a ritual, but once again we enjoy our last moment, a very early breakfast with Costas and Roula just before we leave for the airport. They have become dear friends, people we love and enjoy, people whose trust and affection have become so important to us. We drink coffee and eat a bit of toast, then we are off. It is too fast — as if this whole semester has vanished and all that is left are memories.

But there is a sort of postscript. We fly to Athens for a few days of tourism, museums, the Acropolis visible from our hotel window, and a festive holiday scene that is bursting with color and joy all over the city. Athens provides a very interesting perspective on Cyprus. It is a major European city, teeming with energy, cosmopolitan and metropolitan. Athenians more resemble Parisians than Nicosians in their style and verve, in the pace of life, in the hustle and bustle of a major-league city. It renders Nicosia provincial. That is, Athens makes Cyprus into the extended small town with village roots that it surely is. And that, of course, is part of the charm of Cyprus. It is knowable in some sense, even as we encountered its marvelous complexity; intimate in scale and close knit in personal relationships. Like my village in Ohio, people in Nicosia honk at each other's cars, run into each other on the street and at the same parties and cultural gatherings. It is normal to meet people you know in Cyprus, sitting at cafes, waiting on line at restaurants, walking up the ramp for a football game.

And Athens is a frolic of yule-time folderol. Several streets just spitting distance from our hotel are closed to traffic and at this time of the year are filled to overflowing with shoppers and strollers who make their way between a phalanx of plastic toy hawkers, faux-Peruvian musicians dressed as native Americans, frozen-tableaux men and women in white pancake makeup, and any variety of sketch, portrait, and caricature artists who would be as at home in Venice, California as they are here.

We delight, however, in the men whom I have dubbed Black Santas. They line the street, too, these Africans selling knock-off leather goods which they display on white sheets spread on the sidewalk. But every once in a while, as if by silent alarm, they quickly snatch the four corners of their sheets, gathering their wares into makeshift white bundles which they hoist over their shoulders, and as if one they virtually melt into the crowds. Black Santas, white toy-bags slung over their backs, they bend under the burden, and vanish.

The Green Line Opening: 2010-11

3 | 5 | 2010

Hard to believe I'm back in Cyprus. After a 24-hour sequence of flights, I arrive at the spanking new airport in Larnaca. I think I'm in Athens for the Olympics, I say to myself, as I walk and walk and walk down marbled corridors encased by stainless steel and glass walls. They have gone from the temporary warehouse structure of the 1950s, one with blank walls and a stand-up coffee bar, into the Miami Beach 2.0 model. It is vast and sleek and empty. I wonder if the pols in the capital have bet too heavily on a mass tourist invasion. Or do they know something that I don't, and are betting against the house? But, what a house it is.

I hire a car and drive through the black night to Nicosia. The signs now call it Lefkosia, and through the ever-expanding onset of jet lag I successfully get the right-handed, stick-shifted car to find its way home!

Costas and Roula welcome me back — the best way they know, of course — by offering food. We are contemporaries, but I feel like I've come to visit my grandparents. Roula, despite the late hour of my arrival, can't do enough for me — "some fruits?" She bustles in the kitchen first, then in the spare room I'll stay in, then back to the kitchen. Costas sits. He has just returned from a business jaunt to Romania to oversee his group of Timberland Stores. And as he talks about the world "crisis" I remember how keen an analytical sense he has. Just as Roula reveals her domestic graciousness, so Costas his business acumen. It has been two and half years since we've seen each other, and it has taken less then a half hour to come into focus. I ponder the sense of continuity this reveals. This is nowhere more evident than the next morning, my first back in Cyprus.

The call to prayer at 6 am, followed by more drugged sleep, and then a breakfast fit for a king — platters of toast and sliced meats, yogurt, smoked salmon, anari (a kind of sweet cottage cheese) and lots of coffee, first Nescafe Gold (a delicacy in their household) and then "real" Cyprus coffee. I can't believe how good it feels to be with them. It is the ritual breakfast that D and I have with them each time we leave Cyprus. Now it is my homecoming. D will not arrive for another week, till the start of her spring break.

Athena the pharmacist

I walk around the neighborhood that first morning, saying hello to Athena the pharmacist who remembers the time she gave me a flu shot, and then to the local grocer who supplied the turkey for our Thanksgiving celebration in 2005. "Where have you been?" he asks, gesturing to the women who staff his market, "I thought you would have been back sooner." He grins. He's very busy and I know I have about three sentences to explain my appearance. It goes like this: The American cultural attache has invited D and I to give a series of workshops and classes on U.S. Black History month. They have paid our expenses and this allows us the luxury of our return. We are to work with our old teacher friends in the Association for Historical Dialog, the "Bi-Communal" group, some of whom have already visited us in Ohio to participate in several teacher training programs during the summers. Last year, four of them came with us to the low country of South Carolina where they learned about the African origins of African-American culture. It was a great experience for all of us. But all of that is too much to convey — I tell the grocer only that I'm back for a short visit this time. He waves me into the store, pointing to the peanut butter that he knows I'm after.

It is already summer to me. Temps in the 70s, and I work up a sweat walking about. The Cypriots, of course, all think it is late winter and are bundled up with scarves and fashionable leather boots as they stroll down the city streets. I'm undecided about what to do this first evening in Cyprus. Costas and Roula have already taken me to a souvlaki lunch of gargantuan proportions, all seven grandchildren in attendance. The irrepressible Constantinous sticks his face close to mine and immediately charms me. "Hi, Peter." He goes to an English school now, in second grade, and reaches up to give me the same high-five I taught him five years earlier when he was a power-ranger.

He is doe-eyed and sweet, this little boy whom we have known almost all his life.

I remember the drive from the airport, right-handed car staying to the left, the pitch-dark night. Better get back on the horse, I say out loud to myself. I've been in Cyprus for less than 24 hours and the idea of driving around intimidates me. So, I Jedi-knight my inner vision and imagine the way to Deftera. And with one small detour I get there, just as the sun is setting, unharmed. I remember to turn right at the "Snatch" store (we did think it a funny name five years ago), but I should have waited one more street. Still, there it is, Irene's restaurant, the so-called Panic Room, and even before I turn the corner I smell the souvlaki grilling. Irene looks up, then lights up and starts babbling in Greek. I have worked hard to learn more of this confounding language the past year. I am almost finished with the second year of CD-based language lessons. I hear myself saying, "yes (ne) I arrived yesterday. I am here for three weeks." So far so good. But after that all I have are the pat tourist phrases — "The green bus. Does it stop at the school?" or "Mr Andrei is in his office. He will come to the telephone in a moment, can you wait?" I'm stuck in the vise of not fully comprehending the torrent of words that flow out toward me, and of searching, like a slow version of the first Google, for a couple of words that I can string together to get around the subject for which my vocabulary is too thin. Yet somehow over coffee we manage to converse. It's hardly real sentences, but still a miraculous conversation where I learn that the "other" coffee shop across the street is closed, that her father, Andreas will be over in a minute, and that Andrea is well and happy and wants to see me. If I will sit and eat something — haloumi, souvlaki, a beer, anything — Andrea will appear.

And she does. She's the same yet different. Older, of course, more adult in the way her face has formed, yet still slight, even delicate. But these changes are superficial compared with what she tells me about. Two years ago, the fourteen year old Andrea wanted only to talk about "boys and getting married." Today she engages me in a discussion about overcoming the Turkish Cypriot-Greek Cypriot divide. She's eloquent on the subject, speaking of the humanity of all Cypriots, on the way that nationalism divides peoples. I think as she talks that this is somehow the fruits of the bone-marrow transplant from so many years ago, that it is her rearranged DNA talking to her heart.

I offer to introduce her to my bi-communal teacher friends after she tells me about an informal group of Greek-Cypriot and Turkish-Cypriot students that she meets with. I'll bet the two groups, student and teacher, don't know about each other. I hope they can come to the film series I'm hosting these next two weeks at the Fulbright Center in the Buffer, aka Green, aka Dead Zone. It would be gratifying to bring more people of good will together.

She hugs me goodbye. It feels very satisfying to see her again. When D arrives in a week we will return for more talk, more souvlaki, and more photos. I drive back to the city in the dark, feeling tickled that I have re-mastered the wacky reverse-image British form of driving.

3 | 7 | 2010

I think it's time to see about the new checkpoint. Just after we left in late 2007, the new political leaders of each side agreed to pursue a process designed to spark reunification. Their very first act, on I was sure would open the gates of trust based on trade, was to open the main shopping corridor, Ledra Street, that connects the northern and southern halves of the city. The Green Line, in 1974, severed this commercial artery. It became impossible for Turkish Cypriots and Greek Cypriots to stroll the 100 meters to the other side. Instead they had to walk at least 2 kilometers, outside the old Venetian walls of Nicosia, to cover the same distance. And now, it is open. Flash your passport, stamp a faux visa, and you are in and out within seconds. The tourist Greek-Cypriot Ledra street, McDonalds, Swatch, t-shirts and ice cream now leads smoothly to the Turkish-Cypriot Ledra Street that is as much bazaar as it is pedestrian mall. Open air stalls selling Puma and Dolce-Gabbana knockoffs, fragrant spices, and the usual Pashmina scarves squeeze in next to each other surrounded by the aroma from a thousand cups of Turkish coffee.

I walk to the Buyuk Han, closed because it is still Sunday morning, and then across town, on the very same streets that D and I walked our first day in the north (or the north) five years ago. The old man with his fruit cart is nowhere to be seen, but I have not doubt that he is still there.

It takes ten minutes to reach Cem's shop. A man sits at a desk repairing an old carpet. Cem and Seray, however, are nowhere to be found. Seems they have moved to Kyrenia, a seaside town on the north coast of the island. A Turkish Cypriot materializes, out of almost thin air, to drive me to the new shop and new home that Cem and Seray have created for themselves.

When last I saw Cem he had just received his spiritual blessing from his leader, his Sheik. Now, he looks and feels and sounds like a Buddhist Monk! He is dressed in loose-fitting black cotton pants, shirt, vest, and socks. His beard is stubby and his eyes longing. "We waiting for child," he tells me proudly. They have been married for almost a year, Cem and Seray, and she has joined him as a Dervish celebrant. He explains that only the righteous have the privilege

Seray

of wearing this black-robed garb. And while he has not yet reached the heightened state of consciousness required of novitiates, the Sheik has bequeathed to him the honor and the responsibility of a truly spiritual man. I'm awe struck. Cem embarked on a five year journey that has witnessed, in some very intimate terms, a quest for a truer self. This one-time political activist-soldier has transformed himself. Or, as I prefer to think, recovered his old self.

"We play music now," his voice at stage whisper. "I play Kannun. We have two friends, play flute." The music is mystical, floating, sensual — the kind we have heard at the "demonstrations" of the Whirling Dervishes that we attended. It is the music of the poet Rumi, of inner peace and devotion. As Cem talks about it, garbed in black, it feels real, authentic. There is not a word about the grandeur of Turkic culture, of lost empires, or Ataturk. This man is changed, even reborn.

And Seray? She too appears in black, with her face almost bright white, lips red. She too has converted. In fact, only after she converted did the Sheik give her his blessing to marry. But unlike Cem, she remains the same vivacious young woman. I take pictures and she clowns — draws tear tracks down her cheeks, mugs, crosses her eyes. She is as externally joyous as Cem is spiritually centered. And they seem like much more of a couple now, as if they fit. No longer the older-wiser man of the world who has captured the heart of his assistant, Cem and Seray seem to complement each other on equal footing.

I wish I could stay longer. But the morning slips away and their friend drives me back to north Nicosia so I can walk back down the new Ledra Street, into the South (or, the south). I pass the Weaving Mill only a few hundred meters from the checkpoint. It seems deserted. I wonder what has happened to Leo and Sotoria, my old friends turned antagonists. I will have to come again one late afternoon when they are sure to be there — if in fact they are still there.

But the day is still young. And while I am fogged over by jet lag, I soldier on. Costas and his sons, Michael and Yiorgos, will take me to a football game. Michael's wife Vangalou piles us into her brand-new Lexus four-wheel drive and we move out.

The modern Nicosia stadium remains without a semblance of parking, so we rough-ride up and down ravines, through mud-fields and over streams of water that are hubcap deep. I have always thought of Vangalou as shy and retiring. No more. She drives like a daredevil, or perhaps like a cowboy. "Yahhooow" she calls out as we cut in front of a pickup truck that has stalled out in the mud. She yanks the wheel sharply to the left and the Lexus hops the curb and is driving down the sidewalk. "See, we have a new lane," she calls out proudly. After something like ten minutes in the brush we emerge about 200 meters from the stadium. The car is covered with mud, but she is beaming. We look behind us and there are yet thousands of cars stuck in the gridlock that she so deftly avoided. In retrospect this was the highlight of the game.

The family team "APOEL" wins 1-0 against the very team from Limassol that they played in that angry riot-filled match five years ago. I wear the orange ball cap that Vangalou gave me then — she is a team fanatic — and I'm accepted by the fans in the stands without blinking. Of course, the ever-present issue of "hooliganism" has not vanished from Cyprus football. To prevent crowd disturbances they have erected a steal-mesh screen about 40 feet high at each end of the stadium, effectively sealing off the areas where the fanatics of each team sit. The idea is to isolate these rebellious kids from each other and the rest of the otherwise peaceful fans. But, it works hardly better that it did five years ago. Just as the game ends we watch as a group of 100 or so teenagers, in the pale orange shirts favored by APOEL fans, run toward the exit ramp at the other end of the stadium. The newspaper reports the next day that three Limassol kids had been hospitalized after the ruckus. The two teams issue statements faulting the security forces on hand.

3 | 9 | 2010

I meet Rena Chopalrou for lunch outside the school where she teaches in South Nicosia. It is a stone's throw from the newly opened Ledra Street check point and sits on a lovely square. Several cafes, an old Orthodox Church and the school itself — all constructed from the yellow-gold sandstone of Colonial Nicosia — share this shaded and sheltered space.

I have not seen Rena since the summer of 2008, when she came to Ohio with ten other Cypriot participants in our Teaching American History project at Kenyon College. She is a primary school teacher, as is her husband Yiorgos, and is as intellectually and politically intense (and funny!) as anyone I have ever met. The mother of three-year-old twins, Rena sits on boards of several activist groups, including the Association for Historical Dialogue; she writes political commentary for Greek Cypriot and British Cypriot newspapers; and is a tightly wound ball with layers of energy and exhaustion. "I'll buy you lunch today," she tells me. "You'll buy the whiskey later." I don't quite know how she does it, all of it in several languages.

We have somehow, almost from the beginning, connected. I really like her directness and political energy, and we both seem to like bull-shitting about films and art. I sent Rena one of my aunt Sylvia's paintings (she is a naif-abstractionist) after she saw one in my home in Ohio. We huddle over plates of spaghetti and beans at a cafe literally between the walls of two old Nicosia buildings. Rena is committed to working in the forum of educational policy as a means of enhancing some form of reconciliation. She travels to Greece often, to international conferences, where she worries about textbook objectivity and about the images of the "other." But today she is distressed at the way in which conventional politics in Cyprus co-opts all forms of dissent. I tell her a bit more about the energy of the U.S. Civil Rights Movement in the 1960s, about the way some of the leaders found to mobilize ordinary people (like me) to get the attention of the Federal Government. I'm thinking of Johnson's sponsorship of the Civil Rights Act of 1964 when he said, "And we SHALL overcome." I can see Rena processing this, wondering about what issue, where, how to find the way to galvanize outrage to produce change. "But how can we do this?" she asks. "I think there are only 12 of us here on this island who believe it." My rhetorical answer. "How many Bolshevik were there in 1903 (I think it was 9), or feminist-suffragettes in 1849?" Rena will introduce me to a Turkish intellectual on Friday who has been asking the same questions. Stay tuned.

3 | 11 | 2010

Today is my first film showing for the Association. But I arrive in the Old City of South Nicosia early and decide to walk down to the Green Line and see if the Weaving Mill is open. I wonder how it might feel to see Leo and Soteria again. Our disagreements two-and-a-half years ago left me hurt, exhausted, and perhaps a bit wiser. I rehearse a small speech that I actually repeat when I see them a few minutes later. Something about the importance of friendship and a hope that we can still be. Inside the Weaving Mill is a tumble of young children — some playing chess, others billiards, still others assembling sandwiches and snacks. It has become, clearly, an after-school center. Soteria glances up and actually smiles, gives me a hug and says "yes, friendship is more important than ideology." And she goes back to the six kids gathered around her, each needing, demanding, questioning. I move to the side and spot Leo crossing the street. He sees me, and his eyes narrow. I say my small speech again, and he virtually repeats word for word what Soteria has said. Then he looks up at me a bit quizzically. "But, I can't remember your name."

I have chosen five films about the civil rights and women's movements — several documentaries and three features. In the back of my mind I wonder if there are any examples from which Cypriots can learn. For all of its inner conflict and rhetorical flourish, the civil rights movement from 1955 to 1965 really did accomplish something remarkable — and it did so through mass mobilization and action. This evening's film, "Salt of the Earth," is a clumsy but daring 1950s film about an Hispanic-American strike in New Mexico that sputters, and almost dies. The miners' wives save the day by taking over the picket line, forcing the men to care for the children and do the laundry. The Anglos in power cave in the face of mass action. It is a 30s film made in the 50s, at the height of McCarthyism/HUAC black list, that NO ONE saw for the next twenty years. The 20 or so Greek and Cypriot teachers hate the first half-hour (as I imagined they might) which unwinds very slowly, but gradually they take to the story, to the narrative of overcoming. We sit and talk about it for an hour and I see the lights in their eyes turning on — some view the film as neo-realist, some as feminist, and others as a tract of almost agit-prop. It is, in fact, all three.

3 | 12 | 2010

D is supposed to leave Ohio today and arrive in Cyprus tomorrow. She emails me that something is not quite right — seems the name on her passport does not match the name on the ticket that I purchased in November. I am completely stricken. Her legal name, her passport name, is Dorothy Rose Elder. I used D. Rose Elder. Surely the airlines, customs and the TSA will understand? A few phone calls will clear it all up, won't they? No, they won't. There is nothing to be done, they all tell me, except for D to present herself at the airport and hope for the best. I call and tell her screw it, if they won't let you on just buy another ticket and we'll deal with it afterwards. I really hate this, hate the anxiety, and the responsibility I feel for messing up. Is is noon in Ohio now and I expect to hear from her in a few hours. Some inner clock is ticking and my cell phone sits on the table and there is absolutely nothing I can do.

3 | 13 | 2010

She made it through, no sweat. TSA just said don't do it again. I pick her up at the airport and drive back to Nicosia, for the first time able to admire the spring here. What I first saw, in August five years ago, as desert — dry, arid, foreboding — is now lush and green with flowers lining the highway all the way from Limassol to Nicosia. D and I talk non-stop, news from home, news from here.

I tell her about all the semi-political conversations I have had so far — long talks with Rena on the one hand and Costas on the other. The issue of a "solution" to the Cyprus question seems as remote as ever. But both of them — one on the left the other on the right — also see that both presidents, Talat in the north and Cristofias in the south, have made real progress. They are both Communists, but that has a very wry meaning in this part of the world and seems to come down to a mistrust of NATO and a willingness to engage with Cuba. My friends here mistrust them. They don't understand why they are not moving forward with even more vigor; they think that the US and Great Britain are pulling strings behind the scenes, and what they really can't abide is the presence of several hundred thousand Turkish "settlers" in the north who likely outnumber the Turkish Cypriots. They both say that the moment has passed, a moment defined by 2004 and the Annan Plan that the north supported and the south defeated at the last minute due to complex machinations on the part of the past President of Cyprus, Papadapolous. In some grossly ironic gesture, Papadapolous' casket and body disappeared last week, snatched from the cemetery that is just outside the village of Deftera. It turned up a few days later in another cemetery, supposedly the scheme of several jailed gangsters to somehow shorten their sentences. Beats the hell out of me.

In any event, it appears that after two years of weekly or monthly talks the two sides have agreed on a federal structure with a rotating Presidency; on terms and conditions of citizenship for Turkish residents in the north; and on the principal of compensation for lost property. But there are new elections for President in the north and Talat is behind in the polls. On top of this, Rena cries betrayal. Cristofias, worried about his own reelection possibilities next year, just announced there will be no settlement piecemeal, but only a comprehensive one. In other words, all the compromises don't mean anything unless and until there is a comprehensive and full solution. She now feels dispirited, like many who have had such high hopes for reunification. A sense of resignation resonates with many people with whom I talk. And in contrast to five years ago, when everyone wanted to talk about reconciliation, today it is a subject that remains unspoken unless I raise it.

3 | 15 | 2010

The exception is Costas, who once wound up, just keeps spinning.

Today the subject is the British. "I will tell you," he glances around the room to see if anyone else is listening, "the English are bastards." We are alone on the porch of his apartment, and he likes it when I describe it as a "Florida Room." His hands flutter as he talks about growing up in a small farming village on what is today the runway of the airport in the north. A Turkish-Cypriot family on one side, a Greek-Cypriot family on the other, and the police station in between is how he remembers it — a politically telling, symbolic placement that resonates with today's memory of the good old days. You see, he continues, "they had, the British, only one policy. 'Divide and Conquer.' They only knew about power, about how to hold the Empire by telling factions of local peoples different stories about the others." I understand that Costas grew up under British control of Cyprus and that the movement for National Liberation in the 1950s directed armed rebellion against them. But this gentle and sweet man does not forget or forgive. "I am," he leans back and peels an orange, "only a business man, not a man of politics." Then he takes a deep breath. "But the British, they have made shit of my country."

The fact of the two large British bases on Cyprus, twin Guantanamos, both "sovereign," feels much less charming in this light. Yes, they have cute English street signs and old-fashioned expressions ("boots" and "chips" and what not), but the British army, navy, and air-force are a real presence here on Cyprus — not exactly a counter to Turkish military occupation in the north, but a reminder that neither part of this island is entirely under the control of its own people or government. As I did five years ago, I reflect on the psychology of this condition. If the so called "imagined community" has no integrity, then what? It evokes strong senses of incompleteness and powerlessness to people who have so much at stake over the question of identity. To that extent, then, some Cypriot behavior is clearly compensatory. As I thought five years ago, "hooliganism" at football games, sometimes complete with Greek flag waving, seems to me a form of cultural acting out. What they really need here is the World Wrestling Federation. Imagine a weekly pay-per-view smack-down between Nikos the Giant Greek and the Terror of Turkey, none other than our old friend Dervish.

The only change that I can detect so far is this: Both peoples, Greek and Turkish Cypriots, are today more inclined than ever to see themselves as a coherent people — not a nation, nor an ethnicity (nation in Greek anyway, ετη–νικοσ). But, in good dialectical fashion, they view the Turkish "settlers" in the north as the "other." They view them (whose demographics include poverty, large families, and a proclivity towards criminality) as the source of real discontent. Listen carefully and you hear Malthusian arguments all over again.

3 | 16 | 2010

D spoke today at a different university, a private, for-profit one that seems like DeVry back in the States. This is more usual than not on Cyprus — these business colleges acquire the designation University by agreeing to conform to certain governmental standards, and transform themselves from the Cyprus college of business graphics to Frederich University. It feels very foreign to me, but then again, it is a way that entrepreneurship takes place where the state underfunds public education. D is passionate, as always, talking to these students' hearts with stories of feminism and development from her decade of experience in Ghana.

After the talk someone introduces me to Nicoletta, a live-wire Greek Cypriot academic who completed her Ph.D. in educational theory at the University of Illinois, Chicago. One of her teachers was Bill Ayres, an American elementary education theorist and a former leader in the movement that opposed U.S. involvement in the Vietnam War. He is known for his 1960s activism as well as his current work in education reform, curriculum, and instruction. In 1969 he co-founded the Weather Underground, a self-described communist revolutionary group that conducted a campaign of bombing public buildings (including police stations, the U.S. Capitol Building, and the Pentagon) during the 1960s and 1970s in response to U.S. involvement in the Vietnam War. Ayres is now a retired professor in the College of Education at the University of Illinois at Chicago, formerly holding the titles of Distinguished Professor of Education and Senior University Scholar. During the 2008 US presidential campaign, a controversy arose over his contacts with then-candidate Barack Obama. He is married to Bernardine Dohrn, who was also a leader in the Weather organization.

Since one of Ayres' old antagonists and now colleagues is a friend from Chicago, I find myself suddenly back in the old disagreements between SDS and the Weather Underground. Talk about the way old wounds won't heal in Cyprus. It's hard to argue how important it is for people to remember the past so as not to be imprisoned by it, when I find myself in much the same dilemma.

Similarly, Nicoletta absolutely insists that the Turkish Invasion remains the issue in the foreground even as she hopes to initiate an oral history project of reconciliation. I had proposed something similar years ago, part of the exercise I did with the Historical Dialogue Group on Photo-Story, and I am very cheered that someone here also is on the same wavelength. Curiously, in this small town that is Nicosia, my new acquaintance knows nothing of this larger group. I invite her to one of the films in my series and hope that I can introduce her to some of my friends. Perhaps something that D and I can both do is widen the circles of friends and colleagues. That would be satisfying enough.

But it does occur to me that perhaps Nicoletta and Ayres and some Turkish-Cypriot friends could create a summer institute at Kenyon College to bring diverse teacher-intellectuals together. I will pursue this idea next week with my old friend, the Fulbright Director Daniel Hadjitoffi. He's always willing to dream along with me.

3 | 17 | 2010

We drive with two Public Affairs Officers of the US Embassy staff to Eastern Mediterranean University. It is in the north, just outside Famagusta. D and I will do a combined talk on the origins of Rock and Roll. This will be fun — it is a subject we both love and know a bit about. Our escort, courtesy of Uncle Sam, arrives because D.'s stay here has an official budget and they shepherd her around VIP-style. Me, I'm just along for the ride.

We drive though the pedestrian check-point, the oldest one, the one we first crossed five years ago, slaloming past barriers, concrete mixers, remnants of barbed-wire and several border patrol stations. I always resented these diplomatic cars that sped past our walks through the Buffer Zone — the Dead Zone — and across the Green Line. Now I am in the car. The Zone is remarkably the same as it was — haunted, eerie with the scars of war, dingy and bleak. Yet it is also changing. Our friends at the Association for Historical Dialog have purchased an abandoned building across the street from Ledra Palace. It will serve as their Home for Reconciliation. They also have a professional staff, Greek- and Turkish-Cypriot administrators and technicians, who have office space in well-appointed temporary trailers sitting behind Ledra Palace Hotel and the Fulbright Center. This is no longer the small room with faded linoleum and rusty filing cabinets I wandered into in 2007, and the best, is yet to come across the street. I can't express enough my admiration for the grit and determination of my local Association friends — Charra, Fez, Marios, Dileck, and Rena — who have stayed with this for many years now and built an organization of considerable presence. They wrote successful grants for 2,000,000 euros to gain this foothold and provide salaries for staff. Remarkable.

At the checkpoint our American guide stops the car and a Turkish-Cypriot consular employee slips in behind the wheel.

She is circumspect — open when approached, focused when ignored. Ipek appears to be in her mid-30s, has almost spiked hair, and speaks with the accented precision of a Cypriot who has learned British English. We drive east toward Famagusta. The fields are green with spring, but not with planting. When we ask Ipek about this she is careful. We, and she means Turkish Cypriots, need to learn to do without, she begins. We like our toys. She glances over her shoulder pointing to the steady stream of aluminum and glass new car showrooms. Moments later she tell us about the abandoned factories in this fertile agricultural plain. They don't make anything anymore. She shows us a small white panel truck covered with signs featuring "Cyprus Cola." They once made that product in north Cyprus; now, they use the truck to distribute Coca-Cola. They

Sandbags in the Dead Zone

have simply not bothered to repaint the truck.

We have become too dependent on Turkey, she continues. We like this prosperous life-style but we, our government in the north, can't even pay salaries. Turkey subvents 2/3 of what the average Turkish Cypriot earns. Something like neo-mercantilism comes to my mind as we talk. The subsidy from Turkey, in effect, undermines the ability to create an autonomous and inventive political economy in the north.

Her analysis is all the more startling when we begin to talk about the "Problem" and the possible "Solution" for it. Of course I am for a settlement, she says, but not the one that the Greeks offer. She favors a federation, she says. She opposes the creation of a single state that would necessarily mean Greek-Cypriot dominance. I am puzzled. This is, as far as I have read and learned, exactly what the Greek-Cypriot government has agreed on in the talks on-going for the past two years. But what I hear from Ipek lies at the heart of the problem — neither side trusts the other. Instead, the rampant spread of rumor and half-truth constantly infringes on the ability for each group to actively pursue common goals. It sounds remarkably like the period of the Annan Plan (2004) when innuendo trumped reality time and time again.

I enjoy her frankness. It is a lovely day, like June in Ohio. High deep-blue skies, clear air, and the string of the Kyrenia mountains sharply carve the sky. These mountains, for the past two weeks covered by what locals have called a Saharan dust storm, now contain the horizon to the north. From my window in Nicosia I can look out and see both halves of the city at my feet. From this highway only an occasional village, a solitary mosque, or a new "super" gas station marks the landscape. It is a long stretch of old Cyprus, what had once been the breadbasket, providing wheat and fruit for most of the island. Today, grass extends to the base of the mountains — untilled, it seems.

As we approach Famagusta this all changes. Clusters of new homes, white concrete Cypriot homes, sub-divisions, have sprouted everywhere. They are almost all new. I wonder who lives there, but decide not to ask. I imagine they are Turkish settlers and these are government homes. Ipek tells us that all the construction jobs are held by Turkish workers.

Later this evening, after an uneventful class in a room with only eight students and faculty, we return to the Fulbright Center in the Buffer Zone. We arrange to meet our old friend Fez Ishak for dinner before the films I will show.

She greets us with her usual warmth and considerable charm. She has just returned from a week in Finland, where she attended a workshop on "child-centered" education. She found herself enthralled by Montessori methods and wants to change the system in the north as fast as she can. Her title is that of "Inspector" at the Ministry of Education. "We will change from Inspector to Advisor," she announces proudly. Fez has come to two of my American History projects in Ohio these past summers. We hope she can return. She is smart and serious and loves a good time. I tell her about Progressive Education, about Dewey and the Laboratory School at the University of Chicago and her eyes light up again. I love the way she is open to new ideas. It is the way she greets life on a daily basis. She is the senior vice-president of the Association and represents, from the Turkish-Cypriot position, a vision of a better future.

3 | 19 | 2010

I show "Guess Who's Coming to Dinner" to the members of the Association. One image that stays with me occurs at the end of the film. After much melodrama the two families, black and white, resolve the issue of interracial marriage and decide to have to dinner together. The camera pulls back from the dining room and we see them through the frame of the doorway, pulling out their chairs, sitting down. There is no sound, only the vision of an American Thanksgiving, as if painted by Norman Rockwell. The bounty of the food, the grace of the figures, and the racial harmony all representing a hope, a dream for a better world. As we discuss this scene its fantasy and fancy overtakes our sense of reality. We sit in a plain room, on metal folding chairs, in one of the two sites in Cyprus, dead center in the Buffer Zone, where Turkish and Greek Cypriots can meet and talk together.

The other place is the Ledra Palace Hotel, just next door to the Fulbright Center. It is no different, this Moorish-Imperial hotel, than it was five years ago. Same chain across the rusted gate, same padlock, same buzzer system, the same British-UN Peacekeepers as residents. "Biggest frat party in Europe" is what one local guy calls it. Same faded yellow walls, scarred marble floors, pitted plywood tables. This central meeting place mirrors the stretch of the Buffer Zone that it dominates — pitted and shelled buildings, a neglected British cemetery, and the all-too-familiar graffiti concerning the horrors of the Turkish Occupation in the north. These all remain. I am to speak at a bi-communal meeting of teachers whose agenda includes questioning the way in which each of their histories has become little more than national propaganda. Four of us are keynote speakers — an Israeli, two Brits, and me. We each have a different take on the question. I am introduced as an "expert," a label that makes me recoil. This is NOT a subject on which I have any expertise. But like the others at the head table, this does not in any way prevent me from sharing some ideas. My half-hour consists of trashing the mythology of the "Greatest Generation," of those in my father's generation who fought the "Best War Ever." I show five minutes of a John Wayne movie (he dies quietly and quite without any blood just as the flag on Mount Suribachi is raised to the tune of "From the Shores of Montezuma.") My rap is that since we Americans learned our history at the knees of Hollywood, film is our text-book. I contrast this 1949 film with the letters my father wrote home from France in the summer of 1944. He tells his parents and my mother that while he's been wounded, its all fine and that he'll recover. Two months later he hints at something far more serious, but doesn't want to worry them. He's participating, I tell these Cypriots, in the mythology of the Best War precisely by sanitizing the real one. My hope is to shed some light on the the way that all cultures use and manipulate history. This is, of course, why the Cypriots have gathered. Perhaps I can show them that they are not alone in wanting to confront the distortions of official history.

Of course, some of the best conversations take place as we stand around and wait for coffee or lunch or just for a session to begin. The next day, a primary teacher from Limasol participated in my workshop on Jefferson and slavery (Sally Hemmings is rarely mentioned in mainstream text books, while there are 85,000 Google entries under her name). This woman tells me, "I hate them. The Turkish Cypriots." This startles me, needless to say. When I ask why she has come to a bi-communal meeting like this, she looks down at her feet, and takes a breath. "I wanted to challenge myself."

My friend Dileck saunters over. She teaches Peace Studies at Near Eastern University in north Nicosia and who has been a participant in two of my summer seminars in America. She just delivered a solid analysis on the increasingly "nationalist" content of Turkish Cypriot textbooks over the past five years. Clearly she is a "liberal" in these matters. But, she is distressed. "Everyone is annoyed with me." I only have to raise my eyebrows. She tells me that she has suggested that perhaps a two-state solution to the "Cyprus Problem" might work. Her colleagues, both Greek- and Turkish-Cypriot, attack her. Someone who teaches Peace Studies ought to support a Federal structure, they say. She is not sure. More importantly, she feels that if this group of Cypriots cannot consider a range of options without condemnation, without the disapproval of "political correctness," then all is lost.

Rana, another Turkish Cypriot, joins us. We stand outside the Ledra Palace Hotel, the sun high in the deep blue sky. Rana is the Project Director for the Association. Turkish-Cypriot and American, she is smart and analytical. She speaks to Dileck, and I listen. "Look," she says. "Here's what the polls show." And she explains that Turkish Cypriots prefer a two-state solution while Greek Cypriots want a single state that they can dominate. "The trick is to convince both that their second choice, a Federated State, American-style with two 'states' and a weak national government, is the best option. That both will have to accept something they don't want in order to achieve reconciliation. A tall political order, I think, in a place where politics is always finding new-old ways to knot itself in complication.

At lunch I sit with a Turkish-Cypriot woman who went to NYU twenty years ago. We exchange "I love New York" anecdotes, until I say something about the extraordinary rise in housing prices in Manhattan. My companion sighs. "All the rich Jews," she tells me, "live in those apartments now." I'm stunned. I don't know what do say and I don't know what to think about what she has just said. I reply, "I don't know about that. I'm just a poor Jew."

Forty-years ago, as a grad student in Paris, I asked a shopkeeper to reconsider the change she had just given me. It was a small charcuterie, and the line at the caisse (a marble-topped counter with an open drawer filled with Franc pieces sitting in tidy rows by denomination) was ten deep. She looked up and said, "What do you take me for, a Jew?" I am so accustomed to passing as a non-Jew, so comfortable (most of the time) with this artifact of my family's Polish-Russian origins, that my radar usually remains mute. In Nicosia, Cyprus, in March 2010, it buzzes back to life.

My lunch partner doesn't blink. But five minutes later, after another woman joins us, she looks up at me and says. "You know, I always admired their sense of family. They remind me of Cypriots." And this at a workshop about reversing the image of the "other."

Yet that evening we experience something like what Rana proposed earlier that day. Zacharolula Malas, a Greek-Cypriot teacher called Zachy, invites 10 of us for dinner. We all worked together in America last summer — three Turkish Cypriots, five Greek Cypriots, and two Americans. It is the nicest evening I can imagine. Food, conversation, friendship — serious talk about any and everything — books, films, politics — all over a meal that covers the table with dozens of dishes filled to brimming with local delicacies. The time passes in a flash. I realize that it does speak to possibilities, to common experiences, to real friendship. It makes me think again of that idealized Rockwell Thanksgiving — a feast of family and friends who care. Yes, of course, it is corny. And yes, it actually reminds me of the last scene in "Guess Whose Coming to Dinner."

3 | 22 | 2010

We are. That is, we are coming to dinner. We call our music friends, Elena and Andros, and invite ourselves. We tell them that we'll bring food. They are now both teaching at a music school they operate — she voice and piano, he bouzouki — and they won't be home this evening till eight. We pick up a half-dozen chicken and beef gyros from the joint across the street from our apartment. It is the best I have ever tasted, the chicken, somehow crisp and juicy and flavorful all at the same time. Five euros gets a pita stuffed with succulent chicken, topped by diced tomatoes, shredded lettuce, and a squirt of tahini. The best.

Elena greets us with wet hair and a weary look in her eye. Her 94-year-old mother is just back from the hospital. Her younger brother, Xenofon, a singer and entertainer, is already at the table beaming. And Andros, her husband, the man who taught D to play five years ago, greets us with hugs and kisses. This is a warm and sweet family. But they live on the edge, now as then, of poverty. Their lives feel very hard, arduous, to us. The have none of the glittering prosperity of our host families and of our teacher friends. It is as close to a working-class Greek-Cypriot family as we encounter. The old taverna where Elena once sang is now closed, and that deprives them of a chunk of income. Andros is legally blind, although he seems able to do almost anything with his hands — building, repairing, as well as playing his instrument. It is another warm moment of sitting around a table and sharing friendship, but the shadow of economic distress hovers close.

Xenofon, Zeno, tells us a wonderful story about a village home he has inherited. It is up in the Trodos Mountains, probably an hour from Nicosia, and is in falling-down condition. It took a battery of lawyers and a sheaf of letters to public officials to obtain clear title. But now he is out of money and the tumble-down structure needs a complete overhaul. Andros finds a laptop and they pull up the photographs of the house. It has a story — of course it has a story, this is Cyprus. It is the house where the whole extended family first came following "the invasion." After 1974, they fled the north and had only this two-room and a "veranda" house in the mountains for shelter. At least a dozen of their family members slept there until, one family component at at time, they secured refuge. Xeno, who only claimed his government housing two years ago, now has found the way to reclaim the family's historic home.

The slides on the laptop skid across the screen, one at a time. And suddenly Xeno pauses. There was another piece of property, he tells us, behind the house. Actually, it was a sliver of government land situated between two village houses. And for years their grandfather had operated a still in this "neutral" zone. Likely he made the local white lightning, Zivania, a completely illegal and commonplace activity up in the remote hills of central Cyprus. Over the last decade, as the property lay abandoned, some neighbors resumed operation of the still. And it has taken as much time and energy as it did to clear the tile on Xeno's part to have the government property and the still returned to his family. So now they have a ramshackle home filled with historic meaning, a still-assembled still ready to brew anew, and a source of stories enough to fill an evening among friends.

3 | 23 | 2010

I am sleepy. I had awakened the day before to watch the U.S. House of Representatives vote on the "landmark" health care reform bill. They voted at midnight — it was 5 am here. I feel much better about these American possibilities too. Yet today we lunch with our friend Daniel Hadjotoffi, the Chairman of the Cyprus Fulbright Commission. D and I both really enjoy his company and, I think, his trust. Our conversation is wide-ranging. Rumors abound that the Limassol football team, which is sponsored by a local wine company, which is owned by the (ruling) Cyprus Communist Party, has suddenly doubled its payroll. The finger points to a set of payoffs that provide Government contracts to the team's ownership. Its as if George Steinbrenner had wrangled ship-building contracts from "W" in 1990 and passed half the profits along to the Yankees, who then signed every free-agent in sight. How absurd.

Daniel, a real progressive, is like our friend Rena a real militant leftist, and disillusioned. The current government was to have been a change from the Tammany Hall-style practices of the past, of the recently departed and exhumed Papadapolous. Instead, it continues those practices under different colors. Item: the Communist President of Cyprus, a man devoted to peace talks with the north, arranges a visit to President Obama. A golden opportunity to talk to the man who talks to the Turks. But on his way to Washington the Cypriot leader stops in Havana, where he opens a new embassy in Cuba. Whatever Obama's new approach to relations with Cuba, it is not a politically astute action on the part of the Cypriot President. The White House cancels the appointment and President Christophias comes home empty-handed. To local Cypriots, this represents a clear sign of ineptitude.

3 | 25 | 2010

This visit draws to a close. The three weeks have flown by. It surprises me to see how rich each day feels, how complex its content. A man from the Embassy yesterday invited us to return next year. "In a heart-beat," said D when he asked if we would like to. If felt to me like a vote of confidence, a way of saying "job well done." Hardly twelve hours later comes an email from the same guy, with a website link. "This is the portal for applications for short-term visits," he writes. "Find a sponsor and go for it." This feels like something less than a vote of confidence.

We meet Rena in a lovely park just off the old campus of the University (a favorite word, πανεπιστεμιο, pan-epistemio) where D and I have taught during our two Fulbrights. It is a charming place of pine trees and walking paths. Rena's twin girls, Demetria and Anastasia, tug at their mother's hand. Clearly they are comfortable here. The girls begin to play and soon we sit at a picnic table with coffee before us. Minutes later, one of Rena's friends, Constantina, joins us. She is a good-natured, good -humored intellectual. A historian of European intellectual traditions in the 19th Century, she sits at the end of the table and rolls tobacco into brown papers. And we talk. NOT about the Cyprus question, but about film. About feminist films. She and Rena are both remarkably well read in American and international film, and our conversation moves very fast. Ignoring the speed bumps, we shift gears seamlessly. Somehow Rena takes us to a still-vibrant Easter ritual in Cyprus, one of burning the image of Judas in the week before Easter. It takes me back to the conversation about "rich" Jews. I am relieved when Rena says she feels the effects of anti-semitism all around Cyprus — the mythos of Jewish conspiracies here, no less than in France, built on fragments of reality and then exploded into fantasy. They talk, Rena reports, about the Jewish attempt to buy Cyprus at the turn of the 20th Century. Actually, as I remind her, a German-Jewish industrialist, the Baron de Hirsch, once bought a tract of land in Cyprus to serve as a home for Eastern European Jews (as he did in New Jersey and Colorado at the same time). In Cyprus the experiment failed after two generations, but clearly it serves as a foundation for the story of the Jewish search for dominance. The four of us talk of Jung and Joseph Campbell and Victor Turner, about the role of theory in cultural studies, of the renunciation of Kant. Rena and Constantina both remind us of a new Cypriot intelligentsia that is both analytically sophisticated and humanistically informed. It is a fully satisfying walk in the park.

Later, we sit with Costas and Roula, eating fruit and drinking coffee in their "Florida" room. Today is a holiday — Greek independence Day (you may remember this from a Delacroix painting) that they still celebrate in the south. Costas is filled with energy, telling us stories again as he first did five years ago. But these are new ones, stories about the mid-1950's struggle for independence against Britain.

Costas grew up on a farm — which is to say, in a village whose residents owned and worked the fields that surround the town. By the age of seventeen he joined EOKA (Ethnique Organization of Kiprus Assoc), a "liberation" movement devoted to freedom from Britain and to enosis, union with Greece. He shows us his EOKA diploma proudly, a certificate of his years in the organization.

Then, as he loves to do, he holds forth. He tells about his wife's role in hiding guns in farm wagons, about the way that the British used Turkish-Cypriot police against the Greek-Cypriot insurgents, and then about the "incident." He was 17. A group of his village friends — they lived north of Nicosia — had boarded a canvas-covered truck for a trip to an undisclosed location. As he pushed himself up and into the back of the truck, he became aware of a pair of shoes — they poked out from beneath a curtain strung up to cover a doorway just to the side of the truck. And Costas noticed that the right foot would tap whenever one of the boys who belonged to EOKA clambered into the truck. Someone, he quickly surmised, was tipping the British off as to the political affiliation of the villagers. In a quandary, caught between hoping to avoid identification on the one hand and risking even more danger by pointing out the supposed traitor, Costas hoisted himself into the truck, all the time keeping an eye on the informing feet. Although he had already joined EOKA, the man hiding behind the curtain (a villager in the pay of the British) did not give him up. To this day, he does not know to whom he owes if not his life, then at least his good health. His "combares" were less lucky. Many ended up in British jails.

Like our friend Daniel, who barely escaped capture and likely death in the 1974 war, Costas remains without hatred for the Turkish Cypriots and still holds out hope for a reasonable settlement. His anger he reserves for the British. Of course, he gives them their due. They built roads, created an effective bureaucracy, and established a business culture that Costas has mastered. But they are, to his mind, still "bastards."

Later that same day, Costas reveals a new side. Roula teases him, reminds him that his father had been a really funny and witty guy, and so are his two brothers. What about you, she asks.

He carves the air with the side of his hand, a Cypriot tomahawk chop, and for a moment he reminds me of Tony Soprano. "Here," he smiles, "here I don't have to be funny. Here I am the boss." On cue, his grandson Constantinous enters. We are sitting in the Florida Room, and Constantinous, bored with the Cartoon Channel, is looking for action. He begins to play Greek hangman with Roula, and Costas leans in to see what's so interesting. Suddenly he takes the pencil from his wife's hand and breaks into a Cheshire Cat grin, ear to ear, as he marks spaces for four letters. "Alpha!" his grandson calls. "Min Gott," says Costas as he marks α in the second and fourth position. Constantinous, eight and tri-lingual, can't repress his laugh. "KAKA" he calls. Suddenly his 71-year-old grandfather transforms himself into a twelve-year-old boy, starts to giggle, pound his hand on the table, and asks us in a kind of stage whisper, "you know what this means?" Indeed. Grandfather and grandson are now brothers, con-

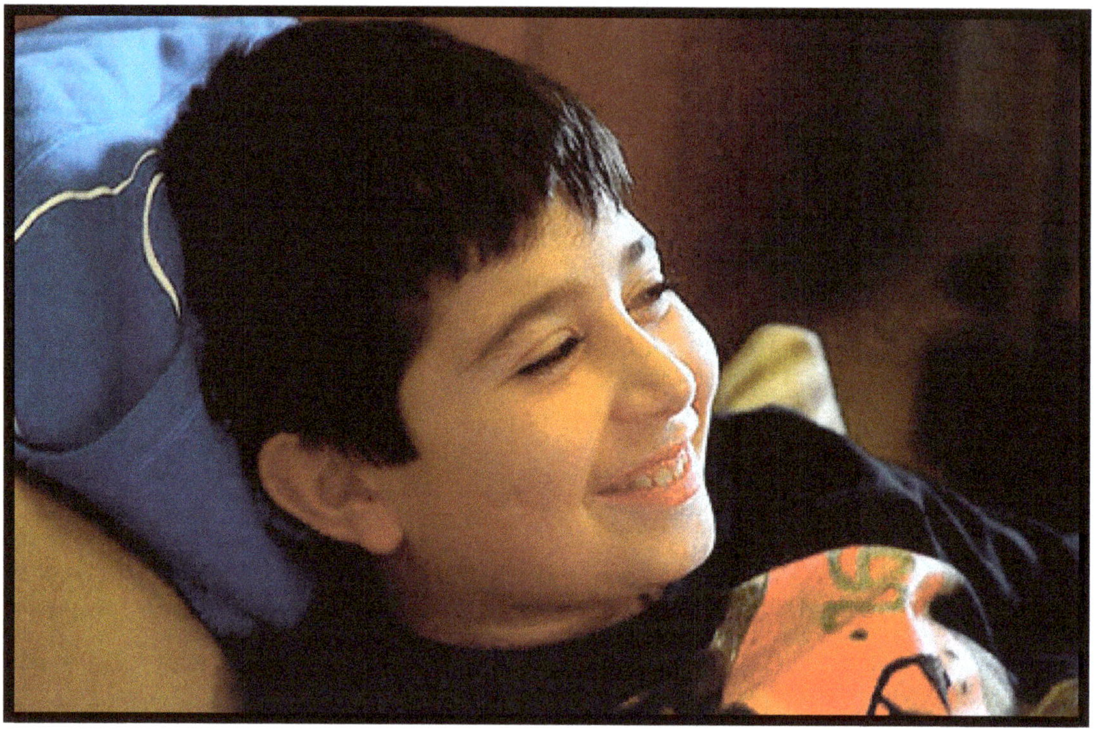

Constantinous and Elena, the taverna chanteusse

spirators in the face of Roula's supposed disapproval. Instead, she laughs too and says something in Greek to her husband that sounds like, "Okay, you have had your fun, now do another word." And he does. This time, he indicates five letters. Constantinous, with great deadpan and foreknowledge, calls out "Sigma!" and again the hand to the head and the "My Gott" as Costas writes, Σ on the first space. Now they both are giggling, eyes twinkling, heads close to each other. "Costas!" Roula calls, as in "I can't believe you." And to the delight of his grandson, this dour accountant business executive writes out σκατα, and I first understand the Greek origins of the word for dirty, "skatalogical," or just "skata."

3 | 26 | 2010

We decide to visit Cem and Seray to say so long. They still talk about coming to visit the US and even have a smart idea about giving birth and hence citizenship to their new baby in California. Who knows, I think privately.

D and I walk up the now fully-opened and functioning Ledra Street, which now allows Greek and Turkish Cypriots to shop and stroll virtually unimpeded along each other's main thoroughfare. What a change in the north. Several new and elegant shops, jewelry and women's clothes, have opened where once only rubble existed. Actually, they have opened where no one, there in north Nicosia, could venture. Likely the location of a "secret" military storage facility — as reported in the (British) Cyprus Mail during the negotiations three years ago. A new, more "western" north Nicosia emerges here (with echoes of Ipek's warnings), it coexists comfortably with the old, we think. A lovely stone carrefour sits at the intersection of several streets that lead up a slight incline to the old Bazaar. The buildings are high enough to bathe this square with dappled light, shadows dancing in a spring breeze, an oasis of respite. It is morning and the shops have just opened on our last day in Cyprus. There, standing in the shade, we find the old blind fruit vendor we met on our very first day five years ago. He speaks only numbers in English, and counts as we place five oranges into the plastic bay he holds up for us. But this time, he is alone. The boy, his grandson, who accompanied him on his rounds then, is no longer at his side.

We carry the oranges to Mustafa, the engineer turned shoe-store owner, just a few streets away. He seems also unchanged and greets us warmly. Sev-

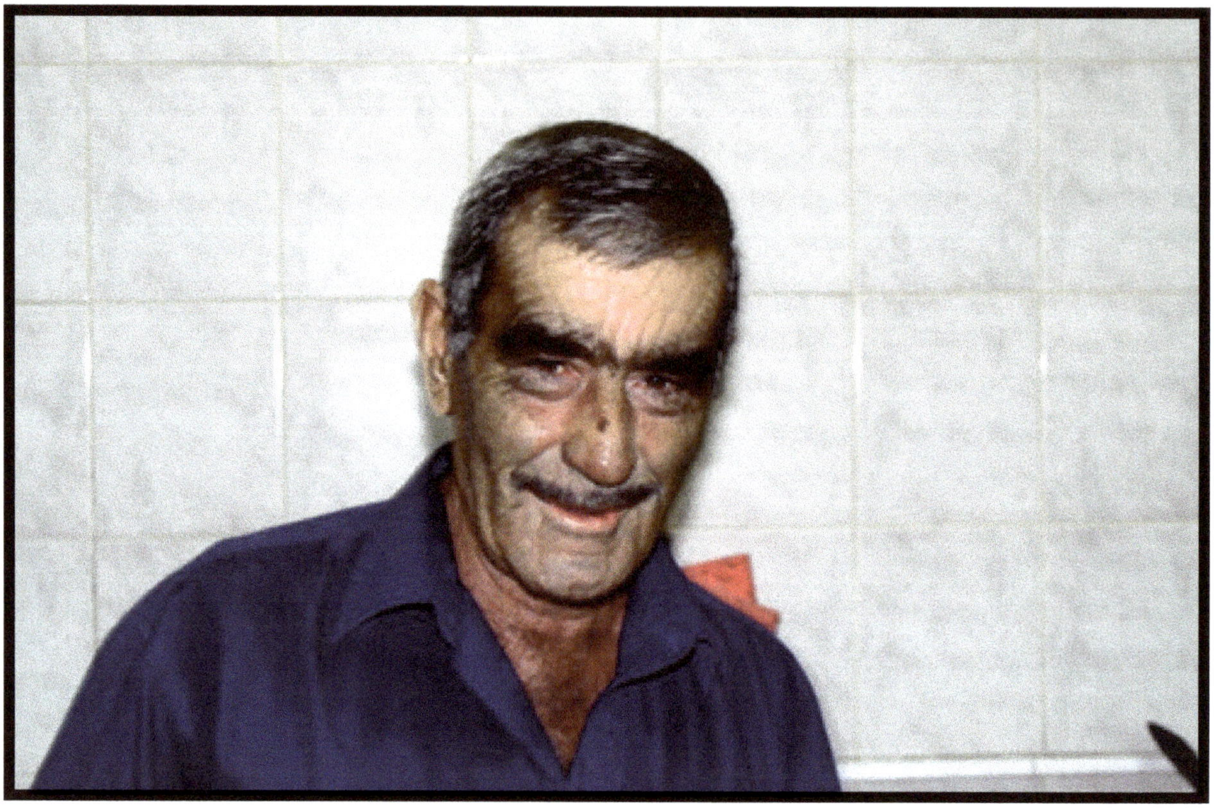

Andrea's grandfather — backgammon and banter

eral men with rich gray mustaches sit on the benches where customers try on shoes. They play backgammon, smoke and banter. As we enter they look up, eyes playing, and greet us warmly. This is still a world of traditional grace and hospitality, where tea or coffee accompanies social and commercial exchange. And while this ambience still also exists in the old part of South Nicosia, it is barely a remnant in the rest of that part of the city. D is wearing a pair of sandals she bought from Mustafa almost three years ago. He beams when he notices them. "I have some new styles for you," he announces and disappears into the storeroom as I rummage through the shelves of heavy black men's shoes that line the interior of the shop. He emerges with two boxes. "Would you like Gucci or Prada?" he asks mischievously. We all know different. But to make sure, he tells us that they are knock-offs, imitations. Fifteen Euros will do the trick and we agree readily, and hand him the oranges. The men wave goodbye and resume their game.

It is only a five-minute walk from Mustafa's shop, through Ataturk Square, and over the Venetian walls to Cem's shop. D has gone ahead and I enter quietly. The shop is empty, filled with carpets and glass, but no one to be seen. I negotiate the steep wooden steps that lead upstairs to a space where Cem and Seray once lived, and where we first met his religious mentor, the Sheik from Los Angeles who has initiated him into the Dervish sect. Cem and Seray and a musician friend sit in this space playing three instruments — Seray a drum, the friend a long wooden flute, and Cem the kannun, an instrument with 75 strings in threes that can all be "bent" on the fly. It is a cross between an auto-harp and a dobro, sitting in his lap as he feathers his finger picks delicately across the strings. It is very much like the mesmerizing, droning music we heard when we watched the whirling Dervishes several years ago. But Cem's group doesn't whirl, they find ecstasy in the moment, in being part of the world spiritually, in reaching a state of mindful peace. The music and the moment cast a spell and sit within us as we listen. It is to me an echo of the call to prayer that awakened me this morning at 6 am, the song floating peacefully over the border of this still-divided city and country. Poetically, I wonder which is more powerful. Politically, I'm sad to say, I know.

Or do I? I leave D turning sheets of handwritten scores for Seray and set out for the Ledra Palace Hotel, five minutes away. I'm going to have a wrap-up with the project directors of the Association for Historical Dialog who have help sponsor my visit.

I arrive around noon at the Association offices behind the Ledra Palace Hotel. The Brit/UN guard opens the lock, releases the chain, and swings the gate open. They know me there now and don't even ask where I am headed. The offices of the Association are humming. Students from American University are in the large classroom listening to a talk about conflict resolution. I stay in the business end of things and talk to Rana and Shirin, the two project coordinators who work for the Association. After several hiccups, once where I announce my insecurities about how things "went," they look at me as if I were crazy. Instead, they talk about next year, about what kinds of projects we might work on together, about how to engage more people in discussion. All the time in my small ego department I'm relieved. They actually think I did a good job! A few minutes pass and then I'm really floored — one of them reaches a hand out from behind the desk and produces a packet. "Here," they say. "We want you to have this." A gold envelope with a card signed by many people, and two books, ones that I will open later. Floored isn't quite strong enough. It's been almost impossible to get feedback here, and suddenly they are showing and not telling and it makes me feel wonderful.

This day, however, is not yet done. We are driving Costas and Roula out to Strovolos, to the main upper-middle class suburb of Nicosia. The family will gather for pizza and wine and coffee on the veranda of Michael's house. Each of the three children live in the same neighborhood, and each is more welcoming than the next. We all dined together at a fish meze restaurant the day D arrived two weeks earlier, and now it is time for our farewell meal.

As the children play karaoke and Wii and the women discuss what the children are doing, the two brothers, Michael and Yiorgos, engage me in a long and intense political discussion. Yiorgos expresses himself in ways that startle me. He is the least conservative of the men in his family, the most Americanized, the most easy-going, the most colloquial and open and warm. Still, for him any solution that compromises too much is no solution at all. He doesn't like the idea of a rotating Presidency, he doesn't trust Turkey over access to off-shore oil, and like his father, he won't have any settlement until and unless the issue of property is solved, and until the "settlers" are expelled. He speaks with such real passion. I feel that if the Yiorgos of Cyprus share this intense negativity, then the status quo will prevail. Of course, it is not my fight, my worry, my cause. But Cyprus has engaged us, and it would be a better place for Cypriots should the Green Line simply disappear. But right now it seems an impossible dream, a hazy ideal, that will take an extraordinary circumstance to shake into reality.

3 | 27 | 2010

Our last day, and we make the rounds. Prailina for coffee with Costas, and then with our old landlord and friend Andreas Koureas. It is lovely to see them all at the same time. But too short at times, just like this whole trip. We move on to Ledra Palace and across the checkpoint to say good-bye to Cem and Seray, and then to the American Embassy to thank our hosts. A day earlier they invited us to return the next year, now they suggest we may need to apply for a grant for local sponsorship. It feels a bit awkward, but there is nothing much to do about it. And then finally, out to dinner with Costas and Roula, to a Japanese-fusion place called Zen where ten-minute Thai back-rubs accompany dessert and coffee. Nice touch! It is the only time in the three weeks that we have been in Cyprus that they allow us to be generous. It has been an intense, intelligent, gratifying stay. We are glad to be going home and sad to leave. Its always that way with Cyprus.

A photographer's studio, untouched since 1974

Keep Walking Toward Peace: March 2011

We've been back for a week on our fourth visit to Cyprus since 2005. Back on Kennedy Avenue, back with Costas and Roula, and back to never-ending discussions about the "Cyprus Problem."

On the very first morning, a beautiful sun-lit Saturday, Costas and I make the rounds of his stores, the Timberland shops he continues to oversee. My head throbs from jet lag, and Costas must see it in my eyes. "Follow me," he orders sweetly but firmly, as we emerge from an inspection of his flagship store in central Nicosia.

We duck down a narrow concrete alley that opens to a postage-stamp-sized patio furnished with three white plastic tables and a random scattering of green and blue plastic chairs. "This is Tacki," Costas introduces me to a genial-looking fellow who emerges from behind a gold-lettered plate-glass window that reads Tacki: Coffee Shop. When I decline a cup of Cyprus coffee, dark and hot and almost bitter, Tacki disappears into the depths of his two-burner kitchen and holds up a pint-bottle of zivaniah. He brings me a soda and pours a good shot for Costas. It is 10 am. Then he reaches into his pocket and pulls out a postcard. "My home," he announces softly. He doesn't even have to tell me that it is in the north, I can read it in his eyes. The setting is a verdant wooded hillside, a village set within the trees, with an ink arrow pointing to a small white square. It is the house he grew up in, the lands where his father's orchards bloomed, and still, almost forty years later, his heart aches and it is the first thing he shows to a stranger.

We settle in, find our bearings, and start the schedule of talks, classes and workshops that the Cultural Office of the US Embassy has pointed us toward. One thing I must say it that in both visits under this program, no one, not a consular official, officer, or attaché, has ever said a word about what we might or might not say. We feel absolutely free to express ourselves on the range of subjects — African-American and Women's history issues — they have invited us to cover.

Dileck, the Turkish-Cypriot woman who has spent several summers visiting our programs, picks me up at the Ledra Palace Hotel checkpoint to drive me to her university. I am going to talk about "West African Culture in African America" and Dileck guides me through the spanking new "city in a city" campus of

Irene and Marios

her university. Near Eastern University is one of a dozen such booming ventures on both sides in Cyprus. It is very cosmopolitan, very "diverse" and, still puzzling to us, very private. A proprietary, for-profit university that, like its counterpart the European University of Cyprus in the south, it seems to double in size every couple of years.

The classroom fills slowly, but soon more than 50 students jam this "American Room" (another gift of the Embassy) to overflowing. And to my delight, at least half of them appear to be African. I do my "West African culture is real and alive in African America" talk filled with examples from some field-work I've done in Ghana, and then ask for questions. The African students, mostly Nigerian, some from Cameroon, ask question after question. It is clear that they are delighted. Finally, a European/American who takes their culture seriously! The talk gives them a sense of validity in an environment where they seen as either random students paying tuition, or as exotic oddities. I find this very gratifying for obvious reasons, and the encounter leaves me very pleased that we have found a way to return to Cyprus, to expand our range of experiences, and enjoy new encounters.

A few days later, at the southern twin, the European University of Cyprus, I ask four young West African men for directions to my classroom. I am to give a talk on Muddy Waters and the blues for a music class, and I'm completely lost in the maze of new buildings. The four young men are huddled on a walkway and are bantering like so many university students do. There is a quality to the voice of the first young man I talk to that tells me he's Nigerian. They all are. When I ask if they are Yourba or Igbo, they break into grins, and give me fives. "Yourba," they announce proudly.

3 | 17 | 2013

We meet several Cypriot friends — Marios, Dileck, and Meltem, all members of the Association for Historical Dialog, at the new Ledra Street checkpoint that connects both sides of Nicosia right up the gullet of its historic main street. We arrange to have dinner together to discuss a project that we first began talking about this past summer in South Carolina — a conference on International Slavery that the Association might host in two years to celebrate its brand new building. Turns out that sugar plantation slavery (perhaps chattel slavery)

Selling fruit in north Nicosia

came to Cyprus in the Fifteenth Century and may well have been a source of the Atlantic Slave Economy that dominated the next three hundred years.

We find El Sobor, the lovely old Spanish/Turkish restaurant in north Nicosia again. It sits just a few hundred meters from the Buyuk Han and in the shadow of the venerable St. Sophia, the Orthodox Church turned Mosque that dominates that neighborhood. We are two Americans, a Greek Cypriot, and a two Turkish Cypriots. Like our "Thanksgiving" dinner last year this warm gathering of friends and colleagues feels right. Very right.

But always in the back of my mind here in Cyprus, I am sifting what I see and hear across the screen of the "Cyprus Question." And for the first time in years, I think I detect something less new than nuanced: the increasing friction between Turkish Cypriots and Turkish "settlers," a designation for both mainland arrivals and army personnel. Sometimes this attitude is revealed in a word or phrase — like those Turks — sometimes in complaints about the economy, meaning the reduction in subsidy from Ankara. A wave of sudden Turkish-Cypriot protests erupted (and remained unreported) in late February, coincident with the massive demonstrations undermining traditional authority in Tunisia, Egypt, Libya, and Yemen in the "Arab Spring" of 2011.

It seems obvious in retrospect that this expression of discontent, thousands of Turkish Cypriots demonstrating against Turkish policy to reduce civil service salaries, is not an isolated phenomenon. Not only did Turkish Cypriots demonstrate but they did so beneath the flag of Cyprus — the Republic of Cyprus which they also claim as theirs. As one report stated:

A group of protesters, whom Turkish officials repeatedly say have ties with Greek Cypriots, staged a demonstration in Turkish Cyprus on January 26, brandishing anti-Turkey placards and chanting insulting slogans against the Turkish intervention in 1974.

This is extraordinary. In contrast to the official response in so many places at the time, the Government of Turkey, via Ertogan the Prime Minister, scolded these Cypriots, telling them to "behave." When the call went out to the web of Greek-Cypriot NGOs devoted to peace and reconciliation to protest in solidarity with the Turkish Cypriots in the north, the response was disappointingly small.

So these contradictory scraps of evidence — Turkish-Cypriot anti-Turkish sentiment and Greek-Cypriot complacency — seem to point in two directions

The demonstration

at the same time. Still, change in attitude, rather than in simple change in policy has to count for something.

Even Yiorgos, the youngest son of Costas and Roula, the American-educated fan of the Cincinnati Bengals, has changed his mind. A full-throated opponent of unification a year ago, he now says something different. "I will tell you, Peter," he puts his arm around my shoulder and I see gray streaking his standing bristles of his brush cut hair, "something will happen. And it will happen soon."

What has changed for him is the discovery of oil and natural gas in the Mediterranean waters shared by Cyprus and Israel. A new prosperity, he thinks, will allow for political generosity where none existed previously. The creation of a common adversary, of an envious Turkey, for Israel, the Republic of Cyprus, and Turkish Cypriots alike promises to change the equation in the region dramatically. Well, who knows. But this does represent a change in attitude.

On the other hand — and here there is always another hand — Rena the firebrand activist teacher and a founder of the Association — tells us a different story. She has just returned from the coastal city of Limasol after a week of leading what we might call "sensitivity training sessions" in a public school there. Seems that there has been a rash of anti-immigrant actions — beatings, taunting, bullying — visited on newly-arrived Palestinian children in that area. The school principal invited Rena to work with his teachers, but she found that many of them lacked the sympathy that she hoped she could mould into a more tolerant actions.

And this too is part of changing Cyprus. The immigrants keep arriving, hoping for a better economic life, EU passports, and a taste of political freedom. But many Greek Cypriots greet them as outsiders, exotic men and women from culturally different backgrounds who seem bent on NOT conforming. And this is what they find so galling. It makes me think that we in America, with all the flaws in our history, have much to teach the world about forging a nation of immigrants.

3 | 19 | 2013

We meet Marios just in front of the new Ledra Street checkpoint, on the traditional main shopping street of Nicosia before the Green Line. He will lead an historical tour of Nicosia, passing in and out of both sides, that he hopes will bring Greek and Turkish Cypriots to a common experience and to a better understanding of each other. We have planned this event well in advance only to have it cancelled or postponed several times. I'm to lead a concurrent workshop on taking photographs and doing oral history. Finally, we have our date and time. I'm really looking forward to this.

I've known Marios for four years, invited him twice to our South Carolina programs, and really enjoy his company, admire his intellect, and appreciate his calming charm. I tell D that I have very low expectations about turn-out given the difficulties we encountered in scheduling. But it turns into a beautiful day, achingly so, with high blue skies, the almost transparent white disc of the moon hanging on the horizon. Everyone arrives about a half-hour late, but lo and behold, the crowd numbers more than 50 Greek and Turkish Cypriots, a handful of "others" including us, and a low-tech film crew that insists on following us from place to place. It takes three hours to walk through the city, over and through the Green line, and in and out of neighborhoods. As people introduce themselves to new acquaintances, I help some with suggestions about setting up a good photograph. A real spirit of cooperation emerges to serve as common ground. I can't help but admire the dedication of the planners and the spirit of tolerance that informs the day. It IS possible, I say to myself more than once.

What Marios shows them is much more than just Greek and Turkish Nicosia. He takes them into ancient Armenian neighborhoods and into a long-abandoned Catholic Church. The real message is that Nicosia (and Cyprus) has ALWAYS been a complex and diverse society, not simply one place that two groups fight over. I feel the germ of a lesson of pluralism starting to form. It's not quite there, but almost!

3 | 22 | 2013

It is time to visit Cem and Seray. They have a new baby girl and have moved back into the apartment above the carpet shop. It is touching to see Cem with his tiny daughter, cooing at her eyes, holding her gently. I imagine that this completes his Dervish transformation into a spiritually-centered man who has renounced much of the materialism (and intrigue) that surrounded him for so long. And Seray seems serene — no less grounded than Cem, but with no need to proclaim it. Still with a brighter than bright smile, she dances before us, her whimsically-formed English more and more fluent every time we see her.

"When you coming back to see us," she asks knowing that the nag drives us crazy. "You can come back, you know. Just like, you know, just like," and she glances over at her doting husband and daughter, "him." Then she grabs the baby from Cem and takes her upstairs for a nap.

"You remember," Cem looks at me with his deep sad eyes. "You ask me question. Now I have answer." I remember the question: why does Turkey devote such time, effort and resources to this tiny speck in the sea? It seems so out of proportion to the meaning of Cyprus. Sure, I know about strategic importance.

It is because if they let Cyprus go, he tells me, then the whole complex of ethnic issues that burn on the Eastern frontier of Turkey become even more problematic. "Kurds," he tells me, his eyes looking out the door of his shop, scanning the street for customers. "And people from Azerbaijan, and OTHERS." The government in Ankara exists on the thin edge of disintegration, he reports. So once again Cyprus is MUCH MORE important than Cyprus. But, in this assessment I also hear the echoes of the greater Ottoman Empire dream, of a Turkey that transcends national boundaries, ethnicity, even language. This at a time when Turkey also appears to hunger after membership in the EU. And clearly, these two visions are in deep conflict.

As if to reinforce the significance and complexity of the region, the local newspapers and the evening local television news — read by men in polyester sport coats and thick wavy black hair — repeat the same story, hour after hour. They show video of British warplanes taking off from one of their two "sovereign" bases for Libya in support of the rebels there. And then hours later, two French-built Bahrain Mirage jets in the operation seek landing rights in Cyprus. Again this divided island is so much larger globally and strategically than its postage-stamp size might dictate — and everyone seems to have an interest in having an interest there.

3 | 24 | 2013

Time to drive again to Deftera. The town that sounds like Monday in Greek, just with a different accent; the town where our old friend Irene has her incongruously-named restaurant, the Panic Room. And where six years ago, we first met Andrea. As always, Irene greets us with great warmth, embracing us, babbling in half-Greek, half-English, "You come back? Poly calla." And we respond in equally fractured Gringlish. What's so wonderful is the human connection that remains between us, even without any facility in formal communication. We somehow manage to compare notes about children, grandchildren, family. Everything except the CQ! Our language simply can't root that issue out of its coma here in the Panic Room.

But I can and do ask about Andrea. I'm hopeful about seeing her, she still owns a tiny part of my heart. But Irene, and then her sister Kiki (who speaks English) tell us that Andrea is studying for her math exam, and that she's waiting to hear from a university in England about next fall. So be it, I say to myself. She's growing up, and more importantly, she's well.

3 | 24 | 2013

Our last night in Nicosia. I write an email to our Association friends and say, "We really want to say goodbye to you all. Let's meet at Brew at 8:30 on Thursday." Brew is a tea-beer cafe that has the feel of the West Village. It's filled with wood tables, soft chairs, stone floor, and candles burning. It is intimate. And curiously it is hidden within the warren of tourist places, souvlaki restaurants, t-shirt shops, Lefkara lace, and other "island delicacies" that mark the tiny alleys and walkways that radiate out from Ledra Street on the southern edge of the Old City. It's the kind of place that our friends seem to like to congregate — a graduate student hang-out where you know you'll run into someone you know.

We park down in the large municipal lot that takes up about half the moat surrounding the southern curve of the Venetian wall, from Phaphos Gate to Famagusta Gate. Up at street level, an assortment of cafes, tobacco shops, Periptero-kiosks, and just plain junk shops dominate the avenue that circles the city just inside the wall. The parking is surprisingly deep down, at least four stories, in the moat. From above, at street level, the cars look small and delicate, hundreds of them. At the place where Ledra Street ends inside the Old City, there stands Nicosia's other old central post-office, a British colonial sandstone building. It's a rendezvous place for Greek Cypriots just as the Central Post Office on Ataturk Square, where Costas went for his mail forty year ago, serves the same function for residents of the north.

We duck into the maze of shops and then down a stone staircase between two buildings across from the Post Office. The streets are so narrow that we have to turn sideways to walk past open-air restaurants with their menus chalked on green slate boards in English, German, and French. To our left the alley opens to hidden a stone patio, an inviting square filled with wooden folding chairs and moist potted plants. It's a kind of oasis in the midst of commerce, where the green door at the other end of the square bids us welcome to Brew.

The cafe is empty save for a waitress draped in a batik skirt and a bartender wearing skinny jeans and a black t-shirt. We find a soft red-cushioned loveseat and order tea, enjoying the quiet. We are both exhausted and exhilarated by two weeks of non-stop talking and teaching. By 9:15, we fear that no one is coming. But fifteen minutes later we are gathered around the same low tables with many of our friends from the Association. Fez, glamorous and sweet, back from Istanbul, her golden hair flowing; Marios, looking like Marlon Brando in black leather, his sly smile always gentle; Rena, intense and full of laughter, a flower in her short dark hair, presenting us with a gift of three Turkish CDs; and Kiriakos, the likely next President of the Association, who engages us all in a discussion about where Cyprus is going.

While there is no consensus in their answer to the question, the intensity of the discussion reveals something very powerful. They are on the verge of achieving the short-term goal of the Association, the creation of the Home for Cooperation. It is to open in less than two months, during the first week of May — with a celebration that will last four or five days and see political leaders, intellectuals, teachers and historians from the region and from Western Europe in attendance. Imagine, I say to myself, how far this project has come. I recall an evening of conversation in 2007 with two "Professional" historians from the University of Cyprus. They wanted to know more about the Association and readily admitted believing that it was "after all just lightweight." The Home for Cooperation is in every sense a true heavyweight. And I'm incredibly moved by the work that these men and women, a generation younger than I, have done. In their own way they have begun a process of political, intellectual and social change on their own terms, and in their own image.

For the first time since 1974, they have coalesced a group of activists around the idea of building for the future. As historians whose trade is the past, they have learned that constant preoccupation with who did what to whom in that past only leads to bitterness and resentment. This is not a traditional revolutionary movement, but it is in its own way revolutionary. A refusal to weigh the past on the scales of justice liberates them to find common ground, to celebrate the cultural, political, linguistic, and religious differences that bind them together. It is a remarkable accomplishment.

The more I think about it, this small intrepid group of teacher-activists has transcended the blind spots of their generation — Cypriots who have grown up with a divided Cyprus as a normal reality. Like Yiorgos, who is their age and who remains open to new ideas and experiences, they have the seeds of the future in their spirit. I feel my own pessimism lift. Two weeks ago I was ready to accept the power of the status quo, and to acknowledge its weight in Cyprus. Now I am no longer sure.

5 | 5 | 2013

The news is startling. It is all over the FaceBook page of the Association, on the Internet, in the English Cyprus News. Not only did the Association complete the renovations of the Home for Cooperation on time, and in time to begin their celebration, but they have sent out a portfolio of photographs. Wearing pearls and a smile, Chara shines with pride and exhaustion — this has taken four years. And next to her, between Chara and Meltem — the leadership of the Association is female — sit the political leaders of the Republic of Cyprus, Demetris Christofas, and the Turkish Republic of north Cyprus, Dervis Eroglu. The meaning can't be more clear. These two late-middle-aged male politicians in gray hair and wool suits, the faces stern, preside over the past. The two women, half their age, these students of the past, have pointed the way to the future. I don't mean this in some vague rhetorical sense, but rather, they can now begin to define Cyprus in terms that once seemed impossible. For the reality I have only just begun to myself understand, is not one of simple division between Turkish/Greek Cypriots, between Greek and Turkish, between Orthodox and Muslim. Rather the social and cultural diversity of Cyprus — Greek, Turk, Russian, Armenian, British, Philippino, Sri Lankan, Yoruba, and Lebanese; Orthodox, Muslim, Jewish, Maronite and Hindu — is its great gift and not its curse. To celebrate and define Cyprus though its diversity means to look for-

Between Chara and Meltem, Demetris Christofas and Dervis Eroglu, and the Home for Cooperation

ward through the accurate, and not the distorted, lens of the past.

Cyprus has always existed as a microcosm of the region. Its complex history, in turn Hellenic, Roman, Byzantine, Frankish, Crusader, Venetian, Ottoman, English, then Cypriot, has led it to the present. The true past, complex and multicultural, reveals a richness of expression and serves as a source of inspiration for the future.

In a world where there are Museums of Barbarism that depict the "other" side as brutal and bloody, or where postage stamps show downtrodden refugees, or where the pilots of Cyprus Air welcome you to Europe's "last divided city," theirs is a truly remarkable achievement. The dozen who began in 2004 became several hundred in two years, and probably several thousand today. And they are all teachers!

I write to Meltem Onurkun, the Professor at Near Eastern University and the Secretary of the Association who shared the honors on stage with Chara. I want to congratulate her on the opening of the Home for Cooperation. In the photograph with Chara she looks radiantly proud. A day later an email appears. Meltem writes that now they can "keep walking toward peace."

Coda: Cyprus December 2013

12 | 5 | 2013

Ghost town Nicosia.

The drive from the airport into Nicosia is uneventful. We pass the familiar landmarks — access roads that lead to ancient Orthodox monasteries, complex roundabouts that challenge my driving on the "wrong" side of the road; and the flora and fauna of the desert landscape. The A2 expressway empties into Nicosia proper from the south by passing through the bottleneck of a major intersection whose traffic lights also mark the start of a broad city avenue — Makarios Avenue.

When we first arrived eight years ago this initial sight shocked us. We expected a peasant society inhabited by donkeys and women robed in black. We were completely unprepared for the modern steel and glassoffice buildings lining the boulevard all the way into the center of Nicosia. Now we are equally unprepared for what greets us. Shops and showrooms, once spanking new and modern, stand empty, brown paper masking-taped over plate glass windows and signs in large red letters that announce "For Rent" or "Available TODAY" It is first disconcerting —like a once beautiful friend who has passed into old age in the blink of an eye—and then simply sad.

We turn onto our old street, Kennedy Avenue, and I squint into the fading light trying to find the large rock-strewn vacant lot that we used as a neighborhood parking place. Instead we pass a brand new building occupying the same space, white stucco, glass, and the familiar green and gold logo of the Bank of Cyprus. The one traffic light on Kennedy turns red and gives us a moment to take in the newest addition to the neighborhood. It allows us to make out the half-dozen shops on either side of the bank that remain empty, the already familiar "TO LET" signs taped to yawning vacant windows. A spanking new building with no tenants, save the branch of the giant private bank that suffered bankruptcy a half year before.

Over dinner an hour later Costas tells us two things that shape our reaction to the new Cyprus. "I lost," and he really smiles without any sign of bitterness, "two millions." And he doesn't need to add the word "Euros." We understand numerically that he's lost almost two and half million dollars of property in the

Makarios Avenue, boarded up

current "crisis." I find it hard to believe that he delivers this information with the same mixture of shock and recognition he normally reserves for a rare defeat by his local football team. "I will tell you more about the haircut later." I think I know what he means but am not sure.

We find it no less challenging to understand the other truth he shares with us this evening. "You know we have a crisis every 40 years." He regards us with a look that I first associated with the story of his loss in 1974. "First, with the war with the Turks. And now this catastrophe. 1974 and 2012." He shrugs as only Costas can — eyebrows and elbows rising in unison.

I have come back to Cyprus to gauge the impact of the Euro-Banking crisis that almost plunged this tiny republic into bankruptcy. And now I understand the profundity of the damage, seeing it in his eyes. It is as serious today as it was in 1974. It takes my breath away to imagine a trauma as powerful today, in economic and social terms, as 1974 had been a generation earlier.

"You got to go there to know there" is a truism I've heard that resonates now. Words like "default" or "bailout" or "fiscal crisis" cannot begin to convey the human tragedy of the moment.

"How can you seem so at peace," I ask, curious and not yet understanding.

"I will tell you." A typical Costas phrase. "It's like this. Either accept and keep moving. Or give in and," and he does a cut across the neck motion with his forefinger, "suicide." And then he really laughs at himself.

It occurs to me that for Cypriots like Costas, the profound losses of 1974 —of property, national identity, and rootedness to traditional society—have provided an example of survival. Like an inoculation, perhaps the old trauma of 1974 offers a kind of psychic immunity to the present.

12 | 6 | 2013

We spend much of the day walking around downtown Nicosia. Where once Makarios Avenue had all the glamour of Madison Avenue — cafes and high-end boutiques — now it has all changed. The disintegration we witnessed yesterday has run rampant, the abandoned hulks of consumer prosperity, the shops and restaurants of Nicosia's center now masked by a Potemkin village of pressboard structures that line the curbs of the boulevard. These pre-fab kiosks will host several dozen craftspeople peddling holiday wares. It reminds me of the yearly event in my own town where candlemakers and coppersmiths vie for limited budgets. But it is a far cry from the Nautica store that Costas owned at the foot of the street, or the electronics shops that sold the latest Xboxes and DVRs. It is early afternoon, a time when professionals and government employees would normally crowd dozens of restaurants and coffee shops. But for a dozen workers wielding nail guns, the street is empty.

This stretch of Makarios runs along the moat that separates modern Nicosia from the Venetian-walled Old City. In recent years, the Municipal council created dozens of urban parking lots in the moat. Today those spaces are filled by a threadbare county-fair carnival of rusty merry-go-rounds and spinning saucers. The carnival sits in the pit that divides the old and new, ready to open this weekend. It seems congruous with the craft fair a few yards away.

Costas and Roula have invited the whole family over for lunch to welcome us back. Their three adult children and spouses and seven children are warm and boisterous. They all speak at least two languages (including English, thankfully). Roula's spirits remain in the same zone as her husband. She cooks up a storm, sets the table several times, and breaks out into a broad grin with every grandson or daughter's hug for their beloved Yaya. Like Costas, she simply refuses to embrace the tragic. Another survivor.

I engage Michael, their eldest son, in a wide-ranging conversation about politics and economics. He confirms what the newspapers have been hinting at for the past 18 months: the banking crisis in the United States that began five years ago triggered a sequence of events that left Cyprus prostrate. Centered on banking and services (providing a plethora of hiding places for offshore Russian, American, and even Israeli companies), Cypriot bankers had invested heavily and almost exclusively in Greek banks. So when the Greek economy swooned into a nose-dive two years ago then dramatically plunged into bankruptcy, Cyprus nearly fell over the cliff with it. The entire economic structure of Cyprus teetered.

The price that Germany, via the EU, extracted for a bailout of the crippled Cypriot banks became known as the "Haircut." This draconian measure lopped off all funds above EU100,000, sweeping away savings account, pensions, and investments. It required all private domestic accounts be drained of assets over 100,000EU.

But everyone seems to know that many at the top of the economic and po-

Costas and Roula and the grandkids

litical food chain had enough warning to move their assets to safe offshore havens before the haircut. In a word, the American folly doomed the Greek banking system and the failure of the Greeks ensured Cypriot bankruptcy. Only Germany had the clout to save Cyprus, but they did so at this unprecedentedly high price. And "why Cyprus?" Michael and several others ask. Why us, the very smallest country in the European Union? Clearly to make an example, a way of showing that the German-dominated economic policy of Europe possessed an iron fist, to borrow Bismarck's imagery.

Michael's own accounting, financial services and management consulting business has been lucky, he tells me. They have not gained a single new client in the past year, but neither have they lost any. And this, he tells us proudly, to a firm that began with two partners and now includes more than 150 employees. He flies to Moscow monthly to work with clients and recruit more business opportunities.

Michael provides the point of view of someone whose business experience and political allegiance normally yields very conservative, conventional thinking. Instead, like his father, his instinct for pragmatism far outweighs anything else. He talks about the moment two years ago when a giant storage facility near the Larnaca airport blew sky high, an explosion felt in Nicosia forty miles to the north. It caused a billion Euros in damages and destroyed most of the Republic of Cyprus' electrical grid.

It turns out that the then-President of Cyprus had agreed to allow Iran to ship armaments and munitions to Syria, likely with the blessing of Russia. When the US protested, the government of Cyprus offered temporary storage. Then the whole shebang blew up, in part because they forgot about the explosives and left them for several years in the warehouse to rot. Boom!

This disaster proved costly not only to the economy but to the presidency. In recent elections, the whole government moved from left to right, from the Communists to the traditional ruling conservatives. Political crisis, economic crisis, social dislocation and distress— when you include an unemployment rate of more than 25%, these add up to a deep depression. The "perception is reality" cliché highlights the terrible loss in governmental credibility, a powerful moral indictment of domestic corruption, and the belief that Cyprus has once again attained the status of scapegoat for the misdeeds of the international power elites.

The current counter-fantasy — again almost universally expressed — holds that this terrible turn of events will soon improve. Why? Geologists have discovered gas and oil in the Mediterranean. The beds, shared by Israel and Cyprus, when exploited by corporate American drilling infrastructure, will ensure a great flow of wealth to the tiny island nation. When? Who knows? But, very soon.

12 | 10 | 2013

We pass through the Dead Zone for the first time. Like everything else on the island of Cyprus, the changes are palpably tough but not completely depressing.

Our friends from the Association for Historical Dialogue really did it. The building, beautifully restored and gleaming, stands across from the dowdy and disintegrating Ledra Palace hotel, still occupied by UN Peacekeepers. The contrast couldn't be sharper — the House for Cooperation (H4C) with a welcoming cafe that opens onto a spacious patio, and the once grand hotel whose bare windows reveal wrinkled towels and drying socks. They have created something alive and lovely amidst the ruins of the dead zone. It is like finding a shoot of spring grass peeking out from beneath the snow and ice of February.

Our friend Fez, a Turkish Cypriot woman we have known since 2007, who has worked with me twice on an oral history project in South Carolina, pulls up in her BMW convertible. Between the car and the designer sunglasses, she is the very image of glamour and sophistication. She works as an "inspector" for the TRNC department of education, in addition to finishing her Ph.D in Educational Pedagogy and raising two children. We love her open and good-hearted honesty. She's a truly caring and compassionate personwho worked for a decade to establish the Association for Historical Dialogue.

We zip through several kilometers of north Nicosia's commercial streets, not far from the house that Costas and Roula left in 1974, now filled with shops, shiny new car dealerships, and a very imposing Casino. This is the new north I think, looks not very different from South Nicosia, from our neighborhood. I had noticed this a few years earlier, but now it seems even more so.

Fez takes us to a modern new restaurant where, as in much of the north, the food is fabulous. Beautifully seasoned, fragrant, and delicious. And she talks. Talks about the way that the teachers in the north have taken pay cuts the last few years, that people are out of work, and the way she feels stifled by the educational system. It's a very interesting dilemma, the conflict between the conventional way of thinking about teaching and new pedagogies of child-centered education. "How can I embrace the new," she asks, "when they change the textbooks yearly and I have to run as fast as I can just to keep up?"

I think about the thousands of American public school teachers trapped by the same dilemma, between innovation and convention, and see the rhetoric of "reform" as a plausible answer. We suggest that the Association could play a role in bringing teachers from both communities together to discuss common goals and problems. But our time together vanishes in the blink of an eye. Fez needs to get back to work. She drops us at the Ledra Palace Hotel checkpoint. Round One.

Around the corner we find our old friends Cem and Seray gathered in the carpet shop. And here too the new reveals itself. Two beautiful small children, now three and one-and-a-half year olds, bring delight to the eyes of their father. They have erased the sadness that he carried in the past, and his gentle way has taken over his being. Seray retains the playful laughter we had come to cherish. But now her facility with English allows her to make fun of Cem's thicker accent and vocabulary lapses.

"You see," she grins as she picks up her eldest daughter, Hatice, "he cannot stand it when I speak better than him."

They take us to a local north Nicosia restaurant owned by some of their friends, a Turkish couple who have lived on Cyprus for more than 20 years. It is about a ten-minute walk from their shop, along the same streets where eight years ago we encountered an old man and his grandson pushing a fruit cart. Then the local shops were threadbare and almost empty. Now the whole area has been paved with flagstones and the streets are reserved for pedestrians. The area lays at the foot of Ledra Street, not far from the newest checkpoint that allows Turkish Cypriots and Greek Cypriots to walk from one community to the other with a minimum of hassle, just by flashing an ID card. The newly transformed district welcomes visitors from the South and has shed its broken-down third world character.

We join the restaurant owners at a long table. The restaurant is empty. They

Cem and Hatice

have arranged to cook for us, made their restaurant into their home, and invited us as guests. We find it a gracious and generous gesture, matched by the wonderful food that graces the table. Cem has arranged to buy a whole salmon, just arrived from fresh Kyrenia, and grilled it to perfection. Combined with savory beans and spicy cous-cous the dinner satisfies in every way. Turns out that Seray cooked much of the food earlier, and now both couples welcome us. Our other family. This time in the north.

I sidle over to the owner, a woman whose daughter sits between us to translate, to ask her about how things are here in north Nicosia. She echoes what I have begun to suspect: that business "is ok. But was much better." The tourists from the South have disappeared and the urban working class of Nicosia doesn't eat at restaurants like theirs. Then her daughter, a recent English language graduate of Eastern Mediterranean University in Famagusta turns the tables. What do I think of the situation and what do I think about Turkey?

I try to be honest yet diplomatic. My disclaimer, that I know too little about current events in Turkey, helps. I say that I hope Turkey can rise to the historic occasion and play a key role in the region, to become the fulcrum of resolution to many conflicts. The faces around at the table beam in approval. They may not all speak English but they sure understand it.

The young woman, Rose, then says to me, "Tell me this. I am born in Cyprus, I am Turkish Cypriot, but because my parents are from Turkey, I cannot enter the South though the checkpoint. Sure, I can fly to Athens and then into Larnaca, but I cannot walk down the street from one side of Nicosia to the other."

I have no answer to this Kafkaesque state of affairs. None.

12 | 11 | 2013

Daniel Hadjitoffi looks rested and healthy. And it's very satisfying to see him again. Turns out that he's no longer the director of the Fulbright program in Cyprus; in fact it turns out he's between jobs. Like how many people here?

Daniel is among the most capable, intelligent, and compassionate persons we've ever met. But today, he's set full-tilt against the economic conditions not only of the present but the past.

A year or more ago he sent me an essay from 2009 that virtually predicted the crash that Cyprus has experienced in 2011/12. His thesis then and now is simple. There is a rule, he smiles ruefully, that a democratic society can tolerate conditions of corruption that do not exceeded twenty percent. And by his calculus, Cyprus has landed way in the red; there are, he postulates, but fifty families in the Republic of Cyprus — an interconnected banking and political elite — who control the country's and the islands' fate.

We needed badly to shine the light of honesty on the darkness of corruption. It would have taken but one — and here I paraphrase Daniel — one honest man to change the conditions of inequality and division that plague Cyprus. Just one.

And why did this not happen? "Simple," his voice grows soft, almost conspiratorial. "Because they fear losing what they have. It is human nature."

It's a stunning indictment, an enumeration of the conditions that account for the Cypriot response to the American/Greek/German euro crisis domino effect. Implicitly, Cypriots are not simply passive victims of great power manipulation, not Lilliputian captives of their own tradition as a powerless state. Rather the combination of self-seeking corruption and inertia provide a political environment that allows the Republic to take the kinds of fiscal risks — think about massive investments in Greek banking and business — that would plunge them into darkness.

And then we shift to the issue of the moment. The discovery of oil and gas. Daniel suggests this may provide both a way out of the current economic crisis (Cyprus as the Norway of the region) but also the key to reunification of the island. Another set of causal links. Energy reserves can provide the common ground where a reunited Cyprus joins forces with Turkey and Israel (and by association, the United States) to extract these vast reserves, then distribute via a new pipeline through Turkey. It's a kind of Grand Bargain that sees all the participants gain something — in fact by giving away illusions of ideology, memory, and mythology. A reunited Cyprus, a new partnership between Turkey and Israel, sustained by American guarantees, will benefit not just the players but also the region. Cyprus can become the rock on which the lever of change will move the world. Or not!

What I have begun to wonder in this context feels much less grand but perhaps just as hopeful. Might the relative equalization of economic conditions between north and South provide a foundation on which to build reconciliation?

12 | 12 | 2013

I've spent most of these last two days in the north. Come to discover it's a Potemkin village there too. Instead of pressboard kiosks much of the "renovation" they have undertaken in the old city there is cosmetic. The Grand Bazaar is clean and freshly painted—and devoid of both charm and customers. They still sell the same Pashmina scarves, "three for 15 E; you choose" but no one comes out of the stalls and puts one around your neck. "You buy?!" they would say; now they just talk to friends on their cell phones. And yes, many of the streets that twist and turn down their version of Ledra Street are clean. But the shops still sell the same Italian designer knock-offs as before. I follow one narrow lane off to the side of the main drag. After about 20 yards it ends at the foot of a massive steel door with a red sign that reads: FORBIDDEN ENTRY atop the logo of a soldier with a rifle cradled in his arms. Turkish Army territory, their side of the Dead Zone, hidden in plain sight. When I try to take a photograph a voice booms out "NO PICTURES."Even here the tourist cleanup barely conceals the presence of the Turkish military occupation.

My old friends, Mehmet and Mustafa, owners of a spice and shoe shop, tell a truer story. They have no business, no customers. It is winter and bitter cold here in Cyprus this week. Their shops are empty and barely heated. "Look," Mustafa tells me, "No Greek tourists. No money. No business." Like Costas he smiles. But unlike Costas, his eyes are dulled by the pain of unsustainable survival. I think of the venerable British Debenhams department store on the other end of Ledra street in the South. The signs at each floor read in Greek, English and Turkish. No Turkish business there either. The two sides of the city really are yoked together, I think, aren't they?

Mehmet seems in better humor. "I pay 30 years for insurance," he tells me, "so now they give me 500 a month." He means Turkish Lira. The exchange rate is about 2.8/dollar. And he manages to live on this pension, sell spices, and acts with an amateur theater troupe that performs all over the north. So he stokes up his burner, conjures a real cup of Cyprus coffee so strong that I'm sure I'll be up all night, and we talk. About his grown son who lives at home but who knows how to use the Internet; about his life on Crete twenty years earlier; about when I might come back and see him again. I wish I knew.

On the way back to the Ledra Street checkpoint I stop at a favorite halvah

Mustafa in his shoe shop, Mehment in his spice shop

shop where they sell this wonderful nutty sweet substance directly out the window from the kitchen. The window is down, but I knock anyway. A man, turns out his name is Ahmed, beckons me it. "We close two years ago. No more halvah." Yet he sits in this empty shop, greeting friends who pass by, in the company of the now dull yellow machinery his grandfather installed almost a century ago. "Three generations," he points to the portraits of his father and grandfather. I snap his picture and I can still remember the fragrance of the ghost halvah.

Later Shirin, who administers the Association for Historic Dialogue, invites us into her office at the new Home for Cooperation. She confirms what everyone has testified to — that the economy of the north is in Intensive Care. But, her explanation is more complicated. Turkish government subsidy has kept the state afloat, provided the cash that created the new car showrooms, and allowed the appearance of prosperity. The reality doesn't jibe. Municipal governments have become bankrupt, ceased services like trash pickup for months, and even had to resort to borrowing money from private sources. The man who owns a private mega university in the city, Near Eastern University, has reputedly bailed out the municipal government of north Nicosia. One of my friends who teaches at NEU has complained for years how poorly the university pays her.

And, the kicker: since the majority of the workforce in the north is employed by the public sector, wages have also dropped dramatically, as much as 20% in recent years. And, at the same time, unemployment expands. How much unemployment? No once seems to know. The English, Cyprus Mail (a reasonably reliable source) reports 17% in the Republic. Others say, "no. it is only 12." Does either number include the array of foreign-born who have done the real labor in the South over the last decade? Many still live in the old city, but the construction jobs that sustained them have dried up. The city now contains skeletons of unfinished buildings wherever one looks. Yet, and I can not fully account for this, Filipinos fill the central section of the old city in the south. The have taken up not only residence but created a mini commercial presence — travel agencies, food markets, and phone-card shops with names like "Little Manila." Undoubtedly many from the Filipinos continue to works as domestics, but by the same token the Sri Lankans who dominated the carting trades a few years ago seem to have disappeared.

12 | 13 | 2013

It snowed last night. We drove to Deftera anyway despite Roula's admonitions, and shivered as Irene bought us a plate of kotopolo souvlaki.

Irene's mother still works at her side, and her smile is as bright as the day (well, another day), but business is slower than slow. We are the only customers present and there doesn't appear to be a rush of take out orders. It feels like a mirror of the rest of the island. And, like Costas, she displays a sense of equanimity in the face of disaster. Her niece, Andrea, home for a few days, tells me on the phone that she is very very busy writing a paper. She's now in her third year of law school in Manchester, England. Quite a journey for this brave young woman. It was she who guided us here to Deftera the first time eight years ago.

By the time we drive back to Nicosia I'm already congratulating myself for a. not honking at anyone and b. not even trying to make a right turn into a right lane. Once again I've somehow managed to conquer the dreaded "roundabouts." The next morning the news shows are full of stories of more than thirty mountain villages cut off from the main roads because of the real snowstorm that extends as far as Cairo and Jerusalem.

12 | 14 | 2013

We run around all day and most of the evening. Our last for this, our fifth visit. Of course, we must find time to have dinner with Elena and her brother Xeno. They announce that they have decided to fight the crisis by opening a small space ("please don't call it a club") where they can sing on the weekends. They experience this economic decline a bit differently from most of our friends. Life has always been on the margins for them and their music reflects the joy and pain of their experiences. Perhaps this is what makes it so compellingly soulful. Elena has suffered many losses in the past two years. Her mother, to whom she had been devoted died in her home not long ago. The toll of care shows dramatically. Elena has lost by her reckoning at least 10 kilos during that time. It's not easy to offer care and support from 5,000 miles away. But, we are pleased to see her son, Panyoties, who has returned to Nicosia on vacation from this third year in art school in England. He's handsome and modern, a contrast to his mother's traditional beauty, and he shares some slides of his art work. An image I'll not soon forget has a woman's face covered by a mask with red splash of color over her mouth. The image, direct and powerful, makes me think of many things—from the silence of hope in Cyprus, to the silencing of women. But, most of it about his mother. About Elena's desperate silence; of the unspeakable things that she has buried deep within. Like so many things on this trip it makes me profoundly sad.

We rush across the Ledra Palace check point to say good-bye to Cem and Seray. They talk more openly now about coming to America and, for the first time, it doesn't sound simply like a fantasy. How their two little girls, who howl with delight when we appear at the shop, have transformed them. Its clear that business is difficult, as it is in much of the north, but for the moment the family has wiped away the sadness.

Around the corner from the shop is a sweet and informal Turkish Cypriot restaurant. We meet two friends from the Association there. Rena, a Greek Cypriot and Dileck, a Turkish Cypriot have both visited us in the US on the same summer project that brought Fez back into our lives. It is really good to see them again, and we share plates of bouriki—sweet, meat, and cheese—as we tell stories about the past year. Recalling the sunshine we shared in South Carolina, I realize it is freezing cold in the restaurant, but the owner, a Turkish Cypriot who speaks fluent Greek and seems to embrace everyone, sets a fire blazing to keep us warm. As teachers both Rena and Dileck are less wounded by the economic downturn. Like Fez they have lost a portion of their salary, but they have income they can count on which as my parents told me recalling the Great Depression, amounts to a great comfort in dire economic times.

Thekla Constantinou. No visit to Cyprus would be complete without seeing Thekla, the fiery secretary of the English Department at the University of Cyprus, where this story first started. She jumps up. "Peter Rutkoff!" She holds out her arms. "You have come back." And then we talk. Or rather then she talks — non-stop for at least a half-hour. And she tells in almost the same words as my friends in the north about the disaster in the South.

How difficult life has become; people have lost their homes and their savings; the wealthy have run off with everything else; her son now has no chance for the university; the government is more corrupt than ever; wages for public servants have fallen and will continue to fall; the university budget is shrinking

Rena and my former Kenyon student Hope in South Carolina

and there is no authorization to replace lost positions. "It is a terrible mess," she announces her voice angry and sharp.

The pain appears universal. From Costas to Thekla, from Fez to Mehmet, from voices in the South and voices in the north, everyone suffers here in Cyprus.

I returned to this island for a "last" visit because I knew a year ago that the final chapter of the book I had already completed, a chapter filled with optimism, would have no credibility without a post-script. But I was unprepared for the reality behind the abstractions of fiscal crisis. No one I have encountered here has been immune. Not Irene, who still presides over the Panic Room, her souvlaki place in Deftera; nor her niece Andrea, now in a third year law program in Manchester, England; or Demos, the icon seller in Lefkara who sat in his shop for a week without making a sale in the ten days before Christmas; nor the north Cypriot woman with a degree in International Relations who sells jewelry at an hourly wage; not the countless Cypriots who cannot and do not pay their rents; nor any of the other Turkish and Greek Cypriots I know and care about in this book.

Yet, at the same time, I can't help but hope. Hope that the current crisis can in fact provide the right conditions for process that will lead to reunification. Might the two communities finally see that they need each other? Might the government of Turkey need a pipeline of gas/oil more than it needs to maintain a force of 40,000 in the north; or the United States see that the survival of Israel is intimately connected to the stability of a united Cyprus and partnership with Turkey?That, as I wrote a year ago, the celebration of a truly multicultural Cyprus can provide the preconditions of a unified country where the divisions of the past, the destructive ideologies of misplaced nationalism, can finally be put to rest.

Seems like a pipe dream. Until during our very last morning, at our traditional farewell breakfast with Costas and Roula. The Sunday edition of the Cyprus Mail announces that the American oil company exploring "Field 12" confirms the probable discovery of billions (yes, billions) of barrels of oil below the seabed. Field 12 is the one shared with Israel. The possibility of a new geopolitical reality might actually be at hand. But, even if the cards all break the right way, will Cyprus emerge as the next Norway? Or the next Nigeria?

Christina clowning

New York City native Peter Rutkoff has been teaching at Kenyon College in Ohio since 1971. He held the National Endowment for the Humanities Distinguished Teaching Chair there from 1999-2001, and from 2009-12 was the Robert Oden Distinguished Professor of American Studies. Peter also serves as the Executive Director of the Kenyon Academic Partnership (KAP), which links the college with a network of thirty secondary schools in Ohio. Students in KAP take dual-credit courses for high-school graduation and Kenyon College transcript credit. Peter's scholarly interests include African-American cultural studies and the African-American migrations, the subject of his book with Professor Scott, *Fly Away: The Great African-American Migrations.* His other non-fiction includes *New York Modern: the Arts and the City* (with Will Scott) and *The Next Hedgerow,* published by this press in 2004. He has also authored several books of fiction, including the recent novel *Irish Eyes* (2012).

www.ingramcontent.com/pod-product-compliance
Ingram Content Group UK Ltd.
Pitfield, Milton Keynes, MK11 3LW, UK
UKHW061955290726
14090UKWH00021B/1235

9 781880 977415